MW00917499

Belle Boyd: The Rebel Spy

By

CW Whitehair

Copyright 2017 by CW Whitehair

Updated Edition: 2023

ISBN: 9781973942177

Contact: cwwhitehair@hotmail.com

Source: *Library of Congress*

Belle Boyd

Table of Contents

Introduction

Belle Boyd was called the *Joan of Arc of the South*, the *Cleopatra of the Secession*, *Belle of the Valley*, *Secesh Cleopatra*, *Cleopatra of the Confederacy*, and the *Siren of the Shenandoah*. Abroad in France, the French newspapers hailed her as *LeBelle Rebelle*, which means "The Beautiful Rebel." Even though Belle Boyd accepted these monikers, the one she would come to admire the most would be the title the Union soldiers gave her: *The Rebel Spy*. In her dramatic memoirs, *Belle Boyd in Camp and Prison*, she proudly referred to this surname more than once as she spoke of her vocation as a Confederate spy.

Belle Boyd was very clever as a spy, even though some of her contemporaries living in Front Royal and Winchester, Virginia, shed a different light on her during that time. She knew how to use her romantic sexual appeal to woo young Union officers like Captain Daniel Keily and Lieutenant Abram H. Hasbrouck, who were far from home and who she preyed upon because of their vulnerability to their military information and lack of discretion. Other Union officers would "sit in the Shenandoah starlight and whisper their most treasured secrets for the privilege of holding her hand and telling her she was beautiful," or if she had any complaints, they would do anything to accommodate her. Belle waged a different kind of war, a different kind of weapon. She "dedicated to the confederate army the only weapon that she possessed...a woman's beauty and a woman's wiles."

The famous Civil War historian and author Carl Sandburg once wrote about Belle's spying activities. She "could have been legally convicted, shot at sunrise, and heard of no more."

Douglas Southall Freeman, the famous Confederate historian and author, endorsed her activities as authentic after years of scrutinizing by various ninetieth-century historians. He wrote, "the renowned

Belle Boyd, one of the most active and most reliable of the many women agents of the Confederacy." Indeed, an endorsement of her spying and covert activities.

Much like Jeb Stuart, who commanded the Army of Northern Virginia's cavalry force, and General Lee greatly depended on for reliable intelligence, Belle was consistent with her information on the Union army's designs and intentions. There is no record that Belle Boyd gave Stonewall Jackson or Turner Ashby one piece of unreliable information. She was as accurate and meticulous with her information as Jeb Stuart was for General Robert E. Lee.

Belle Boyd was constant trouble for Union authorities in Washington and their forces fighting in the Shenandoah Valley. They did not know how to deal with her, nor did the officers in the field. Most Southern sympathizing women were treated with considerable care and respect. Union officers and their soldiers initiated the most proper etiquette, even though most of their husbands were fighting for the Southern Confederacy. Belle took advantage of the gender issue and, in every situation, used it for her benefit and the Southern Confederacy.

By 1862, she was a sensation in the Shenandoah Valley and the rest of the country. Northern newspapers wrote of her and pictured her as the most romantic figure since the "Maid of Orleans." In the South, she was greatly admired by many Southern civilians, particularly women. She was urged to visit their part of the country and increase the spirit and morale. The men of the Confederate army operating in the Shenandoah Valley admired and believed her to be a heroine. The one who became her greatest admirer was Major-General Thomas (Stonewall) Jackson, who had come to worship Jackson, calling him the "Apostle of Freedom."

In 1893, one New England journalist interviewed Belle while she was visiting Boston and wrote, "It may be said that there was not probably a more marked woman in the rebellion than she."

In 2008, I wrote an article for the *Civil War Historian* magazine entitled *Belle Boyd: The Rebel Spy*. Belle Boyd and all that I had come to know of her life and exploits intrigued me and compelled me to investigate the life of a woman who was a spy, author, and actress. I was fascinated by what I read and learned about her exploits as a spy, her ability and style for writing, and her life after the war. I have concluded Belle Boyd was daring, sometimes reckless, learned her art skillfully, and possessed a solid devotion to the Southern Cause that was unquestionable.

Since my feature article for the *Civil War Historian* magazine, I have come across much more up-to-date information on her life and that of her first husband, Samuel W. Hardinge. After the Belle Boyd article was published, a relative of Belle Boyd's family, a local historian from Martinsburg, West Virginia, approached me with infallible proof about the life of her first husband, Samuel W. Hardinge, which shocked me. I took considerable time and effort to confirm his information and discovered that he was correct. That information is included in this book.

The last time a biographer wrote a serious account of Belle Boyd's life was in 1983. Since that time, much more information has been made available to this author, which was not either included or may not have been available to be included in the other two books, *Belle Boyd: The Confederate Spy* and *Siren of the Shenandoah*. For **Belle Boyd: The Rebel Spy**, I used 117 newspaper articles, letters written about Belle, some never published, diaries of soldiers who had interacted with her, and regimental histories.

The other two books written on Belle Boyd do not cover much of her life after the war, just some high points. There is more to her story. I dedicated nearly a third of the project to her life as a theatrical actress, her two marriages after Samuel Hardinge, and her struggles and challenges in life.

I have taken all the information from the original Belle Boyd article and the additional information I have discovered and now present the work in non-fiction book-length.

I have added additional information in the Updated Edition of this book in the text and the Appendix.

Thirty-two-year-old Daniel Keily served in the British navy and the Irish Battalion in papal service and had been decorated by the Pope. He arrived in New York City with Myles W. Keogh (later killed at Little Big Horn) on April 1, 1862. Keily and Keogh immediately received captain's commissions, and served on Brigadier-General James Shields's staff.

Martinsburg, Virginia

Footnote The *Maid of Orleans* was written first by Voltaire in 1730. It was written in 1801 as a five-act theatrical play by Frederick Schuller. The play is based on the life of Joan of Arc. The theme follows the critical events surrounding Joan of Arc's life, including her death, where her honor and reputation were restored.

Belle's Profile

Belle Boyd may have been the most controversial female figure who participated in the Civil War. At seventeen, Belle did not fight the war with weapons like Union and Confederate soldiers, except for one incident. Instead, she used her femininity and sly trickery to deceive and confuse Union officers and enlisted personnel concerning her true purposes. On more than one occasion, she was allowed entrance into Union encampments---dressing very fashionably and displaying her charming appeal, dazzling charisma, and social graces while extracting whatever useful information concerning troop movements, she could pass on to Confederate Colonel Turner Ashby and Major-General Thomas (Stonewall) Jackson.

One of Belle's most significant assets was her ability to appeal to chivalry by flirting her way through the Union ranks with words of compliments, peace, and flattery, and taking advantage of soldiers' vulnerability while listening to their conversations and counting the strength of their forces. She was good at manipulating Union officers or anyone associated with the Union cause to the point one did not know if she was honest and sincere or if she was using them for her gain. Various officers occasionally invited her to ride with them in their carriages, much to the outrage of her conservative female acquaintances. It was all a charade, using her charm and irresistible personality to gain information, an attribute that would help her throughout her life. But she later admitted, she was beginning to experiment in the art of espionage.

Among the Union ranks, some officials knew Belle Boyd was a proven Confederate informant, but she continued to pass freely among them without scrutiny. She was considered by the soldiers and their officers at the war's beginning as innocent and not much of a risk. They all competed for her attention, and she willingly accommodated them. She played on their compassion, their favor, and vulnerability.

One would have to question why the Union soldiers would have continued to allow her unlimited access to their camps. Nonetheless, the most-high ranking Union authorities did not consider her a serious threat until after their defeat at Front Royal, Virginia, during the Shenandoah Valley Campaign of 1862.

Belle Boyd was well educated, an accomplished musician and singer, sensitive to others, independently-minded, adventurous, and possessing bold, reckless bravery that most men would not have been willing to demonstrate. She could be gentle and persuasive one moment, furious, and display her temper the next. Belle was extremely aggressive, sometimes commanding, and stubborn if needed. She resisted authority, and like her mother, she feared no man regardless of their threats. Her temper and stubbornness were her greatest weakness and significantly cost her while on parole at Front Royal, Virginia. Belle was cunning at times; other times, she acted naïve around Union officers and soldiers, but she could also be an individualist.

Belle Boyd possessed essential tools for the espionage game, such as intelligence, perception, daring, and determination. Belle was a brilliant, dominating conversationalist and a romantic with a soft, articulate voice. Belle could be conservative, prim, and proper like most Southern women when the occasion called for it. Still, she could also quickly change and play the role of a lady engaged in self-sacrifice and military drama of self-assertion and courage and knew best by her discernment what would best serve her needs. She was also energetic and physically agile. Belle began riding horses very young and proved to be more skillful than many men.

Another side of Belle was not revealed until twenty-eight years after the Civil War. The war was as difficult for Belle as it was for the ordinary foot soldier in the Union and Confederate armies. She had witnessed men dying and heard their pitiful cries for a wife, child, mother, or father while nursing them in her home or a hospital. Belle witnessed her father's suffering from the effects of serving as a Confederate soldier during the war, her confinement in prison, and countless other scenes she never wrote about or maybe did not want to talk about to anyone. It is much like many veterans today of foreign wars, who hold the terrible tragedies and memories of war deep within

15

their hearts and minds causing emotional scars that last a lifetime. She gave a glimpse of the pain she had and still experienced when near fifty. She told a reporter, "And now when every day something recalls a hidden memory, it all returns to me with such vivid force that I feel almost a sense of piercing physical pain."

During and after the Civil War, Belle loved the attention the Northern and Southern press gave her. During the war, the press criticized and demonized her for her role as a Confederate spy. The Northern newspapers called her the "fastest girl in Virginia or anywhere else for that matter," and they also accused her of being "closeted four hours" with Union General James Shields, wrapping a rebel flag around his head, and committing the same act with Union General Nathaniel Banks. They even wrote that she had a pet crow she trained to say her name, "Miss Belle," and the names "Stonewall" and "General Lee." They accused her of romantic desires for General Jackson, "wanting to share his tent and share his dangers." True or false, Belle loved the notoriety and the attention. After the war, when she became an actress, she still required their attention. Like most notable celebrities of our era, she continued to polarize her society through the events of her life in the newspapers.

Most ninetieth and twentieth century authors and historians cannot make up their mind about Belle Boyd whether she was all she proclaimed to be, or if she was someone who sensationalized her role during the Civil War. Had Belle lived longer, she would have waged a different kind of war against those who have tried to discredit her role as a Confederate spy and claim everything that she did was no more than a bunch of hype to sell her memoirs. There was never a case where any of the officers that she mentioned in her book ever scrutinized or disclaimed any of the information or events that she disclosed.

Chapter 1

Belle's Early Years

Belle Boyd's ancestors were of Scottish heritage. After leaving Scotland, they settled briefly in Northern Ireland before coming to America. William Boyd, Belle's great-grandfather, was the first to journey across the Atlantic Ocean, arriving in Virginia around 1729. His son Samuel had two sons, John, and Samuel. John and Samuel married the Stephenson sisters, Isabella, and Maria, with Samuel marrying the latter; they had a son, Benjamin, Belle's father.

Belle's mother was Mary Rebecca Glenn, whose father was Captain James Glenn of Jefferson County, Virginia. Captain Glenn married Ruth Burns, and the two of them, in 1802, established the estate known as "Glenn Burnie," or "Glennburnie." James and Ruth Glenn had three children, James, Mary, and Frances Elizabeth. Frances Elizabeth married James E. Stewart, a Martinsburg attorney. They moved to Washington, where they lived for some time, before moving to the country village of Front Royal, Virginia. By 1862, their home would be the base of operation for *Belle Boyd: Rebel Spy.*

According to Belle, her birthplace was at her grandmother's home, Mrs. Samuel Boyd, in Martinsburg, Virginia {West Virginia}, in the lower Shenandoah Valley of Virginia. She was born Maria Isabelle Boyd on May 9, 1844, the oldest of eight children. After Belle's birth, her mother gave birth to three sisters and one brother, all of who died in infancy: Benjamin Jr., Anna, Fannie, and Annie. All the Boyd children were buried in Green Hill Cemetery in Martinsburg—Belle's other surviving siblings: Isabelle, William, Glenn, and Mary.

Immediately after Belle's birth, the family moved briefly to Darksville, five miles south of Martinsburg. Her father operated a tavern before moving to Bunker Hill in southern Berkeley County,

Virginia. At Bunker Hill, Belle's father continued to operate a tavern. According to the 1850 census, the Boyd family had moved once more to Martinsburg and rented a log house on East Burke Street. Benjamin entered into a business agreement with his brother John, and they operated a general merchandise store on the 100 block of Queen Street. Belle's father was quite the entrepreneur and had significantly prospered. On February 25, 1853, he purchased a corner lot at the junction of East Race and Spring Street to build a house for his family. Benjamin built a two-story stone Greek Revival-style home where he operated a general merchandise store near the Baltimore and Ohio Railroad. Before the Civil War, the Baltimore and Ohio Railroad was the largest and most important railroad in the United States. It only made good sense for Benjamin Boyd to want to set up a general store near the railroad depot because of its vast opportunity for prosperity. One local historian wrote, "After 1852, it became apparent that Martinsburg was a town of importance and prosperity. Business began to expand." Belle and her family moved into their new home and began the store operation in 1854.

The Boyd family also owned and operated a tobacco farm. This was the one hundred-and-twenty-five-acre farm next to Mary's family's farm, "Glenn Burnie," which she inherited from her father. The Boyd's farm was located between Shepherdstown and Neils, now the community known as Shenandoah Junction.

The family possessed strong Southern values and enjoyed a very close relationship with each other. They were very responsible, tightly knitted, and protective of each other. Benjamin and Mary possessed a respectable standing within the Martinsburg community and a high social standing. They were members of the Martinsburg Presbyterian Church as well as civic leaders. Belle once told a news correspondent from Chicago that she came from a "well-known family of Virginia, having ties among the best in the state." In a later interview with a journalist, she claimed two societies lived in Martinsburg: "the mechanics of the Baltimore and Ohio Railroad and the aristocratic that her family belonged to." Belle came from a family of soldiers who fought in the American Revolution. One family member, James Stephenson, served in the Virginia General Assembly

18

from 1803 to 1825 before serving three terms in the United States House of Representatives.

In another interview with a journalist in Boston after the war, she said that the family's most distinguished friends from Martinsburg and Jefferson County included the "Pendletons, Faulkners, Beckhams, Hughes, Danderidges, Hunters, and Harrisons."

Even at a young age, Belle was high-spirited, often playing pranks on her brothers, sisters, cousins, and the few household servants who lived with the family. She was considered a tomboy, very athletic, climbing trees and riding her horse through the woods. Belle said, "I was at home on a horse's back from my earliest childhood. I was a very little girl when I learned to ride."

Belle was a rebel at heart and very mischievous, even to the point that some called her a "headstrong brat." One mischievous event occurred one evening when her mother and father were entertaining some high state official. Belle was eleven years old and not allowed to eat dinner with the Boyd's guests because she was considered too young by Southern tradition. After dinner, Benjamin and Mary and their guest entered the parlor when they heard an unusual commotion outside their home. When Benjamin opened the front door, Belle lunged through the door riding a white-spotted horse into the dining room. Her father became angry and began to remove Belle and her horse from the house. Belle shouted, "Well, my horse is old enough, isn't he?"

Even though Belle's family was angry and embarrassed at the incident, their guest felt amused and entertained. The state official said, "Surely so high a spirit should not be thoughtlessly quelled by severe punishment! Mary, won't you tell me more about your little rebel?" Even at a young age, Belle Boyd was already a true rebel.

When Belle was not with her cousin Alice Stewart, who she was very close to, she was with her favorite playmates, her next-door neighbors, Virginia, and Betty Doll. At a young age, Belle became very skilled at horseback riding. It was common for a woman to ride sidesaddle, but not Belle; she rode over the saddle like her male counterparts. Belle loved to take horseback rides and be out in the open air, often spending months and weeks at her Grandmother Glenn's home in Jefferson County, where she was away from the confines of living in a town and had nothing but rolling hills and green pastures to ride her horse.

As I wrote earlier, the Boyd family owned a few servants; they were Southern in their acceptance of slavery. One of those servants was Eliza Hopewell Corsey, who Belle called "Mauma Eliza." Some accounts claim Eliza was a runaway enslaved person from the deep Southern states and found refuge with the Boyd family, an issue I intend on addressing later. Eliza was not much older than Belle and was responsible for Belle's welfare. Eliza's relationship became more than just Belle's maid, but also that of trusted confidant, so much so that during the war, she carried information from Belle to Turner Ashby and Stonewall Jackson. Even though it was illegal in the state of Virginia before the Civil War for an enslaved person to be educated, Belle defied the rules and taught Eliza in the evenings by candlelight to read and write. There was a bond that grew between Belle and Eliza that could not be broken or compromised, and because of this, Eliza always held the highest affection, respect, and loyalty for Belle throughout the rest of her life.

When Belle was in elementary school, she did not get along with her schoolmarm, Miss Haven, originally from Brattleboro, Vermont. One day, Miss Haven decided she could not let Belle upset her any longer and decided to expel her from school. Miss Haven sent for one of the Boyd servants to carry her desk and books all the way home and inform her father that Belle would never return to her school again. Ann Elizabeth Riddle, who lived in Martinsburg and was five years older than Belle, recalled the incident many years later: "She was eleven years old and a perfect scalawag, never would obey a rule. I can see Mrs. Haven now with her Drunkard bonnet on, following Belle Boyd and her desk home."

Belle was too independent-minded even at the age of eleven.

In 1856, at twelve, and following Southern tradition, the Boyd family had the wealth to enroll their tomboy daughter in a Baltimore finishing school, hoping to make a lady out of her. At Mount Washington Female College, now Mount Saint Agnes College, Belle studied French, music, literature, and the proper social graces for the period. She had command of several different languages. Belle was attentive and applied well to her studies, but she still found time to be mischievous by writing her initials on a window pane in one of the rooms at the primary school building.

Sometime during Belle's early life, and she does not give a year, she said one of her most incredible experiences was a trip to Eastern Tennessee and the city of Knoxville with her father, who had lost a considerable amount of money and desired to "retrieve his fortunes by migration." On the journey to Tennessee, they rode through the Shenandoah Valley. "We saw the Natural Bridge and took in all the sights of the valley. It was the most charming experience I had ever known," Belle said. The trip for Benjamin Boyd did not bear fruit because he and Belle soon returned home to Martinsburg.

While Belle attended Mount Washington Female College, the United States Supreme Court decided the Dred Scott case. The High Court ruled that an enslaved person had no rights to citizenship whatsoever and was considered the property of its owner. The High Court's decision also meant that if enslaved people were taken to a territory or a free state and escaped, they would still not be considered free citizens but as runaway enslaved people and treated accordingly by law. If there was any question during that time about slavery, the Court's ruling legalized the institution that set off a firestorm between Abolitionists in the North and the Fire-Eaters of the South. The lines between proslavery and antislavery were drawn that much tighter.

Another incident occurred that fueled the flames of the Civil War. In October of 1859, John Brown and twenty-one followers came to Harpers Ferry, Virginia {West Virginia}, to cause insurrection among the enslaved community in Virginia. Harpers Ferry was only seventeen miles from Martinsburg. After Brown captured the United States Armory and Arsenal, and a thirty-six-hour fight with the town's citizens and area militia companies, Colonel Robert E. Lee of the Regular Army and ninety Marines finally captured Brown and his raiders, who had not already been killed or wounded. Belle told a journalist in an interview that "the roads were patrolled and everybody believed you Northerners were coming down to murder us. We women remained at home. It was not considered proper that we should go up to Harpers Ferry to see John Brown. I remember how relieved we all were when we heard the news he was taken and the raid was over." Belle continued, "It was a long time before the alarm subsided and the Negroes were carefully watched."

According to Belle, she did not go back to school "that winter because of the excitement raised by the raid." The growing division, the anger that seethed over states' rights, and the issue of slavery deeply divided the nation to the point that by 1860 there was no turning back from bloodshed.

Belle had her thoughts on slavery, which she recorded after the beginning of the Civil War. She wrote, "Slavery, like all other imperfect forms of society, will have its day; but the time for its final extinction in the Confederate States of America has not yet arrived. Can it be urged that a race, which prefers servitude to freedom has reached that adolescent period of existence, which fits it for the latter condition?" Belle did not cherish nor embrace the idea that her way of life was about to change, but Abraham Lincoln's election had all but insured that concern. Belle was a good debater. On the issue of slavery and state sovereignty, Belle often argued with her fellow school students, some of who came from families involved in national politics, justifying her views.

After finishing school in 1860, Belle wrote a letter to her cousin Willie Boyd, living in Missouri, giving her physical description. She wrote that she was "106.5 pounds, formed beautiful, dark blue eyes, rich brown hair," and white teeth. She wrote that she was "the most beautiful of all your cousins," and she hoped to come west and find a husband, but that did not occur because the war was on the horizon.

While in Washington after completing her studies, Belle visited with her Aunt Francis and Uncle John Stewart, but the Stewarts would soon leave the city because of their Southern sympathies. While in Washington, Belle enjoyed a hectic social life. Belle loved to attend parties and social functions with her mother. She was very outgoing. One of the homes Belle frequented was that of the former governor of Virginia and current Secretary of War John B. Floyd, who later became a Confederate general. On many occasions, the adolescent Belle met cabinet members of James Buchanan's administration, various dignitaries from foreign lands, and influential families from the North and South. She noticed the gaieties and pleasures and the sisterly love and friendship that surrounded the citizens of

Washington. For now, all was well. As was her custom, Belle also attended the theater and political events.

When not socializing, Belle visited the halls of Congress, where she often heard the fiery and deeply divided differences between members of Congress over the social issues of the times. Indeed, some of these debates solidified her resolve for the Southern point of view. Not only did Congressmen represent their constituency, but they also spoke for their Congressional district and culture. Congress was deeply divided over the country's future, and the nation's citizens were just as deeply divided. Belle's home area suffered such division. Belle later wrote about the fears and the passion among the citizens, who were loyal to the Southern viewpoint living in her surrounding area, and how their views were firmly loyal to their Southern culture. Finally, she wrote, "We had not fully recovered from the John Brown raid, and right on top of it came the increasing influence of the Abolitionist, whom we believed would murder us if they had the chance, and their apparent triumph in the election of Abraham Lincoln, the spite of resistance ran high right through our people like lava of the volcano."

On December 20, 1861, South Carolina carried out an earlier threat that if Abraham Lincoln were elected to the presidency of the United States, they would secede from the Union. They were not the only state to secede from the Union. Over the winter months of 1861, six more Deep South states, Georgia, Florida, Mississippi, Alabama, Louisiana, and Texas, followed South Carolina's lead, forming the new Confederate States of America.

By the time Belle returned to Martinsburg, her family had moved to South Queen Street, and her life was quickly changing because of the tensions on the national scene. Martinsburg had grown to a town of over 3,000 citizens. Much like Shepherdstown and Harpers Ferry, Martinsburg's citizens were divided in loyalties to the Union and Southern cause. Belle noticed the community preparing for war, the anxieties that grew with future uncertainties, and the distrust growing among its citizens. Belle wrote," My winter had been cheered by every kind of amusement and every form of pleasure; my summer was about to be darkened by constant anxiety and heart-rendering affliction."

Virginia had not seceded from the Union, but some individuals in Richmond were laboring for secession from the Union. Towns and cities in the North and South, such as Martinsburg, were raising militia companies to protect their communities and if needed, their state. It was the civic obligation of every able-bodied man to join a militia company. This was an obligation that soon was going to affect every family in the North and South. It came on April 12, 1861. Fort Sumter in Charleston, South Carolina, was bombarded and surrendered to South Carolina forces after thirty-four hours. Immediately, President Lincoln called for 75,000 men to put down the rebellion. With this demand, Virginia declined to send its quota of 2,300 men to serve in the Union army and fight against its Southern brethren. On April 18, Virginia voted and seceded from the Union. Belle and her family were now affected by the war.

Immediately Martinsburg, like Harpers Ferry and nearby Shepherdstown, began to see their young men choose sides and enlist for either the Union or the Southern Confederacy armies. At Martinsburg, various organizations were formed to fight for the Southern Confederacy, such as the Wise Artillery, Company B, 1st Virginia Cavalry, and the Berkeley Border Guards, organized on October 31, 1859, after the Brown raid at Harpers Ferry. Belle's father, at age forty-four, was one of the very first to enlist as a private in the Berkeley Border Guards. Her father had been offered an officer's rank because of his standing in the community, but he refused. The Berkeley Border Guards were armed and equipped through donations from Belle and some of the area's ladies. The Berkeley Border Guards comprised some of the best men in the area. One historian who lived during that time wrote, "These heroic men enlisted on both sides. Men equal in intelligence and courage, honesty of purpose and stubborn determination, whose forefathers had fought side by side for the independence of their country during the Revolutionary War; only differing, perhaps, in the circumstances and influences which had educated them into a decided opinion upon the great question then at issue. The state of affairs was not by any means confined to Berkeley and Jefferson Counties, as it was very general along the border, and notably here." The Berkeley Border Guards

24

soon became Company D, 2nd Virginia Infantry, commanded by Captain John Nadenbousch.

Chapter 2

The Civil War: Early Incidents

After the capture and the destruction of the United States Armory and Arsenal at Harpers Ferry on the night of April 18, 1861, all area militia volunteer companies were ordered to Harpers Ferry. Confederate authorities believed that an invasion of Virginia would come through this area. Also, the Confederate occupation of the town was important for disrupting the Baltimore and Ohio Railroad and for dismantling the machinery that had not been destroyed by fire on the night of April 18. The machinery was crated and sent to Richmond, Virginia, to make weapons for the Confederate armies. Belle described Harpers Ferry as it appeared at the outbreak of the war. She wrote, "Harpers Ferry could boast of one of the largest and best arsenals in America, and of a magnificent bridge, which latter, spanning the broad stream of the Potomac, connected Maryland and Virginia."

Confederate forces were daily arriving at Harpers Ferry. At first, Colonel Thomas Jackson, later General {Stonewall} Jackson, was in command at Harpers Ferry but later yielded his command to General Joseph Johnston on May 23. During this time, other than reveille at 5:30 in the morning and constant drilling and learning the skill of being a soldier, war was not a serious reality to the Confederate force at Harpers Ferry. Belle and her family had been experiencing depression, anxiety, and sleepless nights during her father's absence. She encouraged other young ladies who had loved ones serving in the army at Harpers Ferry to join her for a visit. They had no problem obtaining passes, which were needed for anyone who wanted to travel and visit during the war in this area.

When Belle and her friends arrived at Harpers Ferry, they found it was an "animated scene." Belle found many of the officers and men were gay and joyous and not concerned about the reality that a war awaited them and that many of them would die on some battlefield for their cause or carry debilitating wounds and injuries for the rest of their life. Henry Kyd Douglas, who hailed from nearby Shepherdstown, serving as a private in the 2nd Virginia Infantry, and later served as an aide to General Jackson wrote, "Society was plentiful, for the ranks were filled with the best blood of Virginia; all its classes were there. Mothers and sisters and other dear girls came constantly to Harpers Ferry and there was very little difficulty in seeing them. Nothing was serious yet; everything much like a joke." But reality was about to take place.

General Johnston's cavalry scouts along the Potomac River warned him that an 18,000-man Union army under Major-General Robert Patterson, a Mexican War veteran, was approaching the river near Williamsport, Maryland, from Chambersburg, Pennsylvania. Immediately, General Johnston and his 13,000-man army evacuated Harpers Ferry for fear that his lines of communication would be cut off with the Confederate capital at Richmond, Virginia, and Harpers Ferry was indefensible since it was on a peninsula surrounded by two mountains and two rivers.

After evaluating Harpers Ferry in June, Colonel Jackson's brigade marched to Martinsburg with some elements positioned further north toward the Potomac River near Williamsport, Maryland. Jackson and his men were in Martinsburg to destroy train cars, the roundhouse, machine shops, and other Baltimore and Ohio Railroad buildings. As for some of the train locomotives, they shipped them south overland to Winchester, Virginia. While at Martinsburg, Belle had the opportunity to meet Jackson. In an 1893 interview with a Boston journalist, she said Jackson "was an extremely modest man, rather strange and shy in his manner with women."

When Belle found Jackson at the Raemer's Hotel, she noticed ladies surrounded him in the parlor. They were cutting buttons off form his uniform coat and vest. Belle approached Jackson with a bouquet of flowers that she had gathered for the occasion and asked, "Colonel won't you give me a button?"

"Look at me," Jackson replied.

There were no buttons to be found on his uniform coat or vest. Everyone laughed.

Belle gave a good description of Colonel Thomas Jackson. She said Jackson was "not very old, 40 or so, he did not look old, but he was a man with heavy lines in his face. There was a great deal of character in them. He was not your ideal beautiful soldier, but he was a very courteous man, very good, and there was something attractive about him."

One incident during these early days of the war involving Belle occurred on the streets of Martinsburg. Elizabeth Fawver Conley, also of Martinsburg, was known to be loyal to the Union, and her husband served in the Union army, most likely one of the Martinsburg Union companies. Some information that Belle had carried to Jackson; Mrs. Conley also carried the same information to Union forces. Several days had passed when Elizabeth Conley met Belle on the street in Martinsburg. After confronting Belle about the information, Elizabeth slapped Belle on her face. When Jackson learned of the insult, he had Elizabeth Conley arrested. Like Belle, the arrest did not stop Elizabeth Conley from continuing her spying activities and carrying information to Union soldiers during the war.

On July 2, 1861, General Robert Patterson's men began to cross the Potomac River near Williamsport, Maryland, located about eight miles north of Martinsburg. The Union forces were challenged by Confederate soldiers from Stonewall Jackson's First Virginia Brigade, the same brigade that Benjamin Boyd's regiment was assigned. As a result, the Battle at Falling Waters occurred, but it did not last long. Stonewall Jackson's Virginia brigade was outnumbered. Jackson broke off the engagement and slowly withdrew, but he had accomplished what he was ordered to do, and that was to delay the Union army's advance.

Around 10:00 on the morning of July 3, Stonewall Jackson's men marched through the streets of Martinsburg. Their destination was to join forces once more with the main body of the Confederate army under General Johnston at Darksville, about five miles south of Martinsburg.

After Jackson's withdrawal, an incident occurred when Belle and her servant, Eliza, attended to several Confederate soldiers suffering from fever at a hospital while General Patterson's advance Union regiments entered the city. A *Philadelphia Inquirer* correspondent wrote what he witnessed, "The people of the town received the Union troops with quiet, but deep manifestations of joy, ladies, and children thronged the streets in perfect serenity and with laughing joyous hilarity." Belle saw it in another way. She wrote they could "hear the sound of rumbling gun carriages, and the hellish shouts with the infuriated and undisciplined Union soldiers." It was not long before Belle had her first confrontation with a Union officer. Belle and her servant, Eliza, had been attending to the Confederate wounded when the Union army entered the town. Belle stood near a wounded Confederate soldier when a Union captain and two of his soldiers approached. The captain held a Union flag over the beds of the wounded rebels and began to taunt them. Belle scornfully said, "Sir, these men are as helpless as babies, and have, as you may see, no power to reply to your insults."

"And pray," the officer said, "who may you be, Miss?"

Belle did not answer the Union captain.

"A rebel lady," Eliza quickly replied.

The Union officer turned and said while leaving, "a damned independent one, at all events."

Belle and the other ladies nursing in the hospital turned and continued their care of the wounded but found it repulsive and unbearable because of the violent language and actions of the drunken Union soldiers. Belle sought out an officer and pleaded for his intervention. The officer finally gained control of his men and stopped the harassment. It was an episode she never forgot.

Source: *Author's Collection*

Martinsburg, Virginia, 1861

Chapter 3

The Martinsburg Incident

The very next day was July 4, Independence Day. The stars and stripes were flying from some of the Martinsburg homes, "Yankee Doodle" was played in the streets, whiskey flowed freely among the Union soldiers, and news had reached General Patterson's men that Major-General George McClellan had won a series of victories in western Virginia. After a national salute was fired from the Union cannons in the city, the Union soldiers became uncontrollable. They would not obey their officers because of excessive drinking of alcoholic beverages. The Union soldiers began to force their way into residents' homes, destroying furniture by tossing it into the streets and shooting out windows. They left homes despoiled and mutilated. Some women pleaded tearfully with the soldiers, but they continued their physical and verbal attacks on civilians. Belle wrote, "Words from which the mind recoils with horror, which no man with one spark of feeling would utter in the presence even of the most abandoned woman, were shouted in the ears of the innocent, shrinking girls; and the soldiers of the Union showed a malignant, a fiendish delight in destroying the effigies of enemies whom they had not yet dared to meet upon equal terms in an open field of battle."

Belle's home was not spared from the violence. Union soldiers had heard that Belle's bedroom was decorated with rebel flags. A "big Dutchman" {a term used for German soldiers} was among the Union soldiers arriving at Belle's home. At first, the Dutchman confronted Belle outside her home and asked if she was "one of those damned rebels?"

Belle replied, "I am a Secessionist."

When Belle's grandmother knew what occurred outside of the house, she asked Belle to come into the house. "They were afraid because I was so saucy," Belle said later.

As the Dutchman turned and approached Belle's grandmother, he hurled the most abusive language at her. While the confrontation occurred, Eliza heard the commotion, removed the rebel flags, and burned them to protect the family.

When the Union soldiers entered the Boyd's house, Belle's mother could no longer stand the abusive language and stepped forward and said, "Men, every member of my household will die before that flag shall be raised over us!"

The Dutchman became abusive, and according to Belle, "the drunken brute grabbed her and tried to kiss" her mother.

By now Belle stood nearby on the stairway as the incident transpired between the Union soldier and her mother. Belle screamed at the soldier to turn her mother loose, but the soldier just "turned and grinned impudently" at her. Fearful for her family's safety and angry over the soldier's aggressiveness, she produced an 1849 Colt pistol that her father gave her before departing for the army. She fired one shot, mortally wounding the Dutchman in the neck. Belle later wrote, "I could not stand it no longer. My indignation was aroused beyond control, my blood was literally boiling in my veins."

The other Union soldiers threatened to shoot Belle. She said many years after the war: "I just threw open my arms and said men who wear your uniform are cowards, and only those who are cowards shoot women. Now shoot." The Union soldiers turned away from harming Belle.

While the soldier's comrades removed the wounded Dutchman from the house, other Union soldiers prepared to burn the house to the ground. Eliza rushed off to General Patterson's headquarters for help. Finally, a provost detail of guards arrived to restore discipline and order. The Dutchman, who Belle shot, was mortally wounded, and died later. Belle never had any remorse for killing the soldier because of the insults, threats, and perhaps the possibility of rape and death posed to her mother.

Belle did not reveal the Dutchman's name and may not have known his identity. The dead soldier's identity is believed to be

Private Frederick Martin, Company K, 7th Pennsylvania Volunteer Infantry, a ninety-day regiment organized in April 1861, composed mostly of companies from Allegheny County, Pennsylvania. A soldier named Martin was buried in a Martinsburg cemetery on July 7, 1861, and War Department records give no reason for his death. Neither was there ever an official report written about the shooting incident. After searching the Union roster for the 7th Pennsylvania Volunteer Infantry and its history of short service, I could not find any record of a Frederick Martin of Company K. However, I found the name, Fritz Martin. Fritz is commonly used in German instead of the original Frederick. I did not discover any other reports or records surrounding the shooting incident at Martinsburg; it was ignored, even though newspapers reported it, and even they did not give a regiment or name of the deceased victim. The only reason for the Union high command's failure or deliberate suppression for not reporting the shooting or the cause of death of Private Martin could only be the embarrassment it would cause Union authorities in Washington and the Union army at Martinsburg. This shooting incident was a first during the war but not the last time a young lady shot and killed a soldier.

Through the years, some authors and historians have believed that Belle's shooting of a Union soldier is a myth and was imaginary to sell her memoirs. Still, there were Northern and Southern newspapers that printed different versions. One was the Knoxville, Tennessee, *Daily Register* newspaper. On the front page was written an article about Belle Boyd. The publication wrote she was "this fair and fearless Virginia heroine whose daring defense of her father's house and those valuable services have won her from the Northern press the title of the most courageous and dangerous of rebel female spies."

On July 5, another newspaper reported on the Dutchman's shooting: "Miss Belle Boyd, a young lady of this city shot and killed a federal soldier here yesterday when the latter entered and searched her home on South Queen Street. In celebration of Independence Day, the federal soldiers' occupation of the city, under Maj. Gen. Robert Patterson, were given a holiday. The city's streets were filled with soldiers shouting, cheering, and singing. Several of the homes were entered forcibly by the soldiers, one of which was the Boyd home, owned by Mr. and Mrs. Benjamin Boyd."

Shortly after, the commanding officer and several staff officers arrived at the Boyd home and interviewed Belle, Eliza, Belle's mother, and the soldiers who illegally entered the family's home. Patterson inquired into the circumstances surrounding the shooting incident with impartiality and concluded that Belle had acted in self-defense, and did "perfectly right" in the circumstances, and under the same environment, he hoped every Southern girl would do the same.

To protect Belle's family after the shooting incident and to watch her carefully, sentries were placed around Belle's home. Every day an officer inquired if they had any complaints and were always on their best behavior. Belle took advantage of every opportunity to become acquainted with them because they provided information and intelligence. Later when Belle was on the lecturing circuit, she revealed, "It was gay company at our house that year after the Federals came. Their young officers were often on our veranda. I was young and lively, too. So, I just hung about and heard all I could of the Union plans to carry to Jackson." She added later in her memoirs that during this time, her Union acquaintances were opportunities "the rebel spy did not fail to turn to account on more than one occasion." The Union officers were not the only ones who shared the veranda of Belle's house. Instead, she said, "Ward Hill Lemon, Lincoln's law partner, Paul Nicholson of the *New York Herald*, Theodore Davis, *Harper's* skillful artist, were there at times."

During General Patterson's occupation of Martinsburg, while Belle was acting the part of the ministering angel to the wounded in the improvised hospital, she was spying. While engaged in her nursing duties, many scraps of information concerning the movements of the Union army came to her ears. Thus, with impulsiveness and ardor due mainly to her youth, she entered the task with which her name became so prominently identified. Several other ladies acting in concert with Belle had also been picking up scraps of news. They held meetings at Belle's home. The items were bunched together on paper, and the documents were placed in the hands of a trusty house servant for transmission to General Jackson. This routine continued until one day when a messenger was captured by the Union pickets and compelled to disclose their mission.

Belle wrote in her memoirs the covert information she sent to General Jackson was either revealed through an "accident or treachery." Since Belle began her career of spying and espionage, she made the mistake of not sending her messages in cipher, a specific type of coded letters and numbers, which she had not learned this early in the war. Instead, Belle and others wrote out their messages in long hand, which was quickly identified. Belle was specifically arrested and brought to the provost's headquarters. During the Civil War, the provost marshal-maintained law and order among the military and civilian populations. The provost marshal was a judge, jury, and, if need be, executioner in carrying out military law. The provost marshal reprimanded Belle, and then he read the *Articles of War* empathetically. The *Articles of War* declares:

Whosoever shall give food, ammunition, information to, or aid and abet the enemies of the United States Government in any manner whatever, shall suffer death, or whatever penalty the honorable members of the court martial shall see fit to inflict.

When Belle was arrested, she remained calm and did not lose her temper. Instead, she gave the impression she did not understand or realize her offense's gravity. Belle got off easy. Before leaving the provost headquarters at the Berkeley County Courthouse, the provost marshal reminded Belle that the next time the punishment would be carried out. She became angry at the comment but kept her composure and instead curtsied and thanked him. Throughout the Union occupation of Martinsburg, Belle was constantly suspected of spying and aiding the Confederate forces.

The warning from the provost marshal was still not enough. She felt determined to keep up her spying activities and do all she could for the Southern Confederacy. That included systematic pilfering of weaponry, ammunition, and other supplies that could be smuggled out of Martinsburg and South for the Confederate army. Belle wrote, "I had been confiscating and concealing their pistols and swords on every possible occasion, and many an officer, looking about everywhere for his missing weapons, little dreamed who it was that had taken them, or that they had been smuggled away to the Confederate camp, and were actually in the hands of the enemies, to be used against themselves."

Belle's role became less significant, and things were quieter in Martinsburg when the war shifted east to Manassas in Northern Virginia. At Manassas, General P. G. T Beauregard commanded a 22,000-man Confederate army along Bull Run Creek. The 35,000-man Union Army of Northeastern Virginia, under the command of Brigadier-General Irwin McDowell, was threatening them. This initiated a withdrawal of General Johnston's forces to Winchester in supporting distance of General Beauregard. On July 15, General Patterson's army departed Martinsburg. Patterson's army began to advance south through the Shenandoah Valley toward Winchester to try and keep General Johnston's Confederates in the Shenandoah Valley and be unable to reinforce General Beauregard at Manassas.

Belle decided that even though there was a risk in covert intelligence, she would not give up her new vocation. Instead, she would perfect her skills and continue to serve the Southern Confederacy in any way she thought possible. For now, she departed Martinsburg and traveled forty-eight miles south to be with her Aunt Francis and Uncle John Stewart in Front Royal, Virginia, where it would be safe for now.

Although Belle had left town for Front Royal, Martinsburg still had its Confederate spies. Mrs. Charles Faulkner, the wife of Charles Faulkner, the former United States Minister to France, continued to spy. Some Martinsburg residents considered Mary W. Boyd Faulkner and her daughters to be more dangerous than Belle, and Faulkner used her social influence to accomplish her purpose.

Chapter 4

A Nurse & Courier

When Belle arrived at Front Royal, she took up residence in her Aunt Francis and Uncle John Stewart's small cottage behind their Fishback Hotel. Her aunt and uncle had expressed Southern sympathies that made it impossible for them to continue to live in their plush Washington home; Belle was happy with their choice of moving to Front Royal. Fewer than 500 citizens lived in the small village of Front Royal, the county seat of Warren County, Virginia. The village had a goods store, four churches, a courthouse, and many attractive private homes and was the only village of significance in the county.

When Belle arrived at Front Royal, she was amazed at the beauty of the town and the surrounding area. Belle described Front Royal and the surrounding area as a "picturesque village, which nestles in the bosom of the surrounding mountains." The beauty of the Blue Ridge Mountains and the Shenandoah Valley was "far beyond my power of description." For now, Belle and the village's citizens were far away from war except with the news events and some daily reminders of the struggle into which the new Southern Confederacy had entered. In the months following the outbreak of hostilities, many of the women at Front Royal formed sewing societies, making clothes for the soldiers, and were busy preparing food supplies for the soldiers at Manassas. But soon, the reality of the war at Manassas, Virginia, hit home and profoundly affected every man, woman, and child of the Front Royal community.

On July 21, 1861, Generals Beauregard and Johnston consolidated their Confederate forces and defeated General Irwin McDowell's Union army along Bull Run Creek near Manassas. The battle was a decisive Confederate victory due in part because General Patterson was timid and failed to keep General Johnston's Army of the Shenandoah in the Shenandoah Valley. There were many casualties on both sides; everyone knew this would be a protracted bloody conflict. After the Union army retreated in a panic to Washington, the wounded and maimed had to be cared for on both sides. Since the Confederate army was the victor and remained along Bull Run Creek, they shipped the wounded to nearby makeshift hospitals for care. Front Royal, Virginia, was one of those communities where the wounded from both sides were transported and received care.

When the wounded began to arrive at Front Royal, Belle offered her services like many of the men and women of the community. As a nurse, Belle's duties were extremely laborious, lengthy, and trying hours of cleaning and wrapping wounds, feeding the helpless, and coping with the emotional stress of listening to the moans and cries of the wounded and dying. She was doing all she could do for their care. Thomas Almond Ashby, a lad living in the village, wrote his eyewitness account of what he witnessed during those early days of America's Civil War and about the hospitals: "Our Academy building was the first pressed into service. Benches and desks were removed, and beds were established. It was soon overcrowded, however, and the courthouse and two churches were converted into hospitals; and owing to the accommodations still being inadequate, additional quarters were required." Eventually, some vacant lots at the edge of the village where buildings were constructed as hospitals would still not be enough accommodations to house the sick and wounded.

After the battle at Manassas, the wounded and sick were so numerous that all available space had to be utilized. Thomas Ashby wrote, "All of our people, especially the women, were kept busy looking after the needs of this rapidly growing population." When it came to the women of Front Royal, he praised them for their tireless sacrifice and great effort. Ashby continued, "Too much cannot be said about the zeal and faithful serving of our women. They went to the kitchens and prepared dainties, visited the wards, and gave personal attention to the sick, looked after beds and bedding, and in many ways, added to the comfort of the hospital inmates. In their patriotism and unselfish service, no act of self-sacrifice was neglected. But for our women, these soldiers would have fared badly."

While at the hospital and nursing the sick and wounded in Front Royal, Belle heard of the daring exploits of a young girl from Washington by the name of Betty Duval. Betty Duval was a sixteen-year-old fragile-looking girl, remarkable for the sweetness of her temper and the gentleness of her disposition. She became a Confederate courier who carried a message tucked away in her long black hair from the Confederate spymaster, Rose Greenhow, in Washington, about General McDowell's planned attack against the Confederate army at Manassas. Betty Duval eluded Union army pickets, posing as a farmer, crossing the Potomac River, and delivering Greenhow's message to General Beauregard. Betty Duvall's actions and bravery had a significant influence on Belle. Betty inspired Belle because she felt a woman could contribute to the war effort other than nursing and laboring at home, making clothing, and other needed articles for the soldiers. Belle knew she was as bold, daring, and capable of doing the same duty and service for the Confederacy that Betty Duvall had accomplished.

After six to eight weeks of nursing the sick and wounded, Belle returned to Martinsburg to rest and recover her health. By October, Belle felt restless and missed her father. She knew the Confederate army remained encamped at Manassas and resolved to take her mother and visit her father and uncle, Lieutenant John Glenn of the 12th Virginia Cavalry. When they arrived at Manassas, they took up lodging in a large house with some other ladies, who also were visiting with their loved ones. While at Manassas, the bold and daring deed Betty Duval had accomplished before the Battle of First Manassas was still in the back of Belle's mind. Belle became a Confederate courier for General Beauregard through either the connections or influence of Lieutenant Glenn interceding with Colonel Ashby or someone else. Being a courier now meant that Belle was an agent for the Confederate intelligence service.

Civil War couriers carried important dispatches and papers from one officer to another in the army and sometimes endured the dangers of carrying information through enemy lines; they were not the coarse camp women or reckless women seeking adventure. Female couriers were almost always successful and invaluable for information. One time Rhode Island Cavalry {Most likely the 1st Rhode Island

Cavalry} chased Belle for five miles and fired on Belle while she carried information; Belle "escaped by her horsemanship and the superiority of her mount, her horse being and English thoroughbred." Belle recalled one time she came suddenly upon seven men on the road. "They made me dismount, asked me {Belle} where I was going and for papers."

Belle replied she had "no papers and was going home."

The soldiers threatened to search her, and "of course, I {Belle} didn't want that. So. Belle told the officer, "Captain, I've but one little paper that my father told me never to give up except to save myself from death in dishonor."

When Belle gave the Union officer a "small chamois skin bag," he opened it and discovered a Knight's Templars Cross, with a small note that Belle was a Knight's daughter. She must have suspected the officer was also a Mason because he briefly sent his men away, ordered Belle to take a horse, and warned her never to let him see her again.

While Belle smuggled or carried dispatches, she taught her horse Fleeter how to kneel on command to avoid Union patrols. Belle learned the countersigns and passwords to pass through the lines as a courier. This experience taught her how to become a covert agent and gather intelligence; in performing this kind of duty, historian T. C. Deleon believed Belle's daring deeds could be compared to that of "Molly Pitcher" of the American Revolution. One of the most significant efforts of spying and gaining information during the war came from the civilian population. They were a source of information, especially during the early days of the war, and Belle used them. John S. Mosby, who later, during the war, commanded a partisan ranger battalion in Northern Virginia and carried out irregular warfare behind Union lines, learned how valuable and reliable civilians could be when he had breakfast with them after serving on outpost duty near Washington during the early days of the war. Mosby wrote in his memoirs, "In the mornings, I ate breakfast with the local civilians, becoming more and more acquainted with them. They knew the area roads, paths through the wooded areas, the surrounding landscape, and streams. They could also get Northern newspapers. I began to realize the utmost importance they would serve during the war once I received my command."

General Beauregard and Stonewall Jackson, who had been promoted to major general on October 7, 1861, used Belle over several weeks to carry messages for them. Belle was good at courier duty because she knew the location of the Shenandoah Valley from Martinsburg to Harrisonburg and the mountain gaps. Sometimes Belle used a pet dog running beside her to carry the messages in a disguised layer of skin.

While running dispatches for the general officers, Belle also smuggled quinine, a good drug for treating malaria. Like most smugglers, she crossed the Potomac River into Maryland at Pope's Creek, less than two miles wide. The area is the same area that John Wilkes Booth and David Harold used after the Lincoln assassination. In 1943, the Washington *Evening Star* published what one man remembered his mother telling him about Belle: "She {Belle} was one of the 'story' subjects of the tales my mother told me. It was not so much as a Southern spy that my mother spoke of her, but as the bearer of much-needed quinine for the malaria patients of Virginia."

One incident of amusement involving Belle and some soldiers of General Beauregard's army occurred while she was at Manassas. It involved Belle selling some whiskey she had smuggled from the Maryland shore to a soldier, which eventually caused havoc among other soldiers from her home area of Berkeley County. An article appeared in the Washington *Evening Star* on November 6, 1861: "A fight occurred in Beauregard's army, between Borden's Guard and the Wise Artillery, when a number were wounded, including Captain John Q. A. Nadenbush, of the Berkeley Guards, and Captain E. G. Alburtis of the Wise Artillery. The fracas arose in consequence of a woman named Belle Boyd refusing to sell a bottle of whiskey to a soldier. She demanded two dollars for a pint bottle; soldier offered one; Miss Boyd refused to sell; soldier seized the bottle, woman drew a knife; soldier did the same; Wise Artillery interfered in behalf of the woman, and Borden's Guard Artillery for soldier. It was a fierce conflict and was only ended by the interference of general officers. Twenty or thirty were badly wounded."

General Jackson soon commanded the Valley District with his headquarters at Winchester, Virginia, and Belle soon arrived in Winchester.

On Belle's return to Martinsburg, Belle stopped at Winchester. While in the city, she called upon another young lady her age, Kate Sperry. How they knew each other is not of record. In some way, Kate was like Belle. She was high-spirited, opinionated, and often an outspoken rebel who resisted the Union's cause and authority while they occupied Winchester. On one occasion, Kate had been accused by a Union officer of being un-lady like. Kate knew of Belle's notoriety. Her opinion of Belle: "wild, reckless," and a "fast girl she beats all."

On Saturday, October 26, 1861, Belle visited Kate Sperry at her home in downtown Winchester. Kate was not impressed with their meeting, believing Belle was insane by her dress and conversation. Later that evening, Kate committed her thoughts of Belle to her journal, writing, "Belle Boyd from Martinsburg, called this afternoon and of all fools, I ever saw of the womankind she certainly beats all… perfectly insane on the subject of men… a dark green riding dress with brass buttons down the front, a pair of Lieutenant Colonel shoulder straps… a small riding hat with a row of brass buttons on the rim of every state in the Confederacy…a gold palmetto breast pin and a real genuine palmetto stuck straight on top of her head…no brains and you have a full picture of the far-famed Belle Boyd. She is the fastest girl in Virginia, or anywhere else, for that matter. Since the army has been around, her senses are perfectly gone…she is just from Centreville, where the army is now…staid {stayed} there a week, and what with her Staffs, Colonels, Generals, Lieutenants, etc., she is entirely crazy."

Belle always left an impression on everyone with whom she associated. Many young women living in Winchester and Front Royal painted an unfavorable picture of her and drew their conclusions of how she portrayed herself. Belle was not your ordinary conventional woman of the times, who "had been brought up under the institution of slavery and knew little of the hard drudgery of domestic service." Many young women, with whom Belle associated herself in Winchester and Front Royal, had been taught to direct the management of the home and do delicate needlework but not the

42

heavy work around the kitchen and in the house. Mostly trusted servants tended to the house and its duties. Instead, most young women of means played the piano, sang songs, read good literature, and lavishly entertained, primarily only associated with other women of their class in society. Wherever Belle was or whoever she was associated with, she was always the center of attention and very independent-minded, and very outspoken, which was un-conservative for the times. Her personality sometimes caused envy among others of the same gender and age and left an unfavorable impression. Belle had left such an unfavorable impression on Kate Sperry that Belle was still on her mind several days later and still the topic of conversation because, on October 31, 1861, Kate again committed to her journal, "Ella Murphy and I took a long walk this morning and discussed Belle Boyd…came to the conclusion that she's a fine specimen of an addle-brained girl and that the less one associates with her the better morals and everything else."

Winchester, Virginia, was a city with citizens loyal to the Union and acting as spies. How much of Belle's behavior in Winchester was a charade? The Union spymaster, Elizabeth Van Lew, or as she was known, "Crazy Beth," lived in Richmond, Virginia. She was educated like Belle but was an expert at disguising her real intentions. Some believed Van Lew was mentally ill and did not give her too much attention to the activities she pursued. But then, too, I am of the impression also that Belle was at this time amateurish at spying and someone who demanded attention, regardless of how she obtained it, perfecting that attribute for when it came time to return to Front Royal in the winter of 1862 and use it as a weapon against Union soldiers.

After several weeks, Belle returned to Martinsburg. She found Martinsburg was not the prosperous community it had been before the war, but it had changed. One observer wrote, "Business was almost entirely suspended in Martinsburg during the first year of the war, and at times a great deal of distress prevailed, for lack of the necessities of life, which were hard to obtain. Considerable damage was done to buildings, but not as much as would be expected, considering the fighting done here and the length of time soldiers occupied the town."

During the fall of 1861, Colonel Turner Ashby's 7th Virginia Cavalry picketed the Potomac River from Harpers Ferry to Little

Georgetown. During this time, he had his headquarters at Martinsburg. While at Martinsburg, he was initiated into the Masonic order, the same lodge where Belle's father was a member and now a fraternal brother to Ashby. He was "induced to join the Masonic fraternity through his love for the principles of the order that, during the war, was exercised over the men in the army as a vast influence." Belle does not record in her memoirs whether she had seen or spoken with Colonel Ashby. Still, she is likely to occasionally visited his headquarters since Martinsburg remained under Confederate occupation to build the trust needed with her covert activities. Another necessary acquaintance Belle made during the autumn of 1861 was Harry Gilmor, who later, during the war, commanded an independent partisan ranger cavalry organization.

One adventure during the early winter month occurred near Martinsburg involving Belle. One evening, she rode with two Confederate officers, one a relative she did not identify when her young, high-spirited horse suddenly took fright and ran away with her. The horse carried her among some Union soldiers. At first, she felt uncomfortable, not knowing how to handle the situation, but she decided that valor would be the better use of judgment. With her mind determined, she rode to one of the officers, explained that her horse had become uncontrollable, and carried her into their line. The Union officer was courteous and offered to escort her back to her friend and relative, not knowing they were Confederate cavalrymen. He assured her not to fear the "cowardly rebels," which angered her.

Belle's friend and relative were waiting behind some bush when suddenly they appeared and seized the two Union officers. Belle felt amused and said, "Here are two prisoners that I brought you," continuing, "Here are two cowardly rebels whom you hope there was no danger of meeting."

The Union officers asked about Belle's identity. She answered, "Belle Boyd at your service."

One officer shouted, "Good God! The Rebel Spy!"

The two captured Union officers were returned to headquarters and were detained.

Belle does not give a place or area where this incident occurred or the identity of the two Union officers or their assigned unit. But from

October to the end of December, she was in Martinsburg with her family and not at Front Royal, which was behind Confederate lines. However, according to the historian of the 1st Maryland Potomac Home Brigade Cavalry, or as they would be later known, "Cole's Cavalry," the battalion was patrolling the Potomac River near Williamsport, Maryland, eight miles north of Martinsburg. These soldiers could have been attached to this command because these men left Frederick around the first of December for scouting duty along the Potomac River. They were known to scout south of the Potomac River toward Martinsburg. Or the captured Union soldiers could have been officers from the 13th Massachusetts Infantry, who were on picket duty along the river at Williamsport. Even though Belle did not mention it in her memoirs, she rode on a scout with several of Ashby's men, which must have been when the incident occurred.

While Belle was in Martinsburg, her father had returned from the army on sick leave and was, at the end of December, preparing to return to the Confederate army. Benjamin Boyd feared for Belle's safety. With Colonel Ashby's cavalry moving back to Winchester, it would only be a matter of time before the Union army once more occupied Martinsburg. Belle returned to Front Royal to stay with Aunt Francis and Uncle John Stewart.

Source: *Author's Collection*

Front Royal, Virginia

Chapter 5

Front Royal, Martinsburg, & Imprisonment

On January 1, 1862, Belle and her cousin, Alice Stewart, received Miss Lucy Rebecca Buck as a guest at Stewart's home. Lucy came from a prosperous and influential family of Front Royal, who owned the "Bel Air" estate, located on an elevation less than a quarter of a mile east of the village. Lucy enjoyed socializing because guests always filled her home. Belle had never met Lucy until that day. After spending time with Alice and Belle, Lucy was not impressed with her first meeting with Belle Boyd. She spoke favorably about Alice but not Belle. Later that evening, she wrote in her journal, "Mailed my letter and went to Miss Stewart's. Saw Alice, Fannie, Miss Boyd and was introduced to one of the young disciples of Esculapius. Tho' not at all favorably impressed with the two latter individuals, one seemed all surface, vain and hollow; the other rude and evasive. It was my first acquaintance with Alice, and I was much pleased with her. Chatted awhile and had some music, and we then went down to Dr. Brown's, where we spent a most pleasant hour. I never knew the Misses B. so agreeable and friendly." Lucy continued to write, "Felt very much dissatisfied with myself tonight when reviewing the events of the day…there was a consciousness of having compromised my dignity in mingling upon terms of equality and apparent friendship with persons whom in my heart I despise…persons whom I felt to be false and heartless. I never am brought in contact with such persons without feeling a conviction that if forced to confine myself to their society, I shall become as frivolous apparently as they."

During the winter months of 1862, Front Royal and other communities in Virginia had received a reprieve from the horrors of war because both major armies had suspended active campaigning during the winter months. But that did not last long. Both armies,

Major-General George B. McClellan's new Army of the Potomac, which had been in Washington and was reorganized from General Irwin McDowell's old Army of the Northeast, and General Joseph Johnston's Confederate Army of the Potomac {soon to be the Army of Northern Virginia}, who had gone into winter encampment at Manassas were once more on the move. General Stonewall Jackson's small 3,000-man Valley District army had spent the winter in Winchester. On March 11, 1862, they evacuated the city and retreated up the Shenandoah Valley toward Harrisonburg upon approaching a much larger Union army under Major-General Nathaniel Banks.

While General Jackson's army was pulling out of Winchester, Lucy Buck prepared to walk with several lady friends and a gentleman when her cousin Mary and a friend Emma Cloud arrived at the Buck estate. Upon invitation to walk with her, Lucy's cousin and her friend declined to join in on the fun and instead decided to stay at "Bel Air" and "make themselves at home." That evening, Lucy recorded in her journal for March 11, 1862, "So we had a merry walk to town, Nellie, Nannie, Scott, and myself…first we went to pay my bridal call on Kattie Samuels. Found her in her room dressing for dinner…she was looking well…. full of chat and is evidently of the opinion that all the virtues pertaining to manhood are concentrated in one individual…that individual Mr. Samuels. Ah…well-a-day. I hope she may ever think thus, but I feel sad to hear young brides indulging in such bright anticipation as these…I think of the contrast between married life as they imagine it to be and married life as they will find it to be ten years hence."

After leaving Mrs. Boone's residence, Lucy's day changed dramatically. She decided to visit Pollie Haynie at the Fishback Hotel. After entering the hotel, Lucy wrote that she was "seized on my way by Alice S. and Belle Boyd, who insisted on carrying us captive into the parlor…made our escape but were recaptured in Miss Pollie's room and forced in self–defense to comply with their request to sing and play. Our audience consisted of Dr. Dorsey, the young physician and some of the ladies…made Dr. Blackford's acquaintance…not at all favorably impressed."

Lucy did her best to be sociable, singing songs to Belle's piano playing and trying to make the most of the situation. Still, when she returned home, she remained unimpressed with Belle Boyd or entertained but was glad the evening had ended.

The next day, March 11, Lucy Buck recorded in her diary, "Fannie Stewart and her father leaving tomorrow for the South fleeing the enemy." After Stonewall Jackson's army evacuated Winchester the previous day, John Stewart knew Brigadier-General James Shields's Second Division of the Army of the Potomac's Fifth Corps under Major-General Nathaniel Banks would occupy Winchester and the surrounding area. John Stewart decided to take his wife and their daughter, Fannie, and travel to Richmond, leaving their oldest daughter, Alice, Belle, and their grandmother, Ruth Burns Glenn, to stay behind and oversee the hotel's operation. There was much uncertainty among the civilians living in Front Royal after the Union army occupied Winchester, twenty-five miles away. They knew it would be a matter of time before the Union army appeared in their village. According to Thomas Ashby, "the hopes of the people were greatly depressed, and all fully realized the gravity of the situation."

The citizens of Front Royal were apprehensive over the soon-to-be enemy presence in their village. Thomas Ashby remembered, "Many of our people had shipped their most valuable horses, cattle, and other personal property within the Confederate lines, only keeping stock as was needed for farming purposes. Stores and businesses were closed, but our farmers went on cultivating their crops with as much diligence as conditions would permit; for at this stage of the war, we did not know what effect an invading army would have upon the lives and property of our people, whether all rights would be swept away, or our old men, women, and children would be insulted, imprisoned, and maltreated, and our property confiscated."

On March 23, 1862, General Stonewall Jackson's small army came storming back down the Shenandoah Valley. It engaged General Shields's division in a battle at Kernstown, several miles south of Winchester. After fighting all day, Stonewall Jackson's men were defeated by General Shields's men. General Jackson's men retreated up the Shenandoah Valley. However, it would be the only time during the war that the independent command of Jackson would suffer a defeat at the hands of the Union army.

The following day, news spread to Front Royal of General Jackson's defeat at Kernstown. Lucy Buck wrote in her journal, "Twas a miserable Yankee trick, a trap which they had laid for him, for when our little army of 3,000 advanced, it was immediately surrounded by 20,000 {8,000} of the enemy lying in wait for them. Jackson stood his ground manfully and only retired after killing ten to one of the enemy and losing three pieces of artillery."

Belle knew her father was retreating down the Shenandoah Valley with General Jackson's army, and Belle became concerned for her mother's safety since she remained behind Union lines at Martinsburg. She became increasingly alarmed and decided it would be best to return to Martinsburg to look after her mother's welfare as soon as possible. Belle left her cousin Alice and her Grandmother Glenn to watch over the hotel. Belle did not record the day in her memoirs when she left for Martinsburg. Captain David Strother, from Martinsburg and was personally acquainted with Belle, arrived at the hotel in Front Royal with a cavalry patrol on March 27. He kept a diary during the war and did not record a diary entry about meeting Belle at the hotel, where his cavalry patrol had paused for fifteen minutes that day. Surely since Belle and Captain Strother knew each other, there would have been some entry in either Belle or Captain Strother's writings. Therefore, Belle must have already departed for Martinsburg. They would not meet until May 19, 1862, when Captain Strother wrote an entry in his diary about Belle Boyd.

During the Civil War, men, women, and even children had to carry a document known as a pass to travel. The pass, issued by a provost marshal, allowed citizens to move freely from one town to another to visit or transact their business. Since Belle was within Union lines, she quickly secured a travel pass that allowed her to travel from Winchester to Martinsburg with her servant, Eliza. After entering a railroad passenger car for Martinsburg, a Union officer who recognized Belle, suspected her identity after someone had denounced her as a Confederate spy. After introducing himself as Captain Bannon, he asked, "Is this Miss Belle Boyd?"

"Yes," Belle answered.

Captain Bannon politely replied that he was the Assistant Provost Marshal in Winchester. He regretted he had orders for her detainment and she could not proceed until her case had been investigated.

While presenting her travel pass, Belle coldly informed Captain Bannon she and Eliza had permission to "pass on any road to Martinsburg."

Captain Bannon was in a dilemma because Belle had received her pass from General Shields to travel to Martinsburg, but there was an order for her arrest. He did not want to disobey either the order for her arrest or General Shields's permission for her to return to Martinsburg. To be ethical in his duties, Bannon decided to take personal responsibility, detain Belle with the prisoners he was taking to Baltimore, and turn her over to General Dix and let him decide. Belle submitted peacefully but later caused Captain Bannon and his guards some indignation. It happened when a Southern gentleman sat with Belle on the train and gave her a small rebel flag, which she began to wave and shout triumphantly. The Union officer and his men's anger soon subsided, and they began to take it as a joke.

While in Baltimore, Belle was detained at the Eutaw House, a large and fashionable hotel on the northwest corner of Eutaw and Baltimore Street. While detained, she was treated with courtesy and permitted to have visitations from friends. After a week had passed, General Dix, who was usually sympathetic to civilians, could not find any probable cause to detain Belle any long. Dix released Belle from custody and permitted her to return to Martinsburg.

Footnote: Disciple of Esculapius studies medicine and comforts a soldier injured on the battlefield.

Source: *Author's Collection*

Lucy Buck

Source: *Wikipedia*

Eutaw House Hotel

Chapter 6

Other Civil War Incidents

When Belle returned to Martinsburg after her brief arrest in March, she found Union soldiers occupying the town. The provost marshal, Major Charles Walker, Company B, 10th Maine Infantry, knew Belle had returned and immediately placed her under strict surveillance and forbade her to leave the town limits. These restrictions became intolerable for Belle. Belle's mother applied for two passes for Belle and her to travel to Front Royal via Winchester to be with their family. The provost marshal allowed the two women to leave, probably glad to see Belle leave Martinsburg.

Once Belle and her mother arrived in Winchester, they had difficulty obtaining permission to proceed to Front Royal. General James Shields's division had occupied the town and had prohibited all communications with Winchester. After pleading their case, Belle and her mother received permission to proceed to Front Royal from the provost marshal, Lieutenant-Colonel James Fillebrown, 10th Maine Infantry. Companies C, E, G, and I of the 10th Maine occupied the town behind General Banks's main force.

It was dusk when Belle and her mother reached the Shenandoah River near Front Royal. They found the bridge destroyed and no means of transportation but a ferryboat that the Union forces constantly used for their purpose. Through the courtesy of Captain Everhart, he helped them across the river. It was dark when Belle and her mother arrived at the Fishback Hotel, only to discover that General Shields and his staff occupied the premise as their headquarters and residence. Belle found her cousin, Alice, and Grandmother Glenn in the little cottage at the rear of the hotel.

After dinner, Belle sent her calling card to General Shields. He promptly paid Belle and her family a visit. After some conversation,

Belle asked for a travel pass to proceed to Richmond, but General Shields informed her there would be no need to issue her the document because he believed General Jackson's army was demoralized and would be eradicated in a few days, and she could travel to wherever she desired. He must have felt confident to speak so boldly to Belle and her family, but as Belle recorded in her memoirs, "a woman can sometimes listen and remember."

General Shields was an Irishman and a politician who served three different states in the United States Senate before his death in 1878. In 1842, Shields and Abraham Lincoln almost entered a duel until they were talked out of it. James Shields was a marksman; the course of history could have been dramatically changed that day if Shields and Lincoln had carried out the threat.

General Shields had reasons to be happy because, after Stonewall Jackson's defeat at Kernstown, he retreated to the upper Shenandoah Valley to the area of Swift Run Gap. General Banks's army followed Jackson's small army up the Valley and erroneously believed Stonewall Jackson had been whipped and was leaving the Shenandoah Valley. On May 1, General Banks and his army were ordered by President Lincoln from the upper Valley to return to the lower Valley. General Banks and his men went into camp at Strasburg, Virginia, not far from Front Royal, while leaving General Shields's division encamped at Front Royal, arriving there on May 14, according to young Thomas Ashby. General Shields's division would not stay at Front Royal. Instead, they had orders to cross the Blue Ridge Mountain at Front Royal into eastern Virginia and reinforce Major-General Irwin McDowell's Union force at Fredericksburg, Virginia.

General Jackson was not defeated and not about to give up the Shenandoah Valley so easily as Generals Banks and Shields believed, but instead, he was on his way to join forces with Brigadier-General Edward Johnson's 3,600-man Army of the Northwest, which was about the size of a brigade in northwestern Virginia to defeat the Union brigades under Generals Robert Milroy and Robert Schenck. On May 8, 1862, Jackson won a victory over the Union forces at McDowell, Virginia. General Jackson soon returned to the Shenandoah Valley with General Johnson's force. Now with Major-General Richard Ewell's 8,000-man division, which had been

55

watching General Bank's Union army in the Shenandoah Valley, General Jackson's army increased to 17,000 men. They had orders from General Robert E. Lee to keep the Union force in the Shenandoah Valley and impede any efforts to reinforce General McClellan's Army of the Potomac advancing on Richmond.

When General Shields came and paid his respects to Belle and her family, his young aide, Captain Daniel Keily, a young Irishman who later, during the war, became a brigadier-general, accompanied him. Captain Keily was smitten by Belle and, over the next several days while at Front Royal, began to send her flowers and notes, but according to Belle, "these were the days of war, not love, and there are still other ladies in the world besides the rebel spy." Although she did not have romantic intentions, Belle knew she could take advantage of his interest in her and knew there was the possibility of garnishing his information and intelligence to be sent to General Jackson. Belle never mentioned the identity of Captain K. in her memoirs in 1865 because the war still raged, and she wanted to protect his identity. However, young Ashby records a visit that she paid Captain Keily in June 1862 at Ashby's home, which I will address later.

After General Shields and Captain Keily departed from Belle's cottage, they returned to the hotel for a council of war in the parlor. Belle wasted no time and departed for the hotel soon after the officers left the cottage. Whether she suspected their intentions or just stumbled onto the meeting, she immediately took advantage of the situation once she knew the meeting was occurring. Belle knew there was a bedroom with a closet directly above the parlor. Then, inconspicuously, she walked up the stairway. When Belle entered the bedroom, Belle noticed a hole in the closet floor. Whether the Stewarts intentionally placed the hole in the closet floor for spying, Belle was not sure, but she intended on using it for such a purpose. After lying on the closet floor, she placed her ear against the hole in the floor and listened to General Shields and his staff below talking in the parlor for several hours. Belle took a significant risk because martial law is once established whenever an army occupies enemy territory and cities. General Shields's headquarters, the Fishback Hotel, would have been off limits to anyone other than those transacting business with Shields's staff or the provost marshal. If

56

Belle had been caught listening to General Shields's council of war, it could have resulted in dire consequences for her and her family.

When General Shields concluded the council of war sometime around 1:00 in the morning, Belle quickly returned to her cottage and wrote down everything she had heard the Union officers discussing in cipher. The Vigenere method is the cipher that Belle had learned to use. The Vigenere cipher encrypts alphabetic text using a series of letters of a keyword, a simple form of polyalphabetic.

Belle thought about using a servant, most likely Eliza, as her courier but rescinded the idea because she believed any disturbances would alert the Union sentries around the hotel and other nearby areas of town. Instead, Belle took one of the passes she had from time to time procured for Confederate soldiers returning south and had never been used before for her use such as this occasion. After getting past the sentries, she rode across fields, along roads, paths, and marshes through the nighttime darkness until she had covered about fifteen miles.

Finally, she arrived at the home of Mr. M. She did not give his identity because when she published her memoirs, the war still raged. She wanted to protect his identity from possible retaliation. Mr. M. invited Belle into his home when she informed him, she had vital intelligence for Colonel Turner Ashby. Mr. M. informed Belle that Colonel Ashby and his staff were camped about a quarter of a mile away in a wooded area, but as she was about to leave, Colonel Ashby entered the room and was surprised by Belle's presence. Belle remembered his greeting, "Good God! Miss Belle, is this you? Where did you come from? Have you dropped from the clouds or am I dreaming?"

After Belle assured him, he was not dreaming, she told him of how she had overheard General Shields and his officers discussing their plans to destroy General Jackson's army. She gave him the cipher message and departed for Front Royal.

What did Belle overhear during the council of war that General Shields and his staff discussed? First, she must have overheard Shields and his officers discussing their route east to join General McDowell's force at Fredericksburg since they believed General Jackson's army was demoralized and defeated in the Shenandoah

Valley. Secondly, since General Shields's 10,000-man division would be following a route east, they would follow Jackson's army as it moved toward Richmond, possibly trapping the Confederates and destroying them.

General Jackson's army was still in the Shenandoah Valley and was not moving east as Generals Shields and McDowell believed. Jackson knew that General Shields's division was moving east, but where was his division's destination? Was it to join forces with General McDowell or move toward Richmond? What Belle Boyd had overheard confirmed General Shields's destination. That intelligence given to Colonel Ashby now gave Stonewall Jackson enough information that he knew General Banks's army had been significantly reduced in number. A move down the Shenandoah Valley would enable Jackson to carry out General Lee's orders and pose a threat to Washington, keeping General McClellan from being reinforced in his efforts around Richmond. Also, it would be Jackson's opportunity to clean out all Union forces from the Shenandoah Valley. General Jackson could now make plans and march down the Shenandoah Valley, using the Massanutten Mountain {a small synclinal ridge, north to south in the Shenandoah Valley} as a shield to protect his army from detection by Union forces. And Jackson could advance unimpeded to Front Royal, overwhelming any small force located there and have the element of surprise over General Banks's army and its possible destruction.

After Belle left Colonel Ashby, she hurried back to Front Royal, passing a sleeping sentry, who tried to fire his weapon, but she disappeared so suddenly he could not get off a good shot. Then, after a two-hour ride, she returned home safely.

Source: *Warren Heritage Society*

Fishback Hotel

Source: *Warren Heritage Society*

Belle Boyd Cottage

General James Shields

Source: *Wikipedia*

Colonel Turner Ashby

Source: *Author's Collection*

Daniel Keily
(Keily is seated on the right)

Chapter 7

The Bluff

The following day when Belle had risen after her midnight ride to Colonel Turner Ashby, she learned that General Shields and his division had left Front Royal, leaving the 1st Maryland {Union} Infantry, two Companies B and G, 28th Pennsylvania Infantry, two Companies B and D, 5th New York Cavalry, and Battery E, Knapp's Independent Pennsylvania Artillery with two ten-pound Parrot guns. The small 1,000-man force was under the command of Colonel John Kenly, 1st Maryland Infantry. General Shields left them behind to guard a warehouse in Front Royal with $300,000 worth of U. S. Government commissary supplies.

Colonel Kenly and his men went into camp on a hill one mile north of Front Royal. The men of the 1st Maryland were well organized, with two companies being placed in the town and assigned as the provost guards, whose headquarters were established at the Fishback Hotel. Outposts and pickets were detached and stationed on the main roads that led into the village. According to Thomas Ashby, who was disloyal to the Union but had respect for the Union soldiers, wrote, "These Maryland men were well behaved, orderly, and kind to our people, and they created a good impression. At this time, all private property was protected, and, when needed for the use of the army, was paid for. The soldiers paid for the small things, such as milk, pies, cakes, and fruit. There was no disposition to rob or pillage." As for Colonel Kenly, Ashby had the highest regard for him by writing that he was "a gentleman and respected."

Now that Belle had returned to Front Royal, she hoped she would eventually be able to continue to Richmond to see her aunt and uncle, but first, she first sent her mother back to Martinsburg. On May 19, 1862, Belle came across an old family acquaintance serving as a

64

Union army officer: David Strother. Strother was from Martinsburg, and before the Civil War, he was an artist trained in Europe and the United States. Strother worked for *Harpers Weekly* under the pseudonym "Porte Crayon," covering the John Brown trail and the destruction of the Harpers Ferry arsenal at the beginning of the war. In 1862, he received a commission and served as an army captain on General Nathaniel Banks's staff.

Captain Strother arrived in Front Royal from Strasburg on a bright and warm day. After leaving the train, he went to the Fishback Hotel and was amazed at what he had witnessed. He wrote, "On entering the sitting room, I saw to my astonishment a pair of oil paintings, the products of my youth. A young lady came out and spoke to me. It was James E. Stewart's daughter; her father kept the hotel we were in. This revealed the history of the pictures, which I painted about the year 1837 in Martinsburg. Stewart rented my father's house and lived in it. Finding the pictures stored in a lumber room, he asked for the privilege of hanging them up. I gave them to him. Since that time, he has wandered to and fro upon the earth and, lately, for some years, has lived as a clerk in Washington. Dismissed from there, perhaps on account of his Southern proclivities, he has retired to this little secluded village to make a living keeping a tavern. Stewart was a playmate and schoolmate of my earlier youth, and we were also at college together. He was not at home but supposed to be in Richmond."

Captain Strother was amazed to find another Martinsburg acquaintance at the hotel who greeted him, writing, "Miss Belle Boyd also presented herself, looking well and deporting herself in a very ladylike manner. I dare say she has been much slandered by reports. She sported a bunch of buttons despoiled from General Shields and our officers and seemed ready to increase her trophies. The surroundings and polished conversation have softened me strangely, and I feel as if I would be glad to resign."

Captain Strother returned to Strasburg that evening.

Also, on May 19, 1862, Lucy Buck and her friends spent time together and spoke of events in Front Royal and how she could get some letters past the Union lines. Her answer came from one of her friends. Later Lucy recorded in her journal, "Cousin Mary Cloud,

Mrs. Kiger, and Katie Samuels spent the afternoon with us…a pleasant afternoon it was. Katie says Belle Boyd is in town enroute for Richmond and will carry letters through to be mailed for our friends within our lines…will write the boys by her. Poor boys!" When Lucy heard the news, she rushed off to write a letter, hoping Belle would deliver for her.

Before leaving for Richmond, Belle wanted to travel to Winchester. On May 20, 1862, Belle went to the hotel and requested a pass to travel to Winchester from the provost marshal, Major Hector Tyndale, an attorney from Philadelphia serving in the 28th Pennsylvania Infantry. At first, Major Tyndale refused her request but reconsidered his decision to issue the passes to Belle, her cousin Alice, and Eliza the next day.

Belle, Alice, and Eliza were up early and had a carriage prepared for travel, but the passes had not arrived. When Belle went to the hotel to inquire about the passes, she was informed that Major Tyndale and about 130 men departed Front Royal on "a scout." Major Tyndale and his men marched eleven miles south to Browntown, where they learned that some Louisianans had been the previous evening. Since Belle had no passes, this caused an unwanted inconvenience and perplexed her. When her journey to Winchester appeared in jeopardy, an acquaintance she identified in her memoirs as Lieutenant H, whose real identity is twenty-six-year-old Lieutenant Abram Hasbrouck, Company G, 5th New York Cavalry, approached and asked about her problem. Belle explained her case, knowing Hasbrouck could go to Winchester anytime he wanted, and his men were on picket duty that day on the road leading to Winchester. Bell began manipulating him with her pleas of innocence and mercies to intercede on her behalf and help her since he was a friend. The officer hesitated to intervene, and if he knew what awaited him in Winchester, he would have flatly declined to help Belle, but he consented to her request. Belle broke the rules of martial law without the travel passes that were required.

While everyone boarded the carriage to Winchester with Lieutenant Hasbrouck, Lucy Buck and two of her friends, Nellie, and Katie, walked over to the hotel. Lucy wanted to deliver a letter "in person to Miss Belle Boyd." Much to Lucy's surprise, she later wrote, "found a carriage at the door in which was seated the young lady with a Yankee officer...concluded not to entrust my letter with one who appeared upon such familiar terms with those whom we most dreaded, so crossing the street we went on up to see Cousin Mary and spent the day very pleasantly with her." This incident caused Lucy to be that much more apprehensive about Belle's presence and any trust in her to deliver letters in the future, but Lucy did not understand covert operations. To work covertly, one must disguise their true intentions, which means being friends with enemies such as Lieutenant Hasbrouck.

Shortly before arriving in Winchester, Lieutenant Hasbrouck ordered the carriage to halt, where he departed from Belle and her party's company to take care of some business at a Union encampment on the outskirts of Winchester. For some unforeseen reason, whether Lieutenant Hasbrouck's inability to return to Front Royal due to his business or another reason, their journey was delayed until the next day. It may have been on Belle's behalf that they did not return to Front Royal the same day because of a visit she received the following morning.

Belle, Alice, and Eliza stayed the night with friends in Winchester. Early in the morning, a gentleman of "high social position" called on Belle at her friend's house in Winchester, carrying two packages with specific instructions for Belle. Then, he asked, "Miss Boyd, will you take these letters and send them through the lines to the Confederate army?"

After requesting delivery of the letters, the gentleman pointed and instructed Belle, "this package is of great importance: the other is trifling in comparison." And pointed to a little note that he said was "a very important paper: try to send it carefully and safely to Jackson, or some other responsible Confederate officer. Do you understand?" Belle assured the gentleman she would give it her prompt attention and do all he requested.

Who was the mysterious gentleman who appeared at Belle's friend's house the day after she arrived in Winchester? The gentleman was William R. Denny. Before the war, William Denny was a prominent Winchester businessman, and the president of the Winchester and Potomac Railroad. The railroad operated a thirty-two-mile short line from Winchester to Harpers Ferry, where the railroad interchanged with the Baltimore and Ohio Railroad. He was also a lieutenant colonel in the 31st Virginia Militia, a reserve home guard unit. Denny was a known active spy by Southern and Northern citizens living in Winchester. Did Denny possibly know Belle and her covert activities through her cousin, William Compton, who also served in the 31st Virginia Militia and had also taken part in covert activities? She did not reveal the mystery, but again when Belle wrote her memoirs, the Shenandoah Valley Campaign of 1864 was being waged, and Winchester and the surrounding area were at the heart of the fighting between Confederate Lieutenant-General Jubal Early's army and Union Major-General Phillip Sheridan's army. How did Denny know Belle was in Winchester and deliver to her letters and, more importantly, a note for General Jackson? By now, Belle knew who Confederate operatives were in the area during the war and most likely sent her trusted servant, Eliza, to seek out Denny.

After William Denny departed, Belle gave the most critical documents to Eliza to be concealed on her person. If there were problems or trouble with returning to Front Royal, Belle did not believe Eliza would be subject to search. Most servants were never searched and could go anywhere and do as they please without molestation by Union soldiers. Belle wrote on the less critical package, "Kindness of Lieutenant H." and placed it in her basket.

Belle knew her enemies. She knew the provost marshal, Lieutenant-Colonel James Fillebrown, "was never displeased by a little flattery and a few delicate attentions." Belle went to a florist and sent him flowers with a note asking permission to return to Front Royal. She shortly received her answer. Fillebrown thanked her for her compliment and he issued travel passes so she could return to Front Royal.

Belle, Alice, Eliza, and Lieutenant Hasbrouck, who had rejoined them, were near the outskirts of Winchester when two crude-looking men, who later proved to be Union army detectives, approached. One detective called Belle by her name and informed her they had orders to arrest her. When she asked the reasoning, he answered it was "upon suspicion of having letters." She later learned that a disloyal household servant where Belle had visited in Winchester had

68

informed Union authorities. The detectives ordered the coachman to turn the carriage around and proceed to the headquarters of Colonel George Beal, 10th Maine Infantry.

Once they entered Colonel Beal's headquarters, Belle's cousin, Alice, appeared frightened. Belle remained concerned but kept her mind and knew she needed to use her cunningness and brace herself for the interrogation that was to follow.

Colonel Beal wasted no time and got to the point, asking Belle about the letters. She knew if she tried to deny their existence, they would all three be searched, and then she would lose any creditability with the colonel. Belle had placed her hand in her basket and drew out the small package with the inscription "Kindness of Lieutenant H." that was the least important and handed it to Colonel Beal. Immediately, Colonel Beal became angry because of the inscription on the package and asked if this was all she carried.

Belle took her basket with personal effects, turned it upside down with its contents falling on the floor, and invited Colonel Beal to look for himself. After noticing Colonel Beal was angry, she continued to inform him that Lieutenant Hasbrouck did not know that she had written his name on the package of letters. But she had already implicated him, and that, in Colonel Beal's mind, planted the seeds that there might be something more between Belle and the young officer than either admitted.

Lieutenant Hasbrouck turned very pale when he saw his name written on the letters and remembered that Belle had given him the small package, which he carried on his person. When Lieutenant Hasbrouck produced the small package, it contained the same inscription, "Kindness of Lieutenant H." just like the other letters. Colonel Beal became furious. In the package, the young officer unknowingly carried a rebel newspaper, *"The Maryland News-Sheet."* At this point, Belle played both sides of the game by defending Lieutenant Hasbrouck's innocence and hiding from Colonel Beal the most important note to be passed through the lines to General Jackson. William Denny likely knew Union authorities and disloyal servants were watching him and most likely knew Belle could be detained. Hopefully, after reprimanding her for the letters and package, she would be released with the most critical document for General Jackson. But Colonel Beal was not finished. He angrily asked what Belle carried, crumbled up in her hand. At first, Belle acted naïve but decided to play a game of bluff with Colonel Beal and said, "What, this little scrap of paper? You can have it if you wish: it is nothing. Here it is."

Belle approached Colonel Beal to hand him the paper with the most critical information for General Jackson. But fortunately, Colonel Beal ignored Belle and focused his anger on Lieutenant Hasbrouck. She had won what was as good as a military victory on the field. She succeeded in retaining possession of the note for General Jackson and in Lieutenant Hasbrouck's complicity in the whole scheme and turning attention from her. According to his military record, Lieutenant Hasbrouck was dismissed from the service in December 1863 by court-martial, but not for the episode with Belle and Colonel Beal at Winchester. He was court-martial "on the charge of selling government horses." Surprisingly, he returned to active service again on September 20, 1863. This could have only happened if Lieutenant Hasbrouck had been acquitted of selling government horses.

Belle won her release and returned to Front Royal. Still, Union authorities in Winchester sent Major Tyndale a telegram informing him that Belle needed to be watched after the accusations and suspicions brought against her at Winchester. Major Tyndale was already angry with her because of leaving Front Royal without a pass and wanted her arrested, but nothing came of it.

On May 31, 1862, a *Philadelphia Inquire* correspondent wrote an article, later republished in the *Washington Star,* surrounding the event in Winchester: "I have the following statement from an officer who participated in the battle at Front Royal: After you left Front Royal, Belle Boyd made a trip to Winchester in company with a cavalry officer. While there, she was arrested by the military authorities, but with her usual adroitness and assumed innocence she got clear of any charge of treachery, and returned to Front Royal again."

When word got around Winchester about Belle Boyd's episode with Colonel Beal, loyal Union resident, and diarist Julia Chase wrote, "our troops and officers are not half strict enough." Julia Chase believed Belle Boyd should have been detained and imprisoned.

Belle was still free to pursue her vocation as *Belle Boyd: The Rebel Spy*.

Source: *Author's Collection*

Lieutenant-Colonel James Fillebrown, 10th Maine

S
Source: *Wikipedia*

Colonel George Beal, 10th Maine

Chapter 8

The Battle of Front Royal

On May 22, 1862, General Jackson and his 17,000-man army crossed the Massanutten Mountain at New Market Gap and descended on Luray, Virginia, about twenty-four miles south of Front Royal. From Luray, General Jackson used the Massanutten Mountain to shield his army from Union scouting cavalry details and moved as stealthily as possible toward General Nathaniel Banks's 7,000-man force at Strasburg, about twelve miles west of Front Royal. General Jackson hoped to come against Banks's left flank and rear, cutting his line of retreat down the Shenandoah Valley toward Winchester and the Potomac River and destroying his force. But first, Jackson had to eliminate the small Union force at Front Royal.

By the early evening of May 22, Major-General Richard Ewell's division of Jackson's army had marched within ten miles of Front Royal before camping for the night. Thus, the Union forces had not detected General Jackson's force and were still completely in the dark concerning Jackson's army.

The following day, May 23, Jackson's army trudged for hours through rain and ankle-deep mud toward Front Royal with the honor given to Colonel Bradley Johnson's 1st Maryland {Confederate} Infantry to lead the advance of his whole army. This honor was because Stonewall Jackson knew Marylanders were at Front Royal. He wanted to give his only Maryland infantry regiment the honor of being the first fighting organization in combat against their fellow state neighbors.

General Jackson continued to march his men toward Front Royal until they came to a wooded area overlooking the village. Once there, he diverted them onto a narrow path, the Snake Road, connecting them with the Gooney Manor Road, leading into Front Royal and avoiding the Union sentries along the main road. Again, Union sentries did not detect the movement.

Around 2:00 in the afternoon, the Maryland infantrymen surprised and struck the Union sentries about one and one-half miles from Front Royal. The Union sentries were overwhelmed and began to immediately fall back toward Front Royal, firing their weapons as they retreated.

On May 23, Belle had been sitting in the parlor of the cottage and reading to her grandmother and cousin, Alice, when suddenly a servant came rushing in and interrupted, crying the rebels were coming. Belle jumped, opened the door, and ran into the street. Standing in the street, she watched Union soldiers running through the street in confusion. One of the soldiers scurrying around was an officer. Belle stopped him and began to question him about all the excitement. He informed Belle that Generals Jackson and Ewell's troops were on the outskirts of the village, had captured the Union sentries, and were in great force moving toward the village. He also informed Belle that if they had time, they intended to remove as much of the quartermaster stores and the ordnance out of the warehouse away from possible capture by the Confederate forces. Still, if they could not, then they would burn the warehouse.

Belle wanted to garnish all the information out of the Union officer that she could, so she continued to press him for more details. The Union officer revealed to Belle they would fight for as long as possible and then burn the bridges after crossing the Shenandoah River before retreating to Winchester and joining forces with General Banks's command.

Belle raced back into the house and began ascending the stairway when A. W. Clarke, a correspondent for the *New York Herald*, almost knocked her down. Mr. Clarke asked Belle about all the commotions. When Mr. Clarke wanted to know what was happening, Belle jokingly informed him the rebels were coming and he must prepare himself for a visit to Libby Prison in Richmond. Mr. Clarke did not answer Belle but quickly returned to his room to get a small compass and his manuscripts and to depart with the Union forces. When Belle went to her room to get her opera glasses, she passed Mr. Clarke's door and immediately locked him in his room, making him her prisoner.

Belle did not like Clark because of his "extremely distasteful" advances at her, and he "endeavored upon several occasions to intrude his society upon" her. Belle wrote she was "forced more than once to bolt the door of the room," which she and Alice shared, "in his face." After the fight at Front Royal, A. H. Clarke became one of Belle's most prominent critics.

After disposing of Mr. Clarke, Belle raced out to her balcony and noticed the Confederate infantry advancing columns were less than a mile from town. Belle felt concerned because her father still served with Jackson's army on Brigadier-General Robert Garnett's staff and might be involved in the fighting.

The intelligence Belle possessed for Jackson was that Banks had about 4,000 men at Strasburg and a small force at Winchester that could be quickly reinforced by Brigadier-General Julius White at Harpers Ferry and Generals Shields's division, a short distance from Front Royal. General Fremont's 20,000-man army presently operated over the western boundaries of the Shenandoah Valley. Belle knew these Union forces could be easily concentrated against Jackson's army and would also easily outnumber his force. This information is what she acquired from William Denny that was written on the note she held clutched in her hand the previous day at Colonel Beal's headquarters in Winchester. Belle also knew the size of the Union force at Front Royal because she had been through their camps. This information would benefit Jackson and the note, which still had to be delivered. Belle made an error in one piece of that information she recorded two years later in her memoirs: General Julius White was not in command of the Union army at Harpers Ferry. He still served as a colonel in the western theater of the war. He was not promoted to brigadier general until June 9, 1862, when he was transferred east to Winchester. Colonel Dixon S. Miles commanded the Union army at Harpers Ferry in May 1862.

When Belle came down the stairway and raced out the door, several gentlemen who had professed loyalty to the Southern cause stood nearby. She requested that one of them volunteer to carry the information she acquired about the Union troops at Front Royal to General Jackson. They all declined. Belle took the initiative and started toward the advancing Confederate battle line. Belle wrote, "I put on a white sun bonnet and started at a run down the street, which was thronged with Union officers and men. I soon cleared the town and gained the open fields, which I traversed with unabated speed, hoping to escape observation until such time as I could make my way to the Confederate line, which was still rapidly advancing."

Belle was dressed in a dark blue dress with a white apron, which she believed was a sharp contrast in colors, making her an easy target for the Union soldiers to shoot and hit her. The skirmishing was sharp between the 1st Maryland {Union} Infantry, supported by Knapp's Pennsylvania artillery on Richardson's Hill, Colonel Bradley Johnson's 1st Maryland {Confederate} Infantry, and Major Reberdeau Wheat's Louisiana Tiger Battalion on Dickey Ridge.

When Belle cleared the town, the advancing line of Confederates stopped. The "rifle-balls flew thick and fast" around Belle, and more than one struck so near to her feet as to throw the dust in her eyes. The Union soldiers, who were firing from the hospital near the edge of town, began to fire on her because this was the direction the Union sentries were firing. Belle wrote, "numerous bullets that whistled by my ears, several actually pierced different parts of my clothing, but not one reached my body." While Belle made her dash, she was exposed to Union and Confederate artillery, whose shells she could hear whistling and hissing over her head. She was later quoted that she was "too scared to do anything but keep running." A Union artillery shell exploded about twenty feet before her, sending shell fragments in every direction. She fell flat on the ground to protect herself but shortly rose and continued toward the Confederate line with sheer determination and strength. Finally, she came to a fence, which she quickly passed over. She was now among the shouting Maryland and Louisiana infantrymen, praising her for her bravery; she encouraged them to press on toward the village rapidly.

Belle urged the Confederate soldiers to move quickly toward the village. But then she had second thoughts. At first, Belle believed she had made a costly error by urging the Maryland and Louisiana soldiers to press on toward Front Royal because she did not see a main line of supporting columns of infantry. However, that soon changed when she recognized an acquaintance from Shepherdstown, Virginia by the name of Henry Kyd Douglas, now an officer on General Jackson's staff. Jackson and his staff officers were near the Gooney Manor Grade wooded area and determining whether to push toward Front Royal. Captain G. Campbell Brown wrote that Belle was "running like mad down from a hill on our right, keeping a fence between her and the town and gesticulating wildly to us." Jackson sent Lieutenant Douglas to inquire about the urgency from Belle.

As Belle approached Lieutenant Douglas, he began to ask her a question, but she was out of breath and could not immediately comply with his request. When able, she produced the note from William Denny and began to inform Douglas about the strength of the Union force at Front Royal and their intentions to destroy the railroad bridge and the supplies at the warehouse they had been guarding.

Henry Kyd Douglas remembered Belle many years later when he wrote about his war experiences and serving under Stonewall Jackson:

In the early afternoon of the next day, Ewell struck the pickets of the enemy within sight of and negligently near Front Royal. They were driven in, and the small body of infantry supporting them was quickly routed. We stopped to form on a hill overlooking the small town of Front Royal, and the hurried movement of blue coats and the galloping of horsemen here and there told of the confusion in the enemy's camp. General Jackson, not knowing the force of the enemy there was so small or so unprepared by reinforcements for his approach, was endeavoring to take in the situation before ordering an advance.

I observed almost immediately the figure of a woman in white glide swiftly out of town on our right and, after making a circuit, run rapidly up a ravine in our direction and then disappear from sight. She seemed, when I saw her, to heed neither weeds nor fences, but waved a bonnet as she came on, trying, it was evident, to keep the hill between herself and the village. I called General Jackson's attention to the singular movement just as a dip in the land hid her, and at General Ewell's suggestion, he sent me to meet her and ascertain what she wanted. That was just my taste, and it took only a few minutes for my horse to carry me to meet the romantic maiden whose tall, supple, and graceful figure struck me as soon as I came in sight of her. As I drew near, her speed slackened, and I was startled,

78

momentarily, at hearing her call my name. But I was not much astonished when I saw that the visitor was the well-known Belle Boyd whom I had known from her earliest girlhood. She was just the girl to dare to do this thing.

Nearly exhausted, and with hand pressed against her heart, she {Belle} said in gasps, 'I knew it must be Stonewall when I heard the first gun. Go back and tell him that the Yankee force is very small…one regiment of Maryland infantry, several pieces of artillery, and several companies of cavalry. Tell him I know, for I went through their camps and got it out of an officer. Tell him to charge right down, and he will catch them all.

According to Belle, Lieutenant Douglas returned to General Jackson and the rest of his staff and told him everything she had said. Jackson rode forward, and according to several witnesses, who later wrote about the meeting between Belle and Jackson, recorded what occurred. One of them was Brigadier-General Richard Taylor. General Taylor was nearby and overheard everything Belle told Jackson and later recalled in his memoirs:

Past midday we reached a wood extending from the mountain to the river when a mounted officer from the rear called Jackson's attention, who rode back with him. A moment later, there rushed out of the wood to meet us a young, rather well-looking woman, afterward widely known as Belle Boyd. Breathless with speed and agitation, some time elapsed before she found her voice. Then, with much volubility, she said we were near Front Royal, beyond the wood; that the town was filled with Federals, whose camp was on the west side of the river, where they had guns in position to cover the wagon bridge, but none bearing on the railway bridge below the former; that they believed Jackson to be west of Massanutten, near Harrisonburg; that General Banks, the Federal commander, was at Winchester, twenty miles northwest of Front Royal, where he was slowly concentrating his widely scattered force to meet Jackson's advance, which was expected some days later. All this she told with the precision of a staff officer making a report, and it was true to the letter.

79

Another witness, Captain George Campbell Brown of General Ewell's staff, was present at the fight at Front Royal and wrote:

When we first approached Front Royal, even before the Cary drove in the pickets, we saw two or three citizens scampering across the field. Just as our Skirmishers became engaged, Henry Kyd Douglas called my attention to a lady who having made the circuit to the Eastward to avoid the Yankees came running towards us from town. He and A. S. Pendleton rode to meet her, she sent word by them to Gen. Jackson to push on only one Regt. was in town, and that completely surprised if we pressed on, we could get the whole. It was Miss Belle Boyd, who was to my eye very pleasant and ladylike in appearance and certainly had neither 'freckled face,' red hair, or large mouth, as the N.Y. Herald said she had. She seemed embarrassed by the novelty of her position but very anxious for us to push on.

Another witness who claims to have seen Belle Boyd with General Jackson and his staff was Private John Robson, 52nd Virginia Infantry of General Jubal Early's Brigade, General Ewell's Division. Private Robson wrote that Belle was "coming up to the General, who had turned to meet her, she began to talk with volubility. We, of course, could not hear what she was saying nor could even conjecture the impact of her mission, but it was the famous woman spy and scout, Belle Boyd." According to Private Robson, Jackson already knew much but not all the information, which Belle delivered. Private Robson wrote "we only needed Belle Boyd to confirm" the information that General Jackson already had in his possession.

Henry Kyd Douglas did not write in his memoirs that Belle met General Jackson, but General Taylor recalled General Jackson rode with him and his Louisianans. Not only did Belle recall meeting Jackson at this time, but he offered her a horse and an escort to guide her back to safety in the village. Private Robson and Captain Brown confirmed the meeting in their observations when they wrote their memoirs. Lieutenant Douglas recorded in his memoirs that Belle informed him that she must "hurry back, give her love to the boys, and to remember that they had not seen each other on this day." She soon disappeared among the houses, but it would not be the last time that Belle and Lieutenant Douglas would see each other that day.

On Belle's return to Front Royal, she noticed a man, dressed in civilian clothing leaning over a wounded Confederate soldier giving him "something from a brandy flask." The man removed his coat and placed it on the wounded soldier. Belle felt suspicious of the man that had helped the Confederate soldier because she did not recognize him. However, she did not confront him, that would come the following day.

As the Union pickets and skirmishers were moving back through the streets of Front Royal to join with Colonel Kenly's main force and artillery posted on Richardson's Hill northeast of the village, Johnson's 1st Maryland {Confederate}, Wheat's Louisiana Tigers, followed by the 6th Louisiana Infantry entered Front Royal. Town citizen Charles Eckhardt was at the courthouse and watched the Confederate soldiers march past. He quickly returned home, where he found General Taylor's men standing behind his home in battle line formation while the Union artillery fired at them. Eckhardt later wrote, "soon they marched through town, hot for the fight and eager in pursuit."

Lucy Buck wrote her eyewitness account of the fighting at Front Royal at 2:00 in the afternoon: "Going to the door, we saw Yankees scampering over the meadow below our house and were at a loss how to account for such evident excitement on their part until presently Miss B. White rushed in with purple face and disheveled hair crying…Oh my God! The Southern army is upon them…the hill above the town is black with our boys." Lucy continued her eyewitness account, "Leaning out the back window, we saw them, contrabands and Yankees together, tearing wildly by." Soon, according to Lucy Buck, scattered parties of Confederate infantry arrived and charged into the Union soldiers' ranks, when firing one volley the Union soldiers turned around, and it was "every man for himself" as they "scampered out of town like a flock of sheep…such an undignified exodus was never witnessed before."

When the fighting began at Front Royal, young Thomas Ashby was building a dam in a creek with some friends. His first indication that something was wrong was when a known Union sympathizer "scampered along a path near the creek." Ashby and his friends called out to the man, but he did not answer. Ashby quickly headed toward his home on the south side of town when suddenly he ran into the retreating Union infantry running down the street. Ashby was caught in the middle of the fight, recording later in his memoirs, "I heard the whistle of a bullet that passed by me and struck a house nearby; so, I turned on my heels and ran back to the main street, until I came to the house of a citizen whom I knew well, and there I found refuge."

The Union soldiers retreated down the street in significant disorder, "the Confederates following in equal disorder, firing their guns in the most irregular manner, and yelling and shouting like wild Indians. No one was hurt, and the disorder was more like a police riot than a fight between soldiers."

The Confederate forces under General Jackson now had complete control of the village, but the Union force still held Richardson's Hill northeast of the village, continuing to pound effectively the Confederates in a field with their artillery. The Confederate artillery could not respond because their guns did not have the long range like the Union artillery.

After the Confederates had control of Front Royal, Lieutenant Douglas recalled another meeting in the village with Belle in his memoirs, writing, "General Jackson with a semi-smile suggested that I better go with them and see if I could get any more information from that young lady. It took very little time to get into Front Royal and clean it out. The pursuit of the retreating Federals was kept up, and with cavalry, the infantry following as quickly as possible."

While the Union soldiers were retreating, Belle had been standing at an open hotel window with pistol in hand shouting at the Union soldiers, "Go cowards go! Go and tell Abe Lincoln how Belle Boyd betrayed his army."

Douglas wrote about what he witnessed in Front Royal and his subsequent encounter with Belle:

While this was being done, I looked for Belle Boyd and found her standing on the pavement in front of a hotel, talking with some few Federal officers (prisoners) and some of her acquaintances in our

82

army. Her cheeks were rosy with excitement and recent exercise and her eyes all aflamed. When I rode up to speak to her, she received me with surprised cordiality, and as I stooped from my saddle she pinned a crimson rose to my uniform, bidding me remember that it was blood-red and that was her 'color.' I left her to join the General.

If Belle had any additional information on the Union force at Front Royal, she did not disclose it in her memoirs, nor did Lieutenant Douglas disclose it in his memoirs.

As the Confederate forces began to round up Union prisoners and march them through the streets of the village, one of them was A. W. Clarke of the *New York Herald,* who Belle had locked in his room. Clarke had escaped from his room at the cottage by "climbing down two stories by means of the plaza roof and post" and then captured by Confederate soldiers. When he saw Belle, he shouted, "I'll make you rue this. It is your doing that I am a prisoner here." An inflammatory article appeared in the *New York Times* and other Northern newspapers against Belle and her role in the fighting at Front Royal, going so far as to call her "an accomplished prostitute." Belle believed A. W. Clarke was the author of the article, but he could not have been the author since he was held as a prisoner of war by Jackson's men until June 5, at which time he was released.

The 1st Maryland {Confederate}Infantry and the Louisiana Tiger's attack stalled because of the Union artillery. Lucy Buck recalled the shells were falling around her house, which was caught in an artillery crossfire. Lucy and her family were in much more danger than they perceived, and they remained in the "basement where we found some frightened contrabands assembled." But Lucy did not stay in the basement for an extended period. Instead, she wrote, "I could not bear the idea of being entombed ingloriously in the cellar while our deliverers were gallantly endangering their lives in our defense." Lucy and her friend Nellie went to the porch and began to give the soldiers water.

Shortly, General Taylor's brigade came up in support. Colonel Seymour's 6th Louisiana Infantry of General Taylor's brigade was called upon to "outflank the federal artillery from the west,"

83

Colonel Kenly had held Richardson's Hill for two hours, buying time for General Banks to organize a retreat to Winchester, but instead of using the time wisely, General Banks shrugged off Colonel Kenly's assessment as no more than a cavalry raid. Later General Banks reconsidered, but it would be too late for Colonel Kenly and his men.

As the 2nd and 6th Virginia Cavalry approached, Colonel Kenly believed his right rear between the two forks of the river would cut off his line of retreat toward Winchester; his position was untenable. Colonel Kenly escaped over the wagon and railroad bridges, burning them as he retreated. After safely across the river, he posted his artillery guns and infantry on a prominent hill known by the locals as Guard Hill. Guard Hill was a good position for the Union forces because it commanded the two bridges.

Immediately, General Taylor ordered the 8th Louisiana to lead the way across the burning bridge while ordering the rest of the men of his brigade to follow. Unfortunately, many of General Taylor's casualties did not result from combat wounds but injuries from trying to cross the burning bridges.

Colonel Kenly and his small force finally gave up the struggle and retreated, knowing the inevitable was near with the Confederate's effort to cross the bridges. Near Cedarville, Kenly's men were attacked by 250 Confederates from the 6th Virginia Cavalry. However, Kenly and his men fought valiantly, Kenly was wounded, and his command was annihilated.

The Confederate force under Stonewall Jackson defeated the Union force under Colonel Kenly at Front Royal, inflicting 933 casualties, with 750 captured. Only 130 officers and men survived the fight out of the 1,063-man Union force. The Confederates also captured the warehouse with the much-needed supplies and saved the two bridges from destruction. Jackson's total casualties at Front Royal were twenty-six men, and they captured Union artillery and tons of supplies. Front Royal was a one-sided and decisive victory for Stonewall Jackson during the Shenandoah Valley Campaign of 1862.

After the battle at Front Royal, Belle's exploits spread throughout the village, prompting Lucy Buck to write: "Speaking of boldness reminds me of an exploit attributed to Miss Belle Boyd Wednesday. Tis said that she wished some information conveyed to the army about the time of the keenest firing, and not being able to get anyone to go for her, she went herself to a most exposed point, where the bullets fell like hailstones about her riddling her dress. I know not what truth there is in the rumor."

It was more than a rumor when a courier arrived that evening at the Fishback Hotel with a message from General Jackson. Jackson's message read as follows:

May 23, 1862

Miss Belle Boyd,

I thank you, for myself and for the Army, for the immense service that   you   have   rendered   your   country   today.

Hastily I am your friend

T. J. Jackson, C.S.A.

Belle felt tired after she made her flight to the Confederate lines with the information she had in her possession from William Denny and from all she knew of the Union forces' design and position at Front Royal—the day at Front Royal had been rewarding because of her self-sacrificing act of reckless bravery and courage. Other than the message from General Jackson, the cheers, and hurrahs from passing enthusiastic Confederate soldiers greeting her, her father coming through the fight with only a slight leg wound but safe, and Belle's patriotic duty to her country, it all had given her the most excellent satisfaction. She believed she had served her country well on May 23, 1862.

As the wounded were being cared for, Belle's cottage that evening was used as a temporary hospital for the wounded and injured. Even though she felt fatigued, Belle was relentless and attended to dressing soldiers' wounds, alleviating their suffering, and consoling many. Belle had surprised many of her contemporaries with her daring recklessness in running across a field in an infantry crossfire. Now as the news spread about her bravery at Front Royal and reported by

Southern newspapers, she had solidified her position as a *Southern Heroine* and would be spoken fondly of around many Confederate campfires, taverns, public places, and homes in the South. In the North, Belle continued to be demonized by the newspapers, but she would be known by many, especially the Union soldiers, as the notorious and infamous *Rebel Spy*.

Source: *Wikipedia*

Colonel John Kenly, 1st Maryland

Source: *National Archives*

General Thomas "Stonewall" Jackson

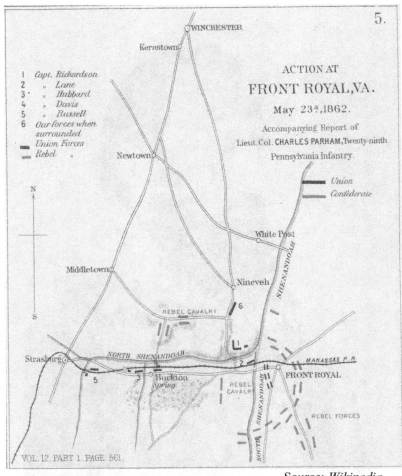

Source: *Wikipedia*

Battle of Front Royal

Source: *Author's Collection*

Henry Kyd Douglas

Chapter 9

General Shields Returns

On the night of May 23, both Generals Jackson and Ewell made their camp at Cedarville. The following day, May 24, Jackson, and his army began earnestly pursuing General Banks's Union army. Jackson planned to hit Banks's retreating army but was not sure of the route the Union force would use. Jackson sent out scouts from Colonel Turner Ashby's cavalry toward Strasburg and cavalry from Ewell's command toward Newtown {Stephen City} to try and determine the Union army's retreat. At the same time, Jackson ordered Ewell's division to march toward Winchester but not to advance so far as to be impossible for recall if necessary.

General Jackson received information from Brigadier-General George Steuart that General Banks's men were retreating down the Valley Pike toward Winchester. Immediately, Jackson sent his forces toward Middletown, which is about twelve miles south of Winchester. During this time, a Georgian from Ewell's division recalled his eyewitness observations while marching toward Winchester. The soldier's account was published in the *Marin Journal* on July 9, 1891, in which he said of Belle Boyd that "from Fort (Front) Royal to Winchester we saw her a few times on the march either riding with Jackson or some of his staff. After the capture of Winchester, we pushed on to Martinsburg, twenty-two miles toward the Potomac. We missed her when we left Winchester." Belle does not record this information in her memoirs, but this Georgia soldier vividly remembers seeing her. I believe the soldier's observations are valid from all I have read and studied about Belle. You may, too, will understand why Belle would be daring enough to do something like this when I write of another eyewitness account surrounding Belle in a later chapter.

While Belle remained in Winchester, another incident involved her the brief time Jackson's troops held the city. At Winchester, Belle learned that Jackson's men had captured a suspected Union spy. When she went to the provost marshal's headquarters, she asked to see the spy and be alone with him after recognizing the man from Front Royal. After Belle revealed her identity to the spy, she told him she knew he was a Union spy. Belle informed him that she had witnessed his Good Samaritan deed at Front Royal involving a wounded Confederate soldier. However, she warned him if "he had any papers, to give them" to her. Belle reassured him that he did not need to fear her betrayal. At first, the man denied he carried any incriminating papers. Finally, the man admitted he had papers in his clothing. Belle went and asked the provost for the man's clothing, and then she ripped them open and found papers that would have doomed the man. She later said, "If I hadn't seen him do what he did to that wounded Confederate soldier, I would have felt right that he suffers, but I couldn't after that, and so I destroyed the papers and reported nothing found. Of course, he was cleared as a spy and, after a time, let go." After the incident, every year, Belle received a Christmas box, and a card inscribed, "From One Who Remembers." Belle always believed it came from the Union spy.

At around 3:00 in the afternoon, General Jackson's men began to encounter the rear guard of General Banks's army near Middletown, Virginia. Brigadier-General Richard Taylor's Louisiana brigade was nearby and attacked the Union column. Around 4:00 in the afternoon, the Union rear guard column received reinforcements, but chaos began with Confederate cavalry, artillery, and infantry hitting them, causing the wildest confusion.

On May 25, General Jackson attacked General Banks's Union force at Winchester, but after a two-hour fight, the Union forces retreated through Winchester. In his *Official Report* to Secretary of War Edwin Stanton, Banks wrote that his "column suffered serious loss in the streets of Winchester. Males and females vied with each other in increasing the number of their victims by firing from houses, throwing hand grenades, hot water, and missiles of every description." After leaving Winchester, Banks and his men fled toward Martinsburg and other soldiers toward Harpers Ferry along the Potomac River.

Before the Union forces gave up Winchester, a gentleman of Southern sympathies visited Lieutenant-Colonel Fillebrown at his office before leaving the city. When asked by the Southern gentleman how the Union forces got caught in this trap and did not know of Jackson's army's approach, Lieutenant-Colonel Fillebrown pointed at the flowers he had received from Belle and answered, "That bouquet did all the mischief: the donor of that gift is responsible for all this misfortune."

While General Jackson's army moved beyond Winchester to drive the Union army from Virginia soil, he sent his old brigade, now under the command of Brigadier-General Charles Winder, to threaten Harpers Ferry. On May 30, Winder's men were recalled from the Harpers Ferry area and marched back toward Winchester, where Jackson's army began retreating up the Valley. Why was Jackson retreating? President Lincoln had become concerned over Jackson's recent victories and his Confederate army hovering along the Potomac River. President Lincoln was unsure if the Confederates would cross and threaten Washington. He called for General Banks to take the remnant of his army and attack Jackson's rear. Simultaneously, General Freemont approached from the west and General Shields from the east. They planned to cut off Jackson's army and possibly destroy it as it moved south through the Shenandoah Valley.

While General Jackson's army escaped, General Shields's First Brigade, commanded by Brigadier-General Nathan Kimball, neared Front Royal. The 12th Georgia Infantry, commanded by Colonel Z. T. Conner, knew they were vastly outnumbered and began a retreat from Front Royal to rejoin Jackson's army. On Friday, May 30, Thomas Ashby wrote, "we were thrown into the greatest uneasiness by the sudden breakup of the camp of the Twelfth Georgia Regiment and its march out of the village." After the Georgians departed, their camp was "ransacked by the people of the village" when "a piece of artillery was run up without warning, on a hill one mile south, and a shell was thrown into the camp. Men, women, children, colored and white had come out to plunder the camp but now fled in a panic. Just before leaving the village, the Confederates had set fire to the depot," and hundreds of thousands of dollars-worth of supplies were destroyed. It was not long before Union cavalry arrived in Front

Royal, dashing through the street in pursuit of the retreating Confederate infantry.

The Union cavalry caught up to the 12th Georgia Infantry several miles south of Front Royal, capturing 160 prisoners. According to Lieutenant-Colonel Franklin Sawyer of the 8th Ohio Infantry, he recorded "among our prisoners was the celebrated Belle Boyd." Belle's reputation had considerably grown and was widely publicized in the Northern newspapers. On May 31, 1862, an article appeared in the Washington *Evening Star*, written first by a correspondent for the *Philadelphia Inquirer*: "At the hotel in Front Royal on the night of the 18th, your correspondent saw an accomplished prostitute, who has figured largely in the rebel cause, and having seen her but a short time previous at Martinsburg, her presence at Front Royal at a time when the rebels were surrounding it, aroused suspicions that she meant mischief. She was pointed out to the military commanders there, and her arrest{was}advised. It was now known that she was the bearer of an extensive correspondence between the rebels inside and outside our lines." The correspondent continued writing about Belle's part in the fight at Front Royal: "An hour previous to the attack on Colonel Kenly, Belle went out on a rise of ground south of the town, and was seen to wave her handkerchief towards the point from which the center of the attack was made. Your Correspondent cannot vouch for the strict accuracy of all the fore going, but undeniable of exists here of her treason. Belle now reposes on her laurels in the Confederate camp."

Belle was neither impressed nor concerned about what correspondents wrote for the Northern newspapers. In her memoirs, she wrote, "The Northern journals vied with one another in publishing the most extravagant and improbable accounts of my exploits, as they were pleased to term them, on the battlefield of the 23rd May." In the newspapers, Belle was described as directing the fire of a Confederate artillery battery; another represented her as having, by the force of her genius, sustained the wavering counsels of the Southern generals, and another newspaper had her with a sword in her hand leading an attack against the Union force at Front Royal. Belle was not concerned by the Northern press and their exaggerations of her role in the battle at Front Royal. Instead, she wrote, "I believe that the veracity of the

Yankee press is pretty well known and appreciated, I shall give no more extracts from their eloquent pages."

On May 31, General Shields arrived in Front Royal and released Belle from house arrest. She was now free to do whatever she desired, and almost immediately, Belle returned to her vocation of spying, continuing the characteristics she knew best, manipulation and deception. Her efforts to keep General Shields manipulated and blinded to her true intentions were noticed by other Union soldiers serving at Front Royal. Captain J. B. Molyneux of the 7th Ohio Infantry wrote:

At Front Royal, we captured the notorious Belle Boyd who was suspected of being a Confederate spy, and I think the suspicion was well founded. She was taken to Gen. Shields' headquarters early in the morning before he had his breakfast. While he was quizzing her in his tent his man entered with breakfast on a tray. There was no table in the tent and only two camp stools were already occupied so the woman suggested that he place the tray on her lap, which he did and when he came out his face wore a very broad grin. When asked why he was laughing, he replied 'oh boys, yez ought to see the legs Shields has to his table.

General Shields's force remained in camp on May 31. Because of Shields and his Union army's idleness, it gave General Jackson and his Confederate army another day to escape the three-prong pincer movement that President Lincoln hoped would destroy the Confederate army.

On June 1, General Shields's force marched from Front Royal and advanced toward Strasburg to carry out his part of President Lincoln's three-prong attack against General Jackson, but "Old Jack" as he was known and his army just barely escaped up the Shenandoah Valley.

General Banks and his force arrived at Front Royal shortly after General Shields's division departed. Banks established his headquarters at the Fishback Hotel, where Belle wasted no time in approaching him. Belle requested a travel pass south to visit relatives in Louisiana. Banks teasingly asked, "What will Virginia do without you?"

94

Belle acted naive, knowing very well what Banks was implicating, replied, "General."

General Banks interrupted and answered, "We always miss our bravest and most illustrious, and how can your native State do without you?"

Belle knew General Banks wanted to keep her in Front Royal so he could keep an eye on her, knowing she would carry intelligence and information to Stonewall Jackson or anyone who could get the information to Jackson. For her it was another form of arrest and restrictions since the town was under martial law with the enemy's occupation.

By June 9, 1862, General Shields's division had marched seventy-five miles south of the Front Royal area with General Banks's force to defeat General Jackson's army. Jackson divided his army to defeat the Union forces one at a time, leaving Richard Ewell's division to encounter Banks's force in a battle on June 8 at Cross Keys, Virginia, between Harrisonburg and Port Republic, Virginia. Ewell managed to defeat Banks's force and rejoined Jackson and the rest of the army at Port Republic. On June 9, Shields's force engaged Jackson's army at Port Republic in a day-long battle resulting in a Union defeat. Generals Fremont and Shields's armies retreated to Harrisonburg and Luray.

After the defeat of Generals Banks, Fremont, and Shields's armies, the Shenandoah Valley Campaign of 1862 ended between the major armies. After the Confederate victory at Port Republic, General Lee sent for General Jackson's army to march across the Blue Ridge Mountain and reinforced his Army of Northern Virginia around Richmond to fight against Major-General George McClellan's 100,000-man Army of the Potomac. Jackson had accomplished all that had been requested of him. He had carried out a successful campaign by defeating three Union armies, threatening Washington, escaping possible destruction of his army, and causing 40,000 Union soldiers to be tied up from fighting around Richmond or elsewhere. As for Generals Fremont and Shields, their military careers began to fade, with Shields resigning from the army in March 1863.

There were 1,000 Union army casualties at the battle of Port Republic. One of those wounded was Captain Daniel Keily of

Shields's staff. Keily was severely wounded in the face while leading forward Union soldiers. He was cited for his bravery, went on during the war, and became a brigadier general.

When Captain Keily arrived in Front Royal by ambulance, he was taken to "Oakley, " Thomas Almond Ashby's home, where the Ashby family cared for him.

When Belle heard of Captain Keily's injury and that he was in Front Royal, she dashed off to the Ashby home to visit him. Even though Belle was not fond enough of Keily to have a romantic interest in him, she visited him out of friendliness, politeness, and concern. Belle does not mention Keily's injury or visit with him in her memoirs. However, young Thomas Ashby remembered Belle visiting the Union officer while recovering at his home. Thomas Ashby wrote, "A singular circumstance occurred concerning his {Keily} stay at our home. While confined to his room one afternoon, a young woman accompanied by a German officer, and riding a spirited horse, dashed up to the front door of the house. She sprung from the horse, rushed into the house, and asked the servant where she could find the wounded officer. When told where he lay, she rushed upstairs, and without ceremony, entered his room. This was the then-celebrated Belle Boyd."

In his narrative, Thomas Ashby gave a creditable eyewitness account of Belle's visit to Captain Keily. Thomas Ashby did not write his eyewitness observations until long after the war's conclusion. It was not until 1914 that he wrote his memoirs. As Ashby continued his observations in his memoirs, he changed course while writing about Belle Boyd, discrediting her contribution to the fight at Front Royal and her role as a rebel spy. At the time of the battle at Front Royal, Thomas Ashby was twelve years old. Even though the first part of his narrative is creditable, the rest must be scrutinized because much of it was hearsay. He must have believed what other individuals living in the area perceived of Belle Boyd. Ashby continued his narrative, "she had developed a strong interest in military matters, and, posing as a Rebel spy and heroine, she had already attracted considerable notice by her exploits, but she was not taken seriously by either the Federals or the Confederates. Though professing warm allegiance to the South, she played with both sides a game that inspired no confidence in either; hence she lived in either camp as it suited her purpose and, as far as I know, was never under arrest."

Belle was taken seriously as a spy because she had been, by this time in June 1862, arrested three times by Union authorities, and she was taken seriously by Northern newspapers, who tried to demonize her on every occasion, when possible, in their articles. As for the Southern newspapers, they hailed Belle differently. They hailed her as a Southern heroine because she had defended her family at Martinsburg and was instrumental in the fight at Front Royal, carrying intelligence to Stonewall Jackson. She had successfully manipulated Union officers and their men for information. Belle was a young lady to the Southern newspapers who could be an inspiration to other Southern women and keep the Southern morale at a pitch, especially after the Union army had been victorious earlier in the year in the western theater of the war with victories at Forts Henry and Donelson, Corinth, and Shiloh.

Thomas Ashby continued, "At the time I speak of, she was in the Federal lines and was receiving marked attention from the young officers. On May 22nd, she had ridden into the Confederate lines and had given Jackson information that proved unreliable."

The information Belle gave Jackson as the fighting began at Front Royal was reliable because Brigadier-General Richard Taylor and Captain Campbell Brown testified to that fact when they wrote about Belle in their memoirs, not to mention the eyewitness accounts of Confederate soldiers in the ranks.

Although Thomas Ashby attempts to discredit Belle Boyd, he gives a vivid physical description of Belle as a "young woman of some personal beauty, vivacious, attractive, and spirited in manner and a skilled rider of spirited horses. Nor was she wanting in energy, dash, and courage, but she had none of the genius, inspiration, and religious fervor of the true heroine. She loved notoriety and attention."

Thomas Ashby questioned Belle's womanhood before concluding his thoughts on paper, writing, "so much for Belle Boyd. Her heroism has long faded into the forgetfulness of her generation. She has found no decent place in history." Ashby, like many others, may have been offended because Belle Boyd married three men from the North, two of who fought for the Union during the war, and she had pushed toward reconciliation between the North and South after the war. Many in the South felt betrayed after the war by close association with someone from the North. All one must do is look at Confederate General James Longstreet. In 1868, Longstreet attended the inauguration ceremonies of President Ulysses S. Grant and afterward received an appointment as surveyor of customs in New Orleans. For this act, he lost favor with many Southerners. Another Southern hero who, for a short time, lost favor in the South after the war was Colonel John S. Mosby. Mosby, like Longstreet, pushed for reconciliation. He campaigned for Grant as president and in return, became a diplomat at the U.S. Consul in Hong Kong. Thomas Ashby's remarks do not surprise this author; he may have been, to some extent mirroring the expressions and sentiments of other citizens of the period. As for my own experiences, I remember, at the age of nine, meeting a little lady who was a young child living in the Harpers Ferry area during America's Civil War. Much of what she knew occurred during the war came from her father, who served under Stonewall Jackson. Even at 100, she remembered everything her father told her about the war, and no other version was correct.

Another exciting incident involving Belle occurred in Front Royal after the fight at Port Republic. Captain Frederic Sears Grand D'Hauterille of General Banks's staff must have known Belle because he recorded in his journal, "June 10, reached Front Royal. I met the famous and very handsome rebel spy, Belle Boyd, who gave me the flag waving, which she led the attack on Kenly in May." The flag that D'Hauterille referred to was a Confederate national flag. The statement "flag waving, which she led the attack on Kenly in May" needs to be looked at carefully. When Belle first encountered Confederates as they neared Front Royal on May 23, 1862, she ran toward the Confederate line. According to Belle, she was waving a white bonnet at the Confederate soldiers and urging them to press on. In his eyewitness account, Henry Kyd Douglas of Jackson's staff verified her statement by writing, "but waved a bonnet as she came on." With her written account and another witness's written account to corroborate, there is no mention of a flag.

One might dismiss Captain D'Hauterille's account as a fallacy. Still, another staff officer on General Banks's staff collaborated with his account by the name of Captain Robert Gould Shaw, who later became a colonel and commanded the first African-American Union infantry regiment in America's Civil War, the 54th Massachusetts. Robert Shaw wrote his mother, Sarah, a letter dated July 28, 1862. In his letter, he wrote about Belle Boyd and the flag incident: "Perhaps you have seen some accounts of a young lady at Front Royal, named Belle Boyd. There was quite a long and ridiculous letter about her copied into the *Evening Star* the other day. I have seen her several times but never had any conversation with her. Other men told me that she never asked for any information about our army or gave them the slightest reason to suppose her a spy, and they were probably as capable of judging as the correspondent who wrote about her. She gave Fred D'Hauterville a pretty secession flag, which she said she carried when she went out to meet Jackson's troops coming into Front Royal."

Robert Shaw's letter adds credence to D'Hauterville's account. He must have seen the flag to verify his account. I have found no other written accounts concerning the flag incident. The only possible explanation can be was when Colonel Kenly's Union soldiers retreated through the main street of Front Royal, and as General Jackson's Confederates were entering the main street, Belle appeared from her cottage and used one of her Confederate national flags to encourage the rebels to continue to victory, such as officers did when they took the flag from the color bearer and rallied their men while in battle.

A Union officer, Captain Edwin Marvin, the historian of the 5th Connecticut Infantry, was at Front Royal with his regiment before the fighting at Cross Keys and Port Republic. Like many in his regiment, he did not view Belle as someone who had or could have taken the life of a Union soldier. He wrote on June 4, "Some of the boys met the woman Belle Boyd, a violent rebel. She claims to have shot a Union soldier who insulted her. It is not believed by the boys. They do not believe any soldier has insulted her or that she shot one." He tried to discredit her by adding, "She appears to be the only witness."

Belle appeared to be boastful about shooting the soldier, but no one could imagine her carrying out such an act, which made anything else she might have said irrelevant. But all Belle would have had to do was produce her Grandmother Glenn, who was at the cottage behind the hotel as a witness since she was with Belle on the day of the incident at Martinsburg and witnessed the event.

Captain Marvin continued to write in his regimental history:

While here most of the men saw the notorious Belle Boyd, who was simply known as a good looking brilliant and witty woman, and also an out and out rebel of the rabid kind. Her home was in Martinsburg, which was generally within the Union lines, and she had an uncle living at this place, Front Royal, whom she occasionally visited, which was as generally within the Confederate lines. Some officers connected with General Shields' staff procured passes for her back and forth. Her uncle's principal residence at Front Royal was taken for a time, and the family was allowed to stay on the premises. This gave her opportunities of gathering some information about what was passing from various staff officers with whom she became very confidential, and observations made by herself, which she managed, as she says, to deliver within the rebel lines by long night rides.

Captain Marvin did not believe Belle's war narrative and denounced her as an underrated spy. However, history has proven differently who Belle Boyd was and what she was capable of and did accomplish during America's Civil War. Many officers and soldiers from both the Union and Confederate armies have held different opinions based on their experiences, events, and scenes they had witnessed of *Belle Boyd: The Rebel Spy.*

Chapter 10

The Camps & Smuggling

After the battle of Port Republic, the Union army encamped in and around Front Royal. They were there until June 20. During that time, the Union army lived in expectation and anxious suspense of being attacked by Stonewall Jackson's army since they did not know his whereabouts. According to Thomas Ashby, a "strong guard was kept on the outpost, and every preparation was made for an attack. Jackson's union with Lee was not known until the engagement with McClellan on the Chickahominy was announced."

Belle visited the Union camps just like she had been doing since the beginning of the war. Captain Daniel Keily was not the only Union officer who tried to attract and win Belle's attention and affection; others were also competing, such as Lieutenant William Johnson, 102nd New York Infantry, J. M. Hadley, 4th New Jersey Infantry, and Captain Lewis Stegman, 102nd New York Infantry. On July 9, 1862, Captain Stegman wrote, "Belle think of me when I am gone even as I shall think of you. Lovingly, with friendly heart, lovingly, must think of me even through warfare's fiercest dart."

Another officer Belle attempted to keep in the dark concerning her covert activities was Doctor Robert Montgomery Smith Jackson. When Belle was a nurse in Martinsburg during the early days of the war, she met Doctor Jackson. He served with the 3rd Pennsylvania Infantry then, but now with the 11th Pennsylvania Infantry. In June 1862, she wanted to renew her acquaintance with him, and she wanted to downplay the spying accusations against her and maintain her acquaintance with him. She scribbled on the back of her calling card, "No spy, only a lover of my Country and my Southern Cause for which I am willing to die at any time 'Liberty or Death.'" One correspondent observed this, and his article appeared in the Frederick,

Maryland *Examiner*, writing, "Our young officers, dazzled perhaps, took her out riding often, and she was frequently a habitant of our camps in the Shenandoah."

Another Union officer at Front Royal discovered that many of the officers were smitten by Belle's charm and warmness, writing, that she "soon had crowds of them at her feet." To win their loyalty, she "scoffed at the rebels, and vowed her never-dying love for the Union" and "they believed her, and in her fascinating way, she drew from them all the information about military movements any of them chanced to possess." The officer best concluded his observations of Belle Boyd by writing, "few could resist her spell, few saw her but were led captive."

Belle knew these soldiers were vulnerable and used all her weapons, such as her charisma, empathy, and wiles, to prey on their weakness to obtain information. Belle's cousin Alice Stewart knew the game Belle played with the Union soldiers. On June 11, 1862, Alice wrote that it was a beautiful day "while you are carelessly winning and throwing the hearts of brave soldiers away."

Not all Union officers were fooled by Belle's method of warfare, even though they knew she visited their camps. On July 1, 1862, Major John Gould of the 10th Maine Infantry wrote, "I see that all sorts of rumors of taking of Richmond, which Miss Belle Boyd, who pays us daily visits, reckoned were true." Belle only visited the camps where she could obtain their devotion and where they were willing to talk to receive her attention. Belle hoped, in return, they would divulge some information to try and impress her, which she willingly played along laughingly, deceivingly, and complementing to obtain it.

Major John Gould of the 10th Maine was not the only officer to notice Belle and her activities in the Union camps at Front Royal. The regimental adjutant also noticed and committed to paper his observations:

You have heard or read of Belle Boyd, a lady of considerable notoriety all over the Valley. She is here making smiles at the officers who will look at her. She has been sadly represented by newspapers, but that she is a precious rogue I think no one questions though no one can prove it. She slipped by our Regt's pickets at Winchester before the late skedaddled and was also arrested for having letters upon her. Col. Fillebrown is not going to let her leave the place again, he says, and by contriving to get the story to her that she is to be arrested, keep her, constantly paying her visits and sending bouquets and cherries.

Colonel Fillebrown had already had one encounter with Belle at Winchester before the fight at Front Royal. He had learned some of Belle's wiles the hard way with his experiences with her at Winchester and was determined to keep a vigilant watch over her activities at Front Royal.

Belle was not the only Southern lady who visited the Union army camps, and other young ladies were doing the same thing. A letter was published on July 12, 1862, in the *Philadelphia Inquirer* and later that month, on July 26, in the *Richmond Daily Dispatch*. The article was about how Southern female spies operated:

These women are the most accomplished in Southern circles. They are introduced under assumed names to our officers, so as to avoid detection or recognition from those to whom their names are unknown. By such means they are enabled to frequently meet combinedly, but at separate times, the officers of every regiment in a column, and by simple compilation and comparation of notes, they achieve a full knowledge of the strength of our entire force. Has modern warfare a parallel to the use of such accomplishments for such a purpose? The chief of these spies is the celebrated Belle Boyd. Her acknowledged superiority for machination and intrigue has given her the leadership and control of the female spies in the Valley of Virginia. Well, this woman I saw participating her arts upon our young lieutenants and inexperienced captains, and in each case I uniformly felt it my duty to call them aside and warn them of whom she was. To one, she had been introduced as Miss Anderson, to another, Miss Faulkner, and so to the end of the chapter. She is so well known now that she can only practice her banishments upon her new raw levies and their officers. But from them she obtains the number of their regiments and their force. She has, however, a trained band of coadjutors, who report to her daily...girls age from 6 upward...women who have the common sense not to make themselves as conspicuous as she, and who remain unknown, save her, and are therefore effective. The reports that she is personally impure are as unjust as they are undeserved. She has a blind devotion to an idea and passes far the boundary of her sex's modesty to promo to its success.

During the past campaign in the Valley, this woman has been of immense service to the enemy...she will be now if she can."

Other Southern ladies, who never attained the same notoriety as Belle, also attempted to gain information from Union officers and their enlisted men. Many of these women and Belle stole unattended weapons, ammunition, swords, foodstuff, medicine, or anything else they believed the Confederate army could militarily use. Instead, they sent it south most of the time by a faithful servant.

How did they steal weapons and other items from the Union camps and never get caught? In camp, many soldiers stacked their weapons in a circle in the evening or when unused. They removed their military gear, and other than those on picket duty, they militarily dressed down for the evening. When they visited the camps, many women, such as Belle, were usually dressed in hoop skirts. Hoop skirts were a dome-shaped, light material made of crinoline. Crinoline was a stiff fabric with a weft of horsehair and wrap cotton or linen thread, which appeared around 1830. By 1850, crinoline had come to mean a stiff petticoat or a lightweight steel skirt-shaped structure called the cage crinoline, which many women adopted. Belle and other such women, who were engaged in smuggling during the Civil War, sewed pockets under these skirts to hide their stolen items. Women during the war were rarely searched but, in most cases, were taken at their word. Belle had been engaged in this practice for some time, smuggling quinine across the Potomac River to secessionists in Virginia.

Belle had been successful up until this time during America's Civil War with spying and passing information and bits of intelligence to General Jackson, but her fortunes were about to change. The role

Belle was used to playing would soon be reversed and used against her and present unfavorable consequences for her.

Chapter 11

Deception

After most of the Union army departed Front Royal on June 20, the 3rd Delaware Infantry, commanded by Colonel Samuel Jenkins, remained behind. The 3rd Delaware Infantry was a regiment in the Second Brigade, Second Division, Second Corps of the Army of Virginia, which Major-General John Pope now commanded. According to Belle, the provost marshal at Front Royal was Major McEnnis. Some of Belle's earlier biographers have used the same name, but there is a problem. The problem is that according to the enlistment and muster rolls at the Delaware State Archives, no Major McEnnis served in the 3rd Delaware Infantry. Belle must have been confused or mistaken by the pronunciation of his real name and therefore misspelled it. According to the Delaware State Archives, the officer's real name was Arthur Maginnis, the regiment's major, in 1862.

Belle discovered Major Maginnis and his assistant, Lieutenant Harry Preston, were very courteous and kind and greatly respected, but she found Colonel Jenkins coarse in both manner and appearance. In the courtyard and a few yards from Belle's cottage, the provost marshal pitched a tent serving as his office. From the tent, Major Maginnis carried out his duties. One of those duties was issuing passes to travel south.

While again Union forces occupied Front Royal, Belle continued her social life with the ladies and the gentlemen of the community. On July 5, 1862, Lucy Buck recorded in her diary that Alice Stewart, who she highly regarded, had taken tea with her. Lucy hoped that in the future, Alice could visit her more often. Later that afternoon, Belle arrived at the Buck's home. Someone must have requested music to be played because Lucy later wrote, "Belle Boyd and Mr. Jefferies

106

came over and sat awhile after tea and little I felt like playing I exerted myself and undertook a piece." Lucy's feelings and attitude had not changed toward Belle.

Again, on July 12, Belle visited the Buck family's home. Lucy, who had been sick that day, still entertained guests that evening. Later, she recorded in her diary, "In late evening Belle Boyd, Alice Stewart, and Mr. Jeffries came in. Belle told them all soon after she got here that she and Dr. Bogardus had traced up their relationship and found that they were cousins, and when he came in, they were evidently very well acquainted from the way they conducted themselves." Belle's relationship did not last long with the physician because, by July 24, Lucy recorded in her journal as she sat on her front porch that "Miss Belle Boyd and the Dr. have quarreled, he thinks it 'does not pay' to visit her.'"

Belle consistently applied energy and effort when it came to making friends. If she was your friend, she was your friend, but if Belle was your enemy, she was your enemy. Belle made friends very quickly and naturally attracted the attention of others. This sometimes-caused envy among other ladies who were not so outgoing at establishing relationships so naturally.

While sitting in the drawing room one morning, Belle noticed two Confederate soldiers standing near the provost marshal's tent and sent for Major Maginnis. When Belle asked the identity of the two men, Major Maginnis informed her that they were Confederate soldiers on parole seeking a pass to travel south. When Belle asked Major Maginnis if they could have dinner with her at the cottage, he agreed. The two Confederate soldiers disappeared, but one of them returned. Belle approached him and invited him to dinner, and he accepted. While at dinner, Belle asked the Confederate officer if he would take a letter for her to General Jackson. He agreed. Belle went to her room to compose her letter when a servant named Cassandra stopped Belle and began questioning her about the Confederate officer. Belle confessed she did not know anything about him, but the servant warned Belle, she had seen him among the Union soldiers that day and that he was a spy. Belle did not heed her warning and wrote the letter to General Jackson. A letter that contained much valuable information about Pope's Army of Virginia, the "state of their army, their movements and doings, and matters of a like nature."

After dinner, Belle gave the Confederate officer the letter for Jackson. Then, as she gave him the letter, she asked, "Will you promise me faithfully, upon the honor of a soldier, to take the utmost care of this and deliver it safely to General Jackson? They tell me you are a spy, but I do not believe it."

The Confederate officer swore to Belle he was not a spy and intended to deliver her letter with the utmost honesty and honor. Shortly after the Confederate officer's departure, a Union officer revealed the man was a spy on his way to Harrisonburg, Virginia.

After speaking to the Union officer, Belle realized she had been deceived and made a costly mistake. She had given the Union spy a letter, allowing him to move about Confederate lines unimpeded and without scrutiny. The Union officer warned Belle of the dire consequences of any further misconduct, which could bring her a severe penalty. He recommended she leave for Richmond, and he would help her to get a pass, but fate had ordained otherwise.

Immediately after some reflection on the mistake she had made, Belle hastily wrote a note to Captain Harry Gilmor, who commanded a company of Confederate cavalry scouts, describing the spy and admitting she had been deceived into believing he was a Confederate officer, who would deliver a letter to General Jackson for her. Since Belle could not leave Front Royal, she had to use someone else to deliver the letter. Belle decided to use an elderly Negro man, who was used in what was known in covert activity, as the locomotive. The mail car used to carry her note was an enormous watch with the working parts removed, but if stopped by Union pickets, the elderly man was to inform the pickets that the timepiece was out of order and had "ceased to mark the hours and minutes."

Who was the spy posing as a Confederate officer? He was Charles W. D. Smitley, chief scout, 5th West Virginia Cavalry. Charles Smitley was born in Cumberland, Maryland, on June 6, 1838. Before the war, the twenty-four-year-old Smitley was a millwright. When America's Civil War began, he attempted unsuccessfully to raise a company of Union cavalry in Marion County, Virginia {West Virginia}, where he resided, but hostilities were so significant against the Union that he went to Grafton and enlisted in Company B, 5th West Virginia Cavalry. Smitley proved to be an excellent scout. He was described by the historian of the 5th West Virginia Cavalry as being "a brave, cool, daring man, one fitted for the position he was given; who was loved by all his men and all that knew him, and a gentleman in the true sense of the word."

Charles Smitley's scouting role was different. He was not the type of scout who followed an army trying to determine its position, strength, and design, but he was what was known as a *Jessie Scout*. *Jessie Scouts* were irregular soldiers on the side of the Union who frequently operated in territory held by the Confederate army. The unit was initially created by Major-General John Fremont and named in honor of his wife, Jessie Benton Fremont.

Jessie Scouts wore Confederate uniforms and posed as loyal Southerners intending to gain intelligence and the condition of the opposing enemy. If captured wearing the wrong uniform by the opposing army, the *Jessie Scout* could be executed for spying. It was a risky business for those who were cunning and daring; Smitley was good at his vocation.

In July 1862, Smitley was sent from New Creek, Virginia {West Virginia}, with orders to report to General R. C. Schenck. When he reported to Schenck's headquarters, he was informed by one of the general's aides that Belle was suspected of violating her parole. His assignment was to entrap her. The idea of the entrapment had originally been conceived by Secretary of War Edwin Stanton, who believed that Belle was too dangerous to remain free. Secretary Stanton had received a letter from a concerned surgeon in Front Royal named Dr. Washington Duffee. Dr. Duffee was concerned that one of his fellow surgeon comrades, Dr. Rex, had either fallen in love with the "celebrated Belle Boyd, the Rebel spy" or that she was "anxious to make a victim" of him. Allen Pinkerton, the famous Union detective who had the previous year arrested Rose Greenhow, the Confederate spymaster in Washington, wrote Secretary of War Stanton that Belle "gets around considerably, is very shrewd, and is probably acting as a spy. She is open, earnest, and an undisguised secessionist, and talks secession on all practicable occasions…informant considers her more efficient in carrying news to the rebels of our operations than any three men in the Valley."

According to Frank Reader of the 5th West Virginia Cavalry, when Smitley arrived at Front Royal, he went to one of the prominent citizens of the village under an assumed name. He represented himself as a paroled Confederate officer looking for boarding. Smitley's host was hospitable and communicative, informing him Belle was in town. Smitley acted surprised and eulogized her valuable service to the Southern cause. He soon learned Belle was the sensation of the town, that the intensely loyal Confederates idolized her, and she had a large following of Union officers ready to pay her homage.

Smitley's introduction to the inner circle of Front Royal and his expressed admiration of Belle's exploits as a spy were carried to her by his host's daughter. The same afternoon, he received an invitation from the host's daughter to have tea with him at one of the Southern residences. Smitley arrived, was introduced to Belle, and found her to be a lady of culture, a brilliant conversationalist, an expert with the piano, and rather attractive. Throughout the evening, many young ladies arrived, accompanied by Union officers, and found Belle was the center of attention. Smitley assumed a lofty, patronizing air toward the officers, "but with the ladies was exceedingly bashful and diffident." When "The Bonnie Blue Flag" was being sung and played by Belle on the piano, he stepped forward and "sang the bass, with all the feeling and power of his strong voice, though his heart burned within him to sing, "Down with the Traitors and up with the Stars." This settled the issue of his social status with the Confederates, and afterward, he was one of the "charmed circle."

Smitley stayed in Front Royal for the next several days and earned Belle's confidence to such an extent that she told him boastfully that she was violating her parole from her arrest at the beginning of June and encouraged him to do likewise.

At a party on the third evening in Front Royal, General Schenck's aide, who attended the event, revealed, and taunted Belle of Smitley's identity. Instead of believing the Union officer, Belle "turned a cold shoulder, became incensed at her attention to the scout," and "scornfully resented the accusations against his loyalty."

110

According to Frank Reader's version of events told to him by Smitley, Belle had reflected "on the situation and early the next morning she came to Smitley, greatly agitated and shedding tears like a child."

Smitley did not sympathize with Belle but departed from Front Royal that same day, rode north to Harpers Ferry, and gave the letter and information to Major-General Franz Sigel.

There are two versions of the story of how Smitley deceived Belle and won her confidence. Why are they conflicting? From the very beginning, Belle had grown very fond of Smitley. She had made the first mistake of letting down her guard and suspicions. In doing so, Belle immediately trusted him. She did not listen to Cassandra's warning or the Union officer, who knew Smitley's identity and was teasing her, knowing she would not believe him. Belle wrote in her memoirs, "If I am to recount my moments of glory, then too shall I recount my moments of sadness, fear, and disappointment. Such was the case with my first affair of the heart. A young woman in love does not often heed the warning of others...I being no different. Entrusting a note from General Jackson, to my beau, whom I thought to be a paroled Confederate soldier, I was heartbroken to find he was C. W. D. Smitley, chief of scouts for the 5th West Virginia Cavalry."

Belle wrote that she first met Smitley when she invited him to dinner. Smitley recalls meeting Belle through his host's daughter. We have two different versions of events, but what is sure is that Belle was deceived, blinded by her feelings for Smitley, and the Union scout reversed the roles. Another factor to consider is that Belle may not have included all the events surrounding Smitley because of the embarrassment that she had been vulnerable to him because of her feelings for him.

The letter Smitley carried to General Sigel has never been discovered and is not in the public records. As for Smitley, Belle wrote that he had been captured somewhere along the Rappahannock River and hung as a spy, but she is mistaken. Smitley continued as a scout for the Union army and lived well after America's Civil War had concluded and eventually moved to Burlington, Ohio.

This time, Belle's mistake of trusting someone to carry intelligence for her would be costly because the information that

Smitley had obtained ended up in the hands of Secretary of War Edwin Stanton. Secretary Stanton's plan had worked.

Chapter 12

Belle's Arrest

Belle had been attempting to go south to Richmond for months, only to have her request denied. However, a Union officer promised to help her to secure a travel pass to Richmond or, if she stayed, she would suffer the consequences. If arrested, Belle suspected they would banish her beyond Union lines, and she would be unable to return to the area until after the war's conclusion, but the punishment might be too severe. Hopefully, the Union officer who had promised to secure a pass by Thursday, July 31, would come through on his promise. That way, she could return.

Meanwhile, according to a *New York Tribune* correspondent, Belle traveled to Warrenton on July 26 and visited a wounded captain of the 4th Virginia Cavalry or, as they were also known, the "Black Horse Cavalry." Belle offered to take letters for the cavalrymen to Richmond for three dollars each. This was not Belle's real intention. Belle still had the information and intelligence about the Union army in the area that she had entrusted to Smitley that needed to be delivered, and she knew of the position of Pope's 35,000 men of the Army of Virginia. General Pope's army remained east of the Blue Ridge Mountain, mainly around Sperryville. Belle's cousin, Stephen Boyd, also had the same information about Pope's army and had not been captured; they must have worked together on occasion.

Little did Belle or the Union officer who promised to help Belle secure a pass south know that Secretary Stanton had already decided her fate. On Wednesday evening, July 29, 1862, Belle was on the balcony with her cousin Alice and Lieutenant Preston watching the sunset, talking about the war and the "unhappy state of our country." In the distance, Belle noticed a large body of cavalry approaching her house. At first, she believed it was a scouting party sent out to capture

113

Major Harry Gilmor and his cavalry company. Belle immediately went to her room, wrote out a note for Major Gilmor about her suspicions about the Union cavalry, and then sent the note by a trusted servant before retiring for the night.

The following day after breakfast, Belle looked out the door and noticed several Union soldiers entering the coach-house and dragging the carriage out of the dwelling to their headquarters, where they hitched horses. She had a strange feeling that came over her that, somewhere, this involved her and the entrapment by Smitley. She walked out on the balcony and looked down the street, noticing the Union cavalry she had witnessed the previous day lounging and conversing with each other.

While standing on the balcony, a servant arrived and informed Belle the provost marshal wanted to see her. Belle immediately met Major Maginnis and Major Francis T. Sherman of the 12th Illinois Cavalry from Martinsburg, Virginia {West Virginia}. Accompanying the two military officers was a civilian, who Belle describes as being "Coarse in appearance, with a mean, vile expression of countenance, and a grizzly beard, which, it was evident, had not made the acquaintance of water or a comb for weeks at least. His small, restless eyes glanced here and there with an expression of incessant watchfulness and suspicion. All his features were repulsive in the extreme, denoting a mixture of cowardice, ferocity, and cunning. In a word, his mien was unmistakably that of a finished villain, who was capable of perpetrating any act, however atrocious, when stimulated by the promise of reward money."

The detective who Secretary Stanton sent to arrest and escort Belle to Washington was a man by the name of Alfred Cridge. Cridge was a detective who worked for the United States Intelligence Service. Detective Cridge had been working on Belle's spying activities and had interviewed a German immigrant detective named Eugene Blockley of Alexandria, Virginia. Blockley was aware of Belle's spying activity because he had kept a file on her and reported directly to Allan Pinkerton, who headed up a detective and spy agency. Just before Belle's arrest, Blockley confronted her at the provost headquarters, where Belle shouted while leaving, "I suppose you came to report me again." Blockley was instrumental in supplying

Cridge with much-needed information, which helped to seal her fate. When Cridge came to Front Royal to arrest Belle, he also came to arrest William Dana.

While Detective Cridge and Major Sherman stood nearby, Major Maginnis informed Belle she had been placed under arrest.

Belle acted surprised and angrily cried, "Impossible."

Before Major Maginnis replied, Major Sherman promised Belle she would be shown every courtesy and consideration and this was a harrowing duty for him to perform. When Major Sherman finished speaking, Detective Cridge produced a document:

War Department

Sir,

You will proceed immediately to Front Royal, Virginia, and arrest, if found there, Miss Belle Boyd, and bring her at once to Washington.

I am respectfully,

E.M. Stanton

Before departing, Detective Cridge informed Belle that he must inspect her belongings. Belle asked for a few moments to prepare for her departure. When Cridge said nothing, she walked upstairs, but to her amazement, he followed. When she asked him to be patient and wait, Cridge denied her request and pushed her aside, saying he knew she had papers she wanted to hide. Detective Cridge inspected her clothes first, turning them inside out, and then he went to her desk and portfolio and examine their contents. However, Eliza, Belle's trusted servant, stalled him, gathering as many papers as she could carry, and then she rushed to the kitchen and destroyed them by tossing them into the fire. Most of Belle's documents were destroyed but not all of them. Detective Cridge confiscated some of the documents and a pistol a Union staff officer had given her the previous year.

Detective Cridge also broke into a writing table and removed some of John Stewart's papers, and then he informed Belle they would be leaving in thirty minutes.

As Alice and her grandmother wept, Belle announced she was ready to leave. Belle had asked if Eliza could go with her, but her request was denied. When the time came for Belle to depart, Eliza's grip on Belle had to be broken because she did not want to be separated.

The news had spread through Front Royal about Belle's arrest. Belle wrote, "The streets were by this time filled with soldiers and citizens of the town. As I stepped into the carriage, which for aught I knew was my funeral car, I cast a rapid, but comprehensive glance upon the crowd collected to witness my departure and the demeanor I should sustain under such a trial. Upon many, nay, upon most of the faces that met my gaze, sorrow and sympathy were in unmistakable characters; but there were, nevertheless, some looks the expression of which was that of exultation and malignant triumph."

Lucy Buck was one of those town gazers who turned out to see Belle, writing, "Belle Boyd was taken prisoner and sent off in a carriage with an escort of fifty cavalrymen today. I hope they are going to put her within our lines and keep her there." Lucy's feelings and attitude had not changed concerning Belle. It sounded like Lucy was glad to be rid of Belle.

A young captain serving with the 9th Vermont Infantry recorded in his diary for July 30, 1862: "We searched some houses and found arms and ammunition. The most important capture made was that of the celebrated Belle Boyd, the female spy. She used to enter Sigel and Fremont's lines with perfect ease and impunity whenever she wished, in spite of their efforts to the contrary. They saw she was a wonderfully keen intriguer. She was sent to Washington this morning under a strong guard."

Another witness to Belle's captivity was Private Isaac Walker, 7th Squadron Rhode Island Cavalry. In his journal, he wrote on July 30, 1862, "We went within four or five miles of Front Royal, where we met the Illinois Cavalry {12th}. They had been ordered the day before to go to Front Royal to get a Rebel spy, a woman by the name of Belle Boyd---she was caught by a United States spy, who had been looking

116

for her for about three weeks. Having met them, we returned with them, for we had been ordered to do so."

The spy who had been watching Belle for three weeks was Martinsburg resident Thomas Noakes. When Belle was arrested, letters and a revolver were taken from her before the trip to Old Capitol Prison.

Thomas Noakes was from Winchester, but according to the 1860 census, he lived in Martinsburg, Virginia {West Virginia}. One Rhode Island cavalryman described Noakes as "tall and athletic, brave and cruel, a known Spartan in his indifference to physical comfort, and in many respects a typical Southerner." Noakes was known as a spy and scout, and he could have been spying on Belle and would have been able to identify her. That was why he was with the 12th Illinois Cavalry, but she makes no mention of talking to or seeing him in her memoirs. Before the war, Noakes was a carpenter and married with five children. Noakes was instrumental during the Maryland Campaign of 1862 in guiding 1,500 Union cavalrymen from besieged Harpers Ferry. He survived the war because he is listed on the 1870 census as living again in Martinsburg.

Another Rhode Islander, Sergeant Henry Alvord, remembered the day, July 30, when Belle was arrested, recording in his diary, "The horses, still tired out from the journey in the cars, were saddled, and the squadron, over a hundred strong, went to Front Royal; gone all day."

The Rhode Islanders remembered Belle very well. Sergeant Samuel Pettengill wrote in his memoirs, *The College Cavaliers*:

The first excursion made from Winchester had a touch of romance in it. Belle Boyd, a notorious Rebel spy {and} a native of Martinsburg, was then living at Front Royal. She had been arrested a few weeks before in Winchester, with contraband letters on her person, and paroled to return to Front Royal. The report has reached Washington that she had broken her parole, as she had undoubtedly done on every favorable opportunity, Secretary Stanton sent a detective to Martinsburg, with power to call on Colonel Voss, of the Twelfth Illinois Cavalry, for assistance to re-arrest and send her to the

117

Capitol. Colonel Voss sent a detachment of his cavalry under command of Major Sherman, to Front Royal to execute this order.

At the time of Belle's arrest, the 12th Illinois Cavalry mustered 575 men at Martinsburg; 200 were sent to Front Royal, and the 7th Squadron Rhode Island Cavalry, which joined them later, 146 men from Winchester; in all probability, 346 cavalrymen from both organizations. Why did so many Union cavalrymen need to escort one female spy? The only answer could be as a precaution to deter any Confederate cavalry attempt to free her while transporting her to Winchester and Martinsburg. Many Confederates held Belle in high esteem and admiration; if possible, they would free her. But at the time, Major Gilmor's Confederate cavalry company was one of the few forces operating in the lower Shenandoah Valley.

Again, Sergeant Pettengill wrote, "The route between Front Royal and Winchester was, at that time under ordinary circumstances, very dangerous. A correspondent of the Associated Press, writing from General Pope's Army, 'this route had to be abandoned for trains and travel, except under strong escort, so troublesome had the guerrillas become.' As strong resistance to the arrest of Belle Boyd was anticipated, Major Corliss was sent with his cavalry to aid Major Sherman. But the arrest was affected without difficulty."

When Belle arrived at Winchester, she noticed the curious town citizens watching as the 500 Union cavalrymen escorted her to Brigadier-General Julius White's headquarters, which was one quarter of a mile northwest of town on the Mason farm.

General White was courteous to Belle and informed her that she would spend the night in Winchester and be sent to the commanding officer at Martinsburg the following day, where he would inform her "what is to be done with you." General White already knew what he would do with her because he had telegraphed Assistant Secretary of War Wolcott earlier. Wolcott instructed Detective Cridge through General White to bring Belle to Washington as soon as possible and commit her to the Old Capitol Prison.

Belle asked to lodge with her friends in Winchester for the night, but General White denied her request, answering, "I cannot consent to that. It would take a whole regiment to guard you; for, though the

118

rebel cavalry should not enter town to attempt your rescue, I make no doubt that the citizens themselves would try it."

Belle continued to plead with General White, but it was to no avail. He would allow her to use his tent and she would be safe. As Belle lay down to sleep, she heard the sentries pacing back and forth in front of her tent. Belle felt troubled by what had happened that day and the unknown fate that awaited her.

The following day, Belle was awakened by the sound of several muskets being fired and the sound of the drummers beating the long roll, which meant assembly for the Union soldiers. Belle lit a candle, hoping her day of deliverance had arrived. One of the sentries instructed her to put out the candle, to which she complied. Sergeant Pettengill remembered this night, and after speaking with residents of Winchester, he learned what the true meaning of the gunfire might have represented, writing, "The night she {Belle}spent at Winchester, there was great confusion and long-continued uproar outside the lines. The pickets were assaulted several times on different sides of the camp for the purpose, as it was understood from conversation afterward with the people living in the vicinity, of drawing from the camp a sufficiently large number of troops to make it possible for the Confederates to raid the camp and capture La Belle Rebelle."

Once the Union soldiers were sure there was no longer a threat from the Confederates or sympathetic citizens, they returned to their tents, but not the Rhode Island Cavalry. Sargent Henry Alvord wrote in his journal, "The squadron turned out at 4 a.m., the pickets having been fired upon, and remained in the saddle until 9 o'clock."

At dawn, Belle was ordered to be ready for the journey to Martinsburg. When they rode toward Martinsburg, Belle noticed that her cavalry escort had been reduced to about two hundred men.

Belle and her cavalry escort continued toward Martinsburg until around 8:00 in the morning, when they paused at a farmhouse where she had breakfast. After breakfast, they continued toward Martinsburg, arriving at 1:00 in the afternoon. Belle felt so exhausted and anxious that she experienced a terrible headache. Belle requested of the commanding officer, Colonel Arno Voss, 12th Illinois Cavalry, who was in command at Martinsburg, that she be allowed to go to her home where she could rest and try to recuperate her health, but her request was denied. Belle felt sure that Detective Cridge "imposed and informed the Federal Colonel that Mr. Secretary Stanton would probably take exception to such an indulgence, which would give" her "an opportunity of holding communications with persons inimical to the United States Government."

Detective Cridge went to Belle's home in Martinsburg and went through all her father's personal papers and possessions under the pretense of looking for communications from Belle and her mother. He came up empty-handed.

Now that Mary Boyd knew Belle was in Martinsburg, she took a carriage to the Union camp and was reunited with her daughter. Belle's mother renewed the request to be allowed to take her daughter home for a short visit, but again it was denied. Instead, the Voss permitted the use of a room at the Raemer's Hotel next to the Baltimore and Ohio Railroad depot. Once twenty-seven sentries (65th Illinois Infantry) were posted around the hotel's exterior, three in the passageway to Belle's room and one outside her room, her mother, brothers, and sisters were allowed to visit her. Belle was happy to be reunited with her family for a short time, even though she knew it would only be temporary.

Chapter 13

Belle's Imprisonment

The following morning, Belle boarded a Baltimore and Ohio train in Martinsburg with Lieutenant William Steele, Company C, 12th Illinois Cavalry, and Detective Cridge as her escorts to Washington. While traveling to Washington, Lieutenant Steele thought Belle would be lodged at the Willard Hotel even after their arrival. However, Secretary Stanton's most trusted agent, Detective Cridge, knew differently. Belle was to be taken to the Old Capitol Prison.

The train arrived in Washington at 9:00 in the evening. Belle was surprised that so many people turned out at the railroad station to see the "wonderful spy." Cridge had wired the chief of detectives for the United States Intelligence Service, twenty-six-year-old Lafayette C. Baker, of his arrival. Baker was an agent with an amazing career of narrow escapes, treachery, accusations, disgrace, and conspiracy theories. He was dismissed from his vocation in 1863 but was later recalled to service once more after President Abraham Lincoln was assassinated in April 1865. Baker led the investigation that resulted in the death of Lincoln's assassin, John Wilkes Booth, and the arrest of the Lincoln conspirators.

Lafayette Baker had already met Belle Boyd at Manassas, Virginia, after he was captured crossing the Potomac River and attempting to pass through Confederate lines under the pretense of being a businessman with business in Richmond. While temporarily held in a stockade, Belle posed as a colporteur or a Christian tract distributor. Belle asked if Baker would read one of the tracts, and then she began to ask how long he had been in the area. Baker replied that he had arrived that morning. She asked him to read the tract and pass it on to other prisoners, and then she departed, but not for long. Soon, Belle returned and asked Baker if he "was a Christian?" Baker told

Belle he once was a Christian, but now he felt unsure. Belle came to the point of her visit and tried to deceive him into giving her information:

"The lieutenant thinks you are a spy: I was born in the North but lived among these people {for}seven years. My sympathies are with the Northern people. I am trying to get a pass from General Beauregard {so} that I may visit my sister in New York, who is a teacher in one of the public schools. I will gladly take any message you may want to send to your friends. I think I shall get my pass to-morrow."

Belle's charade did not fool Baker as a tract distributor. Instead, he answered, "I think I shall see my friends before you do."

Belle and Baker's conversation concluded with Belle warmly shaking his hand. Baker recalled, "Two years and a half later, I met my tract friend, who was the famous Belle Boyd." Later that same day, he was taken to General Beauregard's headquarters where again he saw Belle among the officers.

When Belle departed from the train, Detective Baker recognized and roughly seized her, shouting, "Come on! I'll tend to you."

While Baker pushed his way through the crowd with Belle, Lieutenant Steele protested Baker's unmannerly tactics and the abuse but instead, Steele only received Baker's borages of verbal insults. When Belle was placed in a carriage, Detective Baker ordered, "Drive to the Old Capitol."

Even though Lieutenant Steele had been dismissed from his responsibilities, he continued with Belle and Detective Baker to the Old Capitol Prison, located at the corner of A and 1st Street Northeast. The Old Capitol Prison was once the temporary halls of legislation for the United States Congress between 1815-1819, because of the destruction to the original United States Capitol building during the War of 1812. Before Belle's confinement it had already been used as the home to the Washington Confederate spymaster, Rose Greenhow, and John Mosby, who later during the war, led a battalion of partisan rangers in Northern Virginia.

When Belle arrived at the Old Capitol Prison, she was escorted into a small office belonging to the Superintendent, thirty-seven-year-old William Patrick Wood. Wood was from Alexandria, Virginia. Before the war, he was a cabinet and model designer. He is described as short, powerfully built, sloppy in dress, with bluish-green eyes and a fair complexion. Wood portrayed humility but was really a crafty operator, who was dangerous to cross. After President Lincoln's assassination, he became the first director of the United States Secret Service Agency. Wood was given complete and "absolute authority" over the prisoners, but for the most part, he got along well with them.

No sooner had Belle arrived in his office than Superintendent Wood appeared and said, "And so this is the celebrated rebel spy. I am very glad to see you, and will endeavor to make you as comfortable as possible, so that whatever you wish for, ask for it and you shall have it. I am so glad I have so distinguished a personage for my guest."

Superintendent Wood escorted Belle to her cell room, where he gave her a copy of the rules and regulations. Again, he informed her if there were anything she needed, it would be hers for the asking, and then he departed. Belle's cell room had two windows that overlooked Pennsylvania Avenue. Off in the distance, she could see the former secretary of war, John Floyd's home, where she had many fond memories of visiting after she left school and resided in the city with her aunt and uncle. She also noticed the railroad depot, Camp Sprague, which had been changed to a hospital for wounded Union soldiers, and the Negro village known as "Swampoodle."

Belle's second-floor cell room contained a washing stand, a looking glass, an iron bedstead, a table, some chairs, a personal servant, and an unlocked door if she "behaved herself." The only items Belle requested were a rocking chair and a fire in the fireplace. Belle's servant, whose identity she did not reveal, was an "intelligent contraband" who was helpful to her. Even though her door was kept unlocked, sentries were posted throughout the hallway and within shouting distance of each other.

During her confinement at the Old Capitol, Belle discovered the food was plenty and very good. Her meals included beef steak, chicken, corn, tomatoes, potatoes, various fruits, and bread and butter.

Word soon spread throughout Washington that the "notorious rebel spy," Belle Boyd was a prisoner at the Old Capitol. Washington resident, Margaret Leech wrote, "It was late July and the Old Capitol was blanketed in heat and stench and bedbugs, when another female spy arrived at the prison. Belle Boyd was as defiant and theatrical as Rose Greenhow; but she was young and strong and unbuttered, and she played her role of Southern heroine with zest. She was the darling of the Old Capitol."

An inmate of the Old Capitol and future historian, Frank Moore, wrote, "A woman named Belle Boyd, who had been acting as a rebel spy and mail carrier to Richmond from points within the lines of the Union Army of the Potomac, was captured near Warrenton, VA and sent to the Old Capitol Prison at Washington."

Frank Moore is mistaken in several areas in his observation. First, Belle was arrested at Front Royal, Virginia, and not Warrenton. Secondly, she was not within the lines of the "Union Army of the Potomac." Instead, Belle was behind the lines of the Union Army of Virginia under Major-General John Pope's command.

As soon as Northern newspapers received the news about Belle's arrest and confinement, they began publishing headline articles. On August 6, 1862, the *Frederick Examiner* republished an article initially published in the *Washington Star*. The two newspapers published:

The notorious female spy, Belle Boyd, familiarly known as the betrayer of our forces at Front Royal, whereby the gallant command of Col. Kenly was slaughtered and captured, was arrested at Winchester on July 30, and is now confined in Old Capitol Prison. Her admission will convict her of being a spy. She was dressed today in a plain frock, low in the neck, and her arms were bare. Jackson, it appears, is her idol, and she gave vent romantic desires. She takes her arrest as a matter of course and is smart, plucky, and absurd as ever. Being insanely devoted to the Rebel cause, she resolved to act as a spy within the Union lines and managed in diverse ways to recommend herself to our officers. One of the Generals, formerly stationed in the Shenandoah Valley, is mentioned rather oddly as associated with her, and Belle boasts that she wrapped a Rebel flag

124

around his head. Our young officers dazzled perhaps, took her out riding often, and she was frequently a habitant of our camps in the Shenandoah.

Belle was not at the Old Capitol very long before Detective Baker reappeared to interview her on behalf of Secretary Stanton. At first, Baker tried to sympathize with Belle being held in custody, and the proof they had against her was overwhelming, and she might as well confess to her crimes.

Belle wanted to know in writing what the charges were and why she was being imprisoned before making any statement to Detective Baker. Baker granted her request. After Baker asked Belle to "take the oath of allegiance," and she denied to do so, he threatened her, saying, "Mr. Stanton will hear all of this."

Belle became angry and replied, "When I commence the oath of allegiance to the United States Government, my tongue may cleave to the roof of my mouth."

Detective Baker committed everything Belle said to him to paper. He angrily informed her if this was her resolution, she would have to "lay here and die" and "that it served her right."

Belle became furious and replied, "If it is a crime to love the South, its cause, and its President, then I am a criminal. I am in your power; do with me as you, please. But I fear you not. I would rather lie down in this prison and die, than leave it owing allegiance to such a government as yours." After she finished speaking, she requested that he leave. Until she shouted at Detective Baker, she did not realize other inmates, men who gave a loud and resounding cheer for her occupied the other rooms nearby.

Superintendent Wood was a witness to Belle and Detective Baker's conversation, suggesting the two of them needed to leave Belle for now.

No sooner had Superintendent Wood and Detective Baker departed, Belle heard someone cough and she noticed a "minute nut-shell basket" was at her feet. It was painted with miniature Confederate flags. Wrapped around it was a note from an Englishman expressing his sympathies. Belle wrote him a short reply and, when the sentry was not looking, tossed it back to him. Belle knew now she could communicate with someone else nearby.

It was Belle's first day in prison and it had been a trying one for her.

Source: *Wikipedia*

Lafayette Baker

Source: *National Archives*

Old Capitol Prison

Chapter 14

Imprisonment Part Two

Belle's first night in prison was quite an adjustment. She did not know how long she would be at the Old Capitol. Even though efforts were being made to accommodate her and every consideration given, it was not like being back in Front Royal or Martinsburg. For most of the night, she stood at the window watching, thinking, and praying, not knowing what fate confronted her.

The following morning at 9:00, Belle heard a loud knocking at her door by an officer calling the roll. Afterward, Belle's servant arrived and prepared for Belle's breakfast. While the servant was gone, the sentry outside of her door was relieved of his watch. Before leaving, the sentry instructed his relief that Belle was not allowed to come outside her room or communicate with anyone. If she wanted anything, he was to call for the corporal of the guard.

There was an area behind the prison where the prisoners could exercise. They had to pass by Belle's cell room. On her second day of confinement while they passed, Belle recognized several of her old friends and acquaintances, who had formerly belonged to the army in Virginia. Because of these acquaintances, whom she does not identify, her name and fame quickly spread throughout the Old Capitol.

Late on the second evening, Belle's servant informed her that some new prisoners had arrived that day and were placed in the room next to her. Then, at about 11:00 in the evening, the sound of a knife scooping out wall plaster by the individuals in the next room distracted her from reading her Bible. Then, within the next few minutes, she noticed the knife working its way visibly through her side of the wall.

At first Belle was cautious of the individual who might be attempting to communicated with her, but then she took the knife from her food tray and started digging into the plaster wall. Shortly, they had a hole in the wall that was large enough to send notes to communicate with each other. Belle soon discovered the inmates next to her were friends of happier days. Belle wrote in her memoirs "the clandestine correspondence that was thus carried on was, on either side of the wall, a source of much pleasure, and served to beguile many a tedious hour."

Above Belle's cell room was where Rose Greenhow, the infamous Washington Confederate spymaster, had been incarcerated for five months in 1861. Now some gentlemen from Fredericksburg, Virginia, occupied it. Belle liked the challenges and the risks of communicating with her neighbor inmates, such as the prisoners across the hallway from her cell room. Belle was creative. She wrapped her written note around a marble, taking care that the sentry's back was turned when her correspondence started on its voyage of discovery. As for the inmates in the room to her right, the same system applied as the one with the room on the left.

Major Morse of General Richard Ewell's staff and Major Norman Fitzhugh of General Jeb Stuart's staff, who was captured near Verdiersville, Virginia, while carrying important plans of General Lee's intentions against General Pope's Army of Virginia during the Second Manassas Campaign occupied the room on the left. The 1st Michigan Cavalry captured Major Fitzhugh.

The article about Belle, which initially appeared first in the *Washington Star* and again in the *Frederick Examiner*, reached the officials at the War Department and made them furious because of this section of the story they published, "A leading secessionist of Washington visited her in jail today where her quarters are comfortable and gave her luxuries. Some gentlemen likewise waited upon her. She talked with them randomly and with much abandon and said she intended to be paroled." Originally the War Department had ordered Belle held in close custody or solitary confinement, which meant her door was to be permanently closed and no visitations by anyone, including her family.

On the day the Washington newspaper published its article, the War Department began its investigation looking for answers to the allegations and account of the publication. On August 7, Brigadier-

130

General James Wadsworth, the Military Governor District of Columbia, received correspondence from Assistant Secretary of War Peter H. Watson. In his correspondence, Watson wanted General Wadsworth to investigate and determine if there was any truth that Secretary of War Stanton's orders of maintaining Belle under close custody had been violated. Watson requested the names of the people who visited Belle at the Old Capitol from the newspaper's editor, but he was out of the city. The responsibility was placed in Wadsworth's care for the names of the person alleged to have access to the prisoner and the authority under which they were permitted to visit her. Wadsworth was to investigate:

1) *Whether the order committing Belle Boyd to close custody had been violated*

2) *When and by whom, and under what authority every such violation was committed?*

3) *General Wadsworth is to report to the War Department the results of his investigation.*

General Wadsworth acted promptly on Watson's request, sending his aide, Major Clinton Meneely and Mr. Van Buskirk of the Post Office Department to visit the Old Capitol and to determine the truth about whether Belle was in close custody and receiving visitors.

In his return correspondence on August 7, to the War Department, General Wadsworth claimed he had not previously received an order or had knowledge from the War Department about keeping Belle in close custody. After the investigation at the Old Capitol on August 7, Wadsworth informed Assistant Secretary Watson that while at the Old Capitol, Major Meneely and Mr. Van Buskirk had spoken freely with Belle. They also learned that Superintendent Wood had received the order from the War Department, but that he had allowed Doctor Hale, a leading Washington Southern sympathizer to visit her. This must have been the gentleman who the Washington and Frederick newspapers were writing about, but did not either know or reveal his

131

identity. Belle never mentioned the incident in her memoirs or that Superintendent Wood allowed her visit by Dr. Hale.

Later, Major William E. Doster, the provost marshal in Washington, became interested in Belle. He recalled the first time he met her. Belle was eating peaches and reading an issue of *Harper's Weekly*. He found Belle lively, spirited, full of caprices, and a genuine rebel. She complained there was little to do in prison. She requested Major Doster to intercede on her behalf to Secretary Stanton the freedom to walk outside accompanied by an officer, but Stanton denied the request. On the fourth morning of imprisonment, Belle watched the prisoners go to breakfast when a small Frenchman handed her a half-length portrait of Confederate President Jefferson Davis. Belle immediately hung the portrait of the Confederate president over her fireplace mantel. While Lieutenant George "Bullhead" Holmes passed her cell room, he noticed the portrait, charged into her room, and swore violent oaths while removing it. Holmes was known for his frequent abuse of the prisoners. When Lieutenant Holmes departed, he locked Belle in her room. Belle believed her offense was severe punishment by being enclosed in a hot, stuffy room with no freedom. She grew ill and faint, sometimes believing she would die from the oppressive summer heat. At last, Superintendent Wood, observing how pale Belle had become, allowed her door to be opened and, shortly afterward, allowed her to walk daily for thirty minutes with an escort. Even though Belle received every consideration and allowance, she still admitted to being a rebel and her willingness to help in any way the Southern Confederacy.

*　*　*　*

One day in August, while Belle was at the Old Capitol standing in the doorway of her cell room, she noticed an older man with a gray beard and white hair hanging from his shoulders who had trouble ambulating, but she did not know that his heart was full of vigor and spirit. The elderly gentleman was D. A. Mahony, the editor of the *Dubuque {Iowa} Crescent*. Mahony had been imprisoned at the Old Capitol because he used his newspapers to denounce the government's policies and they designated him as a traitor. Belle did

132

not write much about him in her memoirs, but Mahoney remembered her very vividly. In his book, *The Prisoner of State*, which he boldly published in 1863, only to have Secretary Stanton suppress its distribution, Mahony wrote about Belle and her stay at the Old Capitol. He wrote, "Among the prisoners at the Old Capitol was the somewhat famous Belle Boyd, to whom has been attributed the defeat of General Banks in the Shenandoah Valley by Stonewall Jackson."

Mahony remembered the first time he realized a female was a prisoner at the Old Capitol. It was the first night of his incarceration on August 21, when she sang *Maryland, My Maryland*. Mahony was amazed and gratified by the quality of her voice and the emotion Belle exerted in performing the song. Afterward, he had to know who she was, writing, "On enquiring, we were informed that it was Belle Boyd. Some of us had never heard of the lady before, and we were all inquiring about her. Who was she? Where was she from, and what did she do?"

When Belle sang *Maryland, My Maryland*, that one incident touched D. A. Mahony's heart and emotions and left a life-long impact upon him. Mahony, as well as those within the sound of her powerful voice, listened and, at times, were brought to tears by the impact of her emotions which she poured out while singing. Belle had a way of communicating, and her singing was one of those ways. It was the first time Mahony had heard Belle sing *Maryland, My Maryland*, writing:

The words, stirring enough to Southern hearts, were enunciated by her with such peculiar expression as to touch even sensibilities which did not sympathize with the cause which inspired the song. It was difficult to listen unmoved to this lady throwing her whole soul, as it were, into the expression of the sentiments of devotion to the South, defiance of the North, and affectionately confident appeals to Maryland, which formed the burden of that celebrated song. The pathos of her voice, her apparently forlorn condition, and at these times when her soul seemed absorbed in the thoughts she was uttering in song, her melancholy manner affected all who hear her, not only with compassion for her but with interest in her which came near on several occasions bringing about a conflict between prisoners and guards.

Other Confederate prisoners later remembered after Belle was released from the Old Capitol, the powerful impact she had on them when she performed the song *Maryland, My Maryland*. One day at the Old Capitol in 1863, James J. Williamson, who eventually served with Colonel John S. Mosby and many years later wrote the *History of the 43rd Virginia Battalion of Cavalry*, listened to some men singing the song *Maryland, My Maryland*. Another prisoner named Gus Williams was confined on the same floor as Belle in August 1862. Williamson listened to Gus Williams's account of Belle Boyd's time at the Old Capitol and committed it to paper in 1911 when he published "*Prison Life in the Old Capitol*." Gus Williams was sitting on a bench when others were singing *Maryland, My Maryland*. He rose from the bench where he had been whittling a wood stick, advanced toward the group of singers, and said:

When Belle Boyd was here, I was on the same floor. She would sing that song {Maryland, My Maryland} as if it were her very soul was in every word she uttered. It used to bring a lump up in my throat every time I heard it. It seemed like my heart was ready to jump out, as if I could put my finger down and touch it. I've seen men when she was singing, walk off to one side and pull out their handkerchiefs and wipe their eyes for fear that someone would see them doing the baby act

"She left soon after I came in," Williams continued, "I was glad to know that she was released, but we all missed her. Even some of the Yankees, although they wouldn't show it while she was here; but when she was sent away, they missed her sweet singing, Rebel songs though they were. One of them told me it made him feel sad to hear her sing."

D. A. Mahony asked in his book, what offense did Belle commit for her to be imprisoned at the Old Capitol? He wanted to know more about her. Mahony must have found out much of the information about Belle, which he wrote in his book, *The Prisoner of State*, from other prisoners, hearsay, but then too, he was in the cell room {Rose Greenhow's former room} above her room and it did not take him and a companion by the name of Sheward long to discover a hole in a closet where they had been looking around. The hole was directly over Belle's room. Immediately, Mahony opened communications with Belle, which is how he may have discovered some of his knowledge about her to include later in his book. Mahony often tied his note to a thread and drop it down through the discovered opening. Belle returned the compliment. Mahony and Belle regularly exchanged information. Superintendent Wood and Lieutenant Miller prided themselves on being well informed on every occurrence in the prison contrary to the rules, with all their vigilance aided by the presence, as they admitted, of a detective in every prison except for Belle's room. They never discovered the mail system between Belle and Mahony, but later he wrote that it would make an interesting chapter of the Old Capitol history. One story that Mahony wrote about was interesting, and where he got his information, he did not reveal his sources, but I am going to include what he wrote:

When Banks was down the Shenandoah Valley, Belle conceived the idea of playing the part of Delilah. To accomplish this purpose, she gave out invitations to the Federal officers in camp, including General Banks, for a ball to come off some days subsequently. This done, she took a fleet and long-winded horse, starting late one evening, and rode by morning sixty miles across the mountains to where Stonewall Jackson was encamped. She informed that wary officer of her plans, of the situation of the Federal troops, their disposition in camp, the number of the position of their cannon, and in short, of everything she knew about Banks' army. The night of the ball was fixed for just the time it would take Jackson to march his foot cavalry, as his infantry were called by the confederates, to Banks' camp. Belle's arrangements being all made with Jackson rode back the same day, making the hundred and twenty miles in twenty-four hours.

On the night of the ball, Belle lavished her blandishments on General Banks especially. She had procured a large elegant secesh flag, with which she covered the person of the General, and by her

familiarity made him oblivious, it would seem, to all else than the
attentions of his fair entertainer. Meanwhile Stonewall Jackson had
made a successful march, and knowing from Belle's information, the
weak points to the Federal camp, attacked Banks' corps so suddenly
and with such boldness that it was thrown into confusion. A panic
succeed, and Banks suffered not only an overwhelming defeat, but a
disaster, which has never been repaired as ever since the Shenandoah
valley has been in the virtual, if not in the actual, control of the
Confederates."

In D. A. Mahony's above testimony, he must have been writing about Belle's role during the Shenandoah Valley Campaign of 1862. True, she did make a midnight ride to Confederate Colonel Turner Ashby with information that she had overheard during General Shields's council of war at the Fishback Hotel. True, she knew about the strength and design of Colonel Kenly's Union force at Front Royal, and she did play a role in the fight at Front Royal. True, she liked to entertain and host parties fraternizing with Union officers, but Mahony's story was too fantastically inflated. When stories are told and retold over time, they tend to be stretched. They become folklore and myth. Belle never wrote about this incident in her memoirs. However, some newspapers, such as the Washington *Evening Star*, wrote about her wrapping a Union general in a Rebel flag, but it was not General Banks. General Shields was fond of Belle, but even he does not mention Belle or any such incident of flag wrapping in his memoirs where he had a part to play.

It did not take Mahony long to discover that Belle was a celebrity at the Old Capitol. Whenever she took advantage of the privilege of sitting outside of her cell room on a chair where according to Mahony "the greatest curiosity was manifested by the victims of despotism to see her." Mahony wrote the prisoners on the third floor were civilians, who were being detained at the prison. Often, they had a clear view of Belle and were not as heavily guarded as the other prisoners such as Belle. During the evening hours, prisoners were permitted to crowd inside their room doors where they could see and sometimes exchange words with Belle, they cherished her attention.

On Sunday mornings, Belle went to Sunday preaching. According to Belle, Superintendent Wood walked through the hallway shouting, "All of you whom want to hear the Word of God preached according to Jeff Davis, go into the yard; and all of you who want to hear it preached according to Abe Lincoln go into {room} No. 16."

According to D. A. Mahony, on these occasions when Belle attended preaching, "she wore a small Confederate flag in her bosom." Mahony continued:

No sooner would her presence be known to the Confederate prisoners than they manifested every mark of respect which persons in their situation could bestow on her. Most of them doffed their hats as she approached them, and she, with grace and dignity, which might be envied by a queen, extended a hand to them as she moved along to her designated position in a corner near the preacher. We northern Prisoners of State envied the Confederates who enjoyed the acquaintance of Belle Boyd and secured from her such glances of sympathy as can only glow from a woman's eyes.

Gus Williams also spoke about his reminisce when Belle attended the Sunday morning church services at the prison, what he witnessed and the reaction, adoration, and tribute that the ordinary Confederate soldier surrendered to her. Williams said, "And on Sundays, when there was preaching down in the yard, she would be allowed to come down and sit near the preacher. If you could only have seen how the fellows would try to get near her as she passed. And if she gave them a look or a smile, it did them more good than the preaching. You wouldn't hear a cuss word from any of them for a week, even if one of the guards would swear at them or threaten them."

James Williamson also recalled and included in his publication, *Prison Life in the Old Capitol*, a description from Gus Williams about how Superintendent Wood remembered Belle. Wood said, "her face was not what would be called pretty, her features indicated firmness and daring, but her figure was perfect, and a perfect and splendid specimen of health and vigor. She was a good talker, very persuasive, and the most persistent and enthusiastic Rebel who ever came under my charge. Her father sent her, from time to time, large sums of money, most of which was expended for the comfort of the Confederate prisoners at the Old Capitol."

Williamson also gave Belle credit in his book, and believed that with the information about General Banks and the Union army's operation in the lower Shenandoah Valley, Jackson was able to drive them to the Potomac River. Williamson wrote, "On information furnished by her, Stonewall Jackson drove Banks out of the Shenandoah Valley, for which service Jackson sent a special dispatch thanking her."

Belle undoubtedly left an impression on the Confederate prisoners and many Union officers and guards, especially Superintendent Wood. The prisoners knew and discovered firsthand her life, ways, and compassion and she was not the monster and "accomplished prostitute" that some Northern newspapers had portrayed her. Unquestionably, Belle was someone the Confederate prisoners looked up to during their miserable prison conditions and someone who was very patriotic and an inspiration. Through the trials and tribulations, she endured with the male prisoners at the Old Capitol, she was an encouragement, a symbol of integrity, and showed compassion to all of them.

Source: *J. J. Williamson*

Superintendent William P. Wood

Chapter 15

Old Capitol Incidents

When Belle sang, *Maryland, My Maryland*, she often added phrases that caught the sentry's attention by using words that were offensive to the Union sentry since he was the only soldier nearby. This is because Union sentry guarding her cell room door did not always treated Belle respectfully. One day while walking up and down a seven-by-nine area outside of her cell room, she recognized nearby her cousin John Stephenson {Belle's father's side of the family}, a young cavalry officer, who she claimed served with John Mosby, but most probably the 1st Virginia Cavalry since Mosby's command had not organized at the time. Belle disregarded the prison rules and rushed to greet her cousin when a sentry quickly reacted and placed a bayonet between them. The sentry sent Belle back to her cell room, and her cousin was taken to the guardhouse for more serious offenders.

Sometimes the sentries were rude both in word and action toward Belle. One day, a more serious incident occurred. Belle's servant had given her a loaf of sugar. Immediately, Belle thought of the two Confederate officers across the hallway from her cell room and decided it might be good if they could enjoy some luxuries. Belle approached the sentry guarding her room and requested permission to pass it over to them. She received what she believed was an unmistakable consent, "I have no objection."

Belle believed she had the Union sentry's permission and proceeded to hand the sugar to one of the officers when the Union sentry struck her left hand with the butt-end of his musket rifle, and with such a forceful blow that she believed that her thumb was broken. Belle demanded the Union sentry call the corporal of the guard, but the sentry refused.

Belle continued to demand her right to speak with the corporal of the guard, but the Union sentry became furious. According to D. A. Mahony, Belle was "brave and unterrified, and dared the craven-hearted fellow to put his threat into execution." The Union sentry lost control and pinned Belle by her dress against the wall with his bayoneted musket, inflicting a flesh wound on her arm, a scar she carried for the rest of her life.

Because of all the commotion from the angry prisoners, the corporal of the guard soon arrived and relieved the sentry from his duties. It did happen none too soon because if the Union sentry had continued to assault Belle, "he would have been torn to pieces before it could be known to the prison authorities what had happened," according to Mahony. However, Belle did not comment on the punishment she received for the infraction of the prison rules.

Sometimes Belle sat at her barred window and looked abroad upon the city's houses, streets, and citizens. Frequently, Union troops marched by the Old Capitol. Out of curiosity, Belle looked through her window and watched them pass by the prison. When they noticed Belle, they indulged in "coarse jest, vulgar expressions, and the vilest slang of the brothel made still more coarse, vulgar, and indecent by throwing off the little restraint which civilized society placed upon the most abandoned prostitutes and their companions."

Belle took revenge on the Union soldiers by battling them with words by praising President Jefferson Davis and Stonewall Jackson. Belle made inquiries of the Union soldiers, such as, "How long did it take you to come from Bull Run?"

The Union army had been defeated at Bull Run, near Manassas, Virginia, the previous year and fled to Washington in a panic, but she knew her taunting humiliated them.

Belle asked, "Are you going to Richmond?" From the beginning of the war until now, it was the battle cry of the Northern politician "On to Richmond." General McClellan's Army of the Potomac had been before Richmond during the spring and summer of 1862 and could not capture it.

Still, Belle taunted the Union soldiers by asking, "Where is Pope's coat?" Belle was referring to General John Pope, who had his dress uniform coat captured by Jeb Stuart's cavalry at Catlett Station. The coat was displayed in a store in Richmond during the summer of 1862.

The Union soldiers had endured enough of Belle's taunting and one angrily replied, "Hush up you d---b---h, or I'll shoot you."

Belle boldly and defiantly shouted her reply, "Shoot me. Go meet men, you cowards. What are you doing here in Washington? Stonewall Jackson is waiting for you on the other side of the Potomac. Aye, you could fight defenseless, imprisoned women like me, but you were driven out of the Shenandoah Valley by the men of Virginia."

Did the officers of the Union soldiers passing by permit the soldiers to thus insult a female? According to D.A. Mahony, the answer is "yes," and they "participated with the soldiers in uttering the most vulgar language and indecent allusions to the imprisoned woman, and that too, without having the remotest idea of who she was, or of what she was accused." Since Belle's incarceration at the Old Capitol was so highly publicized by the Northern newspapers it is hard to imagine the Union soldiers did not know who she was and why she was detained.

When the marching Union soldiers provoked Belle, she placed a "secesh" flag through the window and left it there until they had all passed the Old Capitol. Then, sometimes when they insulted her, she stepped away from the window, out of sight where she could not hear them.

*   *   *   *

While at the Old Capitol, Belle became reacquainted with a Confederate officer named Lieutenant Clifford McVay. Lieutenant McVay was wounded near Richmond and left for dead by his comrades. He was discovered by Union troops, who took him, prisoner. McVay's condition was such that he could not be removed too far. He had some friends who interceded on his behalf and therefore paroled and cared for by his friends. Since he had been paroled, he did not return to the Confederate army but instead, he returned to his home in Alexandria, Virginia, which was behind Union lines. When Lieutenant McVay was offered the opportunity to take the Oath of Allegiance to the United States, he refused and was sent to the Old Capitol as a prisoner of war.

Lieutenant McVay was in a cell room on the same floor as Belle's but not directly across from her room. Soon Belle and Lieutenant McVay began communicating with each other. Belle and McVay used a marble with a small note tied around it, and they rolled the marble from one room to another with the help of the other prisoners. Sometimes the sound of the marble became so annoying to the sentry that he would look around, but not in time to catch the guilty party. Soon through this method, Belle and Lieutenant McVay cultivated a relationship that ripened into a romance and an engagement. It was not the kind of romance and engagement a couple would generally pursue. Belle did not marry Lieutenant McVay. She did not even mention the affair in her memoirs, but according to historian Louis Siguad, the engagement took place. According to Siguad, a letter written by her aunt by marriage, Susan Glenn, wrote that Belle was about to marry a Confederate soldier named Lieutenant McVay. Belle was most likely flattered and infatuated with McVay's communicating charm, the words, and the admiration he felt toward her. But apparently, it was not the deep-seated love and commitment it takes when a couple loves each other and plans to make a life-long commitment.

Another factor soon influenced McVay and Belle's relationship. Union authorities decided to release her in a prisoner-of-war exchange. General Wadsworth, sent General John Dix at Fortress Monroe a dispatch:

General: I am directed by General Thomas to forward you all the prisoners of war confined in the Old Capitol Prison. Enclosed here with are lists of prisoners forwarded. I forward, likewise, Miss Belle Boyd, a young lady arrested on suspicion of having communication with the enemy. I have learned that she shall be placed over the lines by the first flag of truce, which in accordance with her wishes. No specific charges or information has been lodged against her.

Belle was going home.

143

Chapter 16

Freedom & Celebrity

Soon communications between Belle and Lieutenant McVay slowed and eventually ceased. It all came about one evening while Belle sat outside her room reading. Superintendent Wood appeared shouting, "All you rebels get ready; you are going to Dixie tomorrow, and Miss Belle is going with you." All the prisoners began cheering, and Belle screamed with joy. Belle was being exchanged for Colonel Michael Corcoran of the 69th New York Infantry, who had been captured at the Battle of First Manassas in July 1861. Belle had friends who had been working behind the scenes on her behalf to obtain her release and freedom. Ward Hill Lemon, who was from Berkeley County, Virginia {West Virginia} a law partner of Abraham Lincoln before the war, and the president's bodyguard, was also a good friend of the Boyd family. Years later, Lemon wrote in his memoirs, "The next day, the famous woman spy, Belle Boyd, {whom the humble author of these pages well knew and who was at her respected father's house…Ben Boyd…at Bunker Hill in Berkeley County, Virginia on the night of her birth} was arrested and sent to Washington and afterward released at the instance of the writer through the instigation of friendship for her father and family induced by early association."

D. A. Mahony recalled the reaction from the prisoners when they learned that Belle was among the prisoners to be exchanged, writing:

As soon as it became known in the Old Capitol that she was about to leave, there was not one, Federalist or Confederate, Prisoner of State, officer of the Old Capitol, as well as prisoner of war, who did not feel that he was about to part with one whom he had at least a great personal regard. With many it was more than mere regard. There was more than one McVay who aspired to the enviable position,

144

which the handsome, dashing, and gentlemanly Confederate Lieutenant succeeded in acquiring. Every inmate of the Old Capitol tried to procure some token of remembrance from Belle, and there was scarcely one who did not bestow to her some mark of regard, esteem or affection, as their sentiment and feelings influenced them severely, and as the means at their disposal afforded them an opportunity to manifest their sensibility. While every man who had any delicacy of feeling for the apparently forlorn prisoner, rejoiced at her release from such a loathsome place, and from being subject, as she was continually was, to insult and contumely, there was not overcome him as he saw her leave the place for home.

The following morning, many of the Washington citizens turned out to see the departure of Belle Boyd and the rebel prisoners. Belle and 200 Confederate prisoners were formed in a line across the street from the Old Capitol building.

Belle stepped into an open carriage with Major Norman Fitzhugh, formerly of General Jeb Stuart's staff. Major Fitzhugh assumed the responsibility of escorting Belle to Richmond. When the carriage with Belle and the Confederate officer departed, cheers came from the crowd. After a month of captivity, Belle was free from prison, but she had committed one more rebellious act, that of carrying on her person "two gold sabre-knots for Generals Jackson and Joe Johnston."

Belle rode to the wharves along the Potomac River where the U. S. S. *Juanita* awaited to take her and the Confederate prisoners off to Fortress Monroe. At dawn on August 30, they set sail for Fortress Monroe.

The following morning, the U. S. S. *Juanita* arrived at Fortress Monroe, where Lieutenant Darling of General Dix's staff boarded the steamer. Belle noticed the transports carrying the rest of General McClellan's army back to Northern Virginia, but she did not feel dismayed by the fleet's appearance but happy to be free. After boarding another vessel and riding up the James River, Belle could tell they were getting closer to Richmond when she noticed the "Stars and Bars" waving in the evening breeze from a window at the house of Mr. Aikens after rounding a river bend.

145

When the U.S.S. *Juanita* tied up at a pier near Richmond, Colonel Robert Ould, the Confederate Commissioner of Exchange at Richmond, and his associate Mr. Watson met Belle and the other prisoners and marched them on shore. Colonel Ould knew the extent of how the Northern newspapers had tried to embarrass and demonize Belle by writing that she was a "camp follower" and a "prostitute" and "controversies raged about her chastity." According to Belle's first biographer Louis Sigaud, he wrote, "Had Belle been even the most repentant of all errant Magdalens, Commissioner Ould would nevertheless have refused to admit her." In a letter of reproach to his federal confrere regarding two immoral women sent through by the federals, Colonel Ould said, "Sir: I send back to you two strumpets are but the beginning of a classic of outraged morality." Continuing, Commissioner Ould wrote, "holy feelings, the sanctity of a pure woman's character," and mourned the dishonor cast upon "the purity of a flag of truce." The high-minded Mr. Ould was so angry that he seemed to have considered the affair a possible reflection of his honor. He said sternly, "If I did not believe you were imposed upon, I would be justified in taking this matter as a personal affront."

The same night of Belle's arrival in Richmond, she stayed at Mr. Aikens's house and thoroughly enjoyed his society and that of his family. She found the family to be very hospitable. The following day, she rode in a carriage to the Ballard House, located at 14th and Franklin Street in Richmond, where rooms had been prepared for her reception. The Ballard House was a plush, upscale hotel connected to another upscale hotel, The Spotswood, by an enclosed iron bridge above Franklin Street. The Ballard House was a popular venue for gathering Confederate congressmen, senators, and Northern spies.

On the way to the Confederate capitol, Belle's route took her near the encampment of Company A, Richmond Light Infantry Blues, 46th Virginia Infantry commanded by Captain O. J. Wise, former Governor Henry Wise's son. When her carriage passed by, Company A stood at attention and presented arms in honor of her for her heroic courage and commitment to the cause of the Southern Confederacy.

The Richmond newspapers also announced Belle's arrival. On September 3, 1862, the *Richmond Dailey Dispatch* published; "About two hundred Confederate exchange prisoners arrived in this city yesterday. Among the officers was Maj. Norman Fitzhugh, A. A. Gen. of Stuart's Cavalry Division, a brave officer, who was captured a short time since. Miss Belle Boyd, of Winchester, who has become celebrated from the fear in which the Yankees held her, was also among those who arrived."

After spending ten days at the Ballard House, Belle moved to a boardinghouse on Grace Street owned by a lady she identified by the name of Mrs. W. While I was searching the Richmond civil war archives, there was a Mrs. Elizabeth Wynn, who owned an upscale boardinghouse on Grace Street. Mrs. Wynn is undoubtedly Mrs. W., who Belle was speaking about. While at the boardinghouse, Belle enjoyed the company of society and friends. She was now a celebrity among the residents of Richmond and had now, according to one newspaper, acquired "international fame." By now, everyone had heard of Belle Boyd and her exploits of shooting a Union soldier in defense of her family, her role in the fight at Front Royal, and her imprisonment at the Old Capitol in Washington. Other noted individuals living at Mrs. Wynn's boardinghouse that Belle became acquainted with were General and Mrs. Joseph Johnston, General Louis Wigfall, and his family from Texas. General Wigfall also served in the Confederate senate. One evening while living at the boardinghouse, an officer appeared. The officer was a prisoner at the Old Capitol the same time Belle was imprisoned. He had arrived in Richmond to give Belle a gift from her fellow prisoner comrades. The gift was a gold watch and chatelaine, enameled and richly set with diamonds. A note in the box read, "in token of the affection and esteem of my fellow prisoners in the Old Capitol."

Belle's fame and celebrity had spread while living a short time in Richmond. General Thomas R. R. Cobb knew of her, and while writing a letter to his wife dated September 24, 1862, he mentioned Belle: "Belle Boyd, the celebrated girl, is at an adjoining house." The adjoining house was Mrs. Wynn's boardinghouse.

While Belle enjoyed her freedom in Richmond, the single bloodiest day of the American Civil War had occurred in Maryland along Antietam Creek. What would become known to the Confederate army as the Battle of Sharpsburg and to the Union army as the Battle of Antietam, 23,000 soldiers in fourteen hours became casualties of the war. General Robert E. Lee and the Army of Northern Virginia fought a series of battles from August 9 until September 1 against Union Major-General John Pope and his Army of Virginia at Cedar Mountain, Manassas, and Chantilly while Belle was confined at the Old Capitol. General Pope and his army retreated to the forts around Washington, leaving the way open for General Lee and the Army of Northern Virginia to cross the Potomac River. General McClellan, who had commanded the Union army on the Virginia Peninsula during the spring and summer of 1862, was now given command of the Union army in and around Washington to defend the capitol. He was expected to stop Lee's army. On September 4, Lee's army began crossing the Potomac River in the first Northern invasion, fighting a series of battles against McClellan's Union army from September 12 until September 20 at Harpers Ferry, South Mountain, Antietam, and Shepherdstown before retreating into the Shenandoah Valley.

After the battle along Antietam Creek, Ben Boyd, still serving in the Confederate army, arrived in Richmond to take Belle home to Martinsburg. The *Richmond Dailey Dispatch* published, "Miss Belle Boyd has returned to Martinsburg." Martinsburg was once more in the hands of Confederate troops, and Belle was eager to see her family, but her visit would not be lengthy but short in duration.

The following day after returning home to Martinsburg, Belle rode out to an encampment to visit General Jackson with a friend, who she does not identify. According to Belle, "As I dismounted at the door of his tent, he came out, and, gently placing his hands upon my head, assured me of the pleasure he felt at seeing me once more and free. Our interview was of necessity short, for the demands upon his valuable time were incessant; but his fervent 'God bless you, my child,' will never be obliterated from my memory, as long as Providence shall be pleased to allow it to retain its power."

General Jackson warned Belle that if his force had to leave Martinsburg, it would be expedient for Belle to leave as on previous occasions because the Union forces would soon occupy the town, and she would be arrested and imprisoned since she was on parole and would be violating it by being behind Union lines. General Jackson promised to give her plenty of warning by which her "plans must be regulated."

148

James Power Smith wrote a different account of Belle's visit to General Jackson and an account that must be given creditability. Smith was originally a theological student at Hampden-Sydney College when the war broke out. He enlisted in the Rockbridge Artillery and served in that unit when General Lee invaded Maryland. Still, after the invasion, his life changed when General Jackson one day sent for him and invited him to serve on his staff as an aide-de-camp with the rank of lieutenant. Smith's account of Belle's visit to Jackson is quite different from the one she wrote in her memoirs. Smith wrote:

One day at Bunker Hill, the notable female scout, Belle Boyd, made her appearance on horseback with the escort of a young Confederate cavalryman. She was well mounted, and quite a soldierly figure, and asked to see General Jackson. But the General was averse, and more than once refused to see the young woman, of whose loyalty he was not altogether assured. She was much disappointed and went away quite angry with the aide who had denied her admission to the general's tent. Some days after this she sent a message that if she ever caught that young man in Martinsburg, she would cut his ears off.

Belle's anger and attitude toward Lieutenant Smith over the incident is in character for her.

Why did Belle not write about this episode in her memoirs? Evidently, she wanted to protect her creditability as a Confederate spy. Many viewed Stonewall Jackson as a Southern hero and a great leader of the Southern Cause. Someone of Jackson's stature would not be challenged on any issue. All Southerners greatly honored Jackson, and his word was not to be questioned. One must also look at this from Jackson's point of view. Yes, Jackson must have known that Belle had been honored in Richmond and looked at as a Southern heroine, but she had also been a Yankee prisoner-of-war for a month. Jackson may have considered, what, if anything, did the Union authorities attempt to do to try and break her willpower? He may have thought that Belle being held in prison and its hardships would be too much for a young lady of eighteen to endure emotionally. Did she agree on some deal, such as trapping Jackson to secure her freedom with such little time in prison? All these questions were reasonable for Jackson before placing his trust in her once more. Also, another factor in Jackson's hesitancy was the fact that he read in the Northern newspapers the accounts of and from Southern civilians in the area that Belle had, before imprisonment, been mingling with Union officers while they were in the area. All these questions are legitimate for a commander to ask. Spies and counter-espionage agents were constantly infiltrating both Union and Confederate armies.

In Belle's memoirs, the account she wrote must have taken place on another journey to General Jackson's headquarters. Jackson must have reconsidered and believed Belle was still loyal to the Southern Cause and she could be trusted, and this is the account she used in her memoirs.

Shortly after Belle spoke with General Jackson, he rode to Martinsburg and had tea with her family. The following day, Jackson notified Belle the troops under his command were moving back to Winchester. On October 26, General McClellan's Army of the Potomac began crossing the Potomac River at Berlin, {Brunswick} Maryland, marching south, east of the Blue Ridge Mountains through the Loudoun Valley, once again, Union troops occupied Harpers Ferry. This may have been the timeline in which Jackson warned Belle she needed to leave Martinsburg and move to Winchester. Jackson offered her the use of an ambulance for transportation, which she accepted because, as Belle describes in her own words, it was "the invariable practice of the Yankees, when they evacuated any place, to take with them every horse and mule, without the slightest discrimination between public and private property; and, should circumstances compel them to leave any animal behind, it was in these instances wantonly destroyed."

While at Winchester, General Jackson rewarded Belle. She wrote, "I received my commission as Captain and honorary Aide-de-camp to Stonewall Jackson; and thenceforth I enjoyed the respect paid to an officer by soldiers." Jackson did this to honor Belle for her daring service as a spy and an agent for the Southern Confederacy. Still, it was no more than an honorary position because she did not travel and campaign with the army functioning in an aide's capacity such as Henry Kyd Douglas, Sandie Pendleton, or James Powers Smith.

Certain privileges and respect were due to her because of her captain's rank. First, she was to be shown all the respect and courtesies due an officer in the Confederate army, and secondly, she could assist with any reviews of Confederate troops.

Before her journey to the Deep South, Belle had the opportunity to participate in a review of Confederate troops with Lord Hartingdon from England and Colonel Leslie, and again when Generals Lee and Longstreet reviewed General Wilcox's division. Several newspapers wrote about Belle's honorary position in the Confederate army years after the war ended. The *Wheeling Intelligencer* wrote, "Acting upon General Jackson's advice she {Belle} removed to Winchester in the summer of 1862, and it was there and then she received her commission as captain and honorable aid to the general, and thenceforth enjoyed the respect paid to an officer." When the reviews occurred, Belle attended on horseback and associated with the staff officers. Again, The *New York Times* published another article about Belle's position, "In Winchester, Jackson conferred upon her a commission as Captain in the Confederate army." It must be noted this event occurred in the autumn of 1862 and not during the summer of 1862.

Another event occurred after Belle received her commission and before General Jackson's troops departed from the Shenandoah Valley to Fredericksburg. While Belle was on her way to a troop review near Winchester, she met a young barefooted Confederate soldier painfully trudging along the road. When Belle witnessed his condition, she dismounted, removed her shoes, and the fine cloth gaiters laced at the side, trimmed with patent leather, and made the young soldier put them on his feet. The young soldier's companion told Belle they would not last long to justify the sacrifice. Belle replied, "Oh if it rests his poor feet only a little while, I am repaid. He is not old enough to be away from his mother." Belle must have attracted a lot of attention when she arrived at the review wearing her new Riding Habit presented to her by the Confederate army for her heroism made from gray Confederate cloth and trimmed in black braid with her captain's rank on the collar and yet barefooted.

Belle lived a daring life and one of intrigue and one of adventure. One of those adventures took her back to Martinsburg to visit her family and have fun, but it could have been costly if captured by Union troops. One incident needs to be mentioned. While Jackson's force was still in the Shenandoah Valley near Winchester, General Wade Hampton, who commanded a division in Jeb Stuart's cavalry, was operating in Martinsburg. While Hampton's cavalry operated near Martinsburg, Belle daringly took the risk to pay "many visits" to her home. On one of those occasions, she was almost captured by Union forces. According to Belle, she had arrived in Martinsburg accompanied by a large party. While dancing, Belle and her friends were informed the Yankees were advancing. On more than one occasion, this same alarm was previously broadcasted when she returned home. As on previous occasions, Belle and her friends responded, "Wolf! Wolf!" Only this time, it was a true, and Belle and her friends had little time to escape before heavy skirmishing near the outskirts of the town began to occur. Belle and her friends immediately departed and escaped capture, but it would be the last occasion of seeing her mother for nearly a year.

The Union army now operated east of the Blue Ridge Mountains and slowly made its way south toward Richmond. With the possibility of a new campaign, Jackson's corps was about to leave the Shenandoah Valley. When Jackson's army did leave, it would be the last time Belle would speak to or see him.

Chapter 17

The Deep South

On November 5, while the Union army marched south through Virginia to attack General Lee's army, General George McClellan was relieved of his duty as the commanding officer of the Army of the Potomac. The reluctant Major-General Ambrose Burnside assumed command of the army and his duties on November 9. When it was learned that General Burnside would continue the offensive, General Lee, who had recently recommended Jackson's promotion to lieutenant general, sent for him and the army's Second Corps. On November 22, Lieutenant-General Stonewall Jackson said his last farewell to the citizens of Winchester and began his march toward Fredericksburg, Virginia, and his destiny.

With the Confederate army departing the lower Shenandoah Valley, Belle and some other officers' wives did likewise. Belle had thought about going to Staunton in the upper Shenandoah Valley but decided against it when she learned that there was a smallpox epidemic. Belle and the officers' wives left before the army, leaving behind their baggage, which was transported in one of the ordnance wagons with the army. The ladies continued through the Blue Ridge Mountain to Flint Hill, and then to Culpeper Court House.

When Belle arrived at Culpeper Court House, heavy snow fell, and the wind blew it into drifts. Belle went to the brick home of Mrs. Presley Rixey in Culpeper to seek shelter from the weather. Mrs. Rixey's home was located on spacious grounds on Coleman Street, now Main Street. William "Extra Billy" Smith, a general in the Army of Northern Virginia and the governor of Virginia during the second half of the war had constructed the home. The house was demolished in the early 1930s to construct a new post office. Today the county administration offices are on the Rixey house site.

Apparently, Belle knew about Mrs. Rixey's home to search it out. Mrs. Rixey's home was a favorite starting point for runners of the Union blockade, and it was near the Confederate camps. Belle also must have known Mrs. Rixey entertained many distinguished guests and that her home was popular among Confederate officers during the war.

On that wintery night, Nellie Grey, a young lady of Belle's age, stayed at Mrs. Rixey's home. Nellie was the wife of Dan Grey from Petersburg, Virginia, who was the regimental adjutant of the 13th Virginia Cavalry.

Nellie was in her room when she heard a rapping at her bedroom door. When she opened the door, Mrs. Rixey asked Nellie if she would share her room that night with another lady. Nellie recalled, "The idea of sending anybody out in such weather was not to be thought of for a moment," therefore, she agreed. Nellie quickly dressed and went down to the parlor. Nellie recalled that Mrs. Rixey's parlor "was filled with Confederate soldiers who were there either because they were near the army or because they were waiting an opportunity to run the blockade."

Even though the weather outside was miserable, the atmosphere in Mrs. Rixey's parlor appeared gay, and as usual, several officers of rank were in the room. Nellie recalled she was "busy writing messages to her mother to be sent by a little lady who intended on running the blockade to Baltimore, that she did not catch her roommate's name when introduced by Mrs. Rixey."

Nellie gave an excellent description of Belle. She recalled Belle was "nineteen, perhaps twenty, rather young, I thought, to be traveling alone. True, I was not older, but then I was married, which makes all the difference in the world." Nellie noticed Belle was "well dressed, a brilliant talker, and everyone in the room was attracted to her, especially the men. She talked chiefly to the men; indeed, I am afraid she did not care particularly for the women, and at first, we were a little piqued; but when she said she was devoted to The Cause, we were ready to forgive anything." Belle told everyone in the room she had been a prisoner at the Old Capitol in Washington, and then she showed them her watch the prisoners had purchased for her.

After some time had passed, Nellie went up to the bedroom, fell fast asleep, and did not hear Belle when she entered the room. It was not until the following morning, when the maid arrived to make a fire, that Nellie awakened and recalled, "We woke up face to face in the same bed, and she told me that her name was Belle Boyd, and I knew for the first time that my bedfellow was the South's famous female spy."

When they got up, Belle took a large bottle of cologne and poured it into a washbasin, where she bathed. The cologne was the first Nellie had seen in over a year. It was the last Nellie saw of Belle until she ran the blockade.

That same day at dinner, a servant whispered to Nellie that someone wanted to see her in the hallway. She excused herself and went out to see who was visiting her. Nellie noticed and later recalled, "an abject, pitiable looking creature, a soldier, ragged and footsore." The soldier wore grey trousers patched with blue and a jacket with much "Federal blue." He looked like he belonged to both armies. Nellie again recalled, "His trousers were much too short for him and altogether small. His shoes were heavy brogans twice too large for him, and tied on with strings. He was without socks and ankles showed naked and short between trousers and shoes." It was not until the ragged soldier spoke that Nellie recognized his voice as her brother-in-law, Lieutenant Dick Grey.

Nellie invited Lieutenant Grey to have dinner with them, but because of his appearance, he declined. However, it did not end there. Suddenly the ladies filed out of the dining room into the hallway where Dick Grey and Nellie were still talking. After noticing his appearance, and while the ladies held a council, Mrs. Rixey and Belle took the soldier and fed him a good dinner. Afterward, the ladies contributed articles of clothing for the needy soldier.

After dinner, Dick Grey stood in the hallway ready to return to camp, and Nellie recalled, "Belle Boyd came down the stairway, carrying a large new shawl."

"You must let me wrap you up, lieutenant," Belle said, putting the shawl around Dick's shoulders and pinning it together.

Dick blushed and hesitated, "A shawl like that was too much; it was a princely gift, a fortune."

"I can't let you go back to camp in this thin jacket," Belle said, "while I have this shawl. It is serving our country, lieutenant, while it protects her soldiers from the cold. I may need it? No, no, I can get others where this one came from."

"I have heard many generous deeds like this done by Belle Boyd," Nellie Grey wrote, "She did not spend another night with us. She seemed to feel that she had the weight of the Confederacy on her shoulders and took the afternoon train to Richmond."

Belle did not write about her time at Mrs. Rixey's home or her acquaintance with Nellie Grey. But Nellie remembered it forty-five years later when she recited her life experiences to Myrta Lockett while they had tea and knitted in front of a fireplace.

Nellie recalled that Belle was going to Richmond. Belle wrote in her memoirs that she was going to Charlottesville, where she "remained some time." She may have gone to Richmond and then returned to Charlottesville or vice versa. But she does not leave a record of her experiences or whom she visited while in Richmond or Charlottesville.

*   *   *   *

Sometime after Belle arrived in Charlottesville, she became anxious to rejoin her mother in Martinsburg. Belle knew returning to the lower Shenandoah Valley would be unsafe because of the risk of being captured by Union troops and again imprisoned in Washington. So, she decided to write General Jackson and ask for his opinion, which would be the wisest decision to consider. She was more than willing to run the risk of capture, but she would abide by his decision.

General Jackson sent an answer, and his letter is below, written verbatim:

Head-Quarters, Army of Virginia
Near Culpeper Court-House

January 29th 1862

My Dear Child,

I received your letter asking my advice regarding your returning to your home, which is now in the Federal lines. As you have asked for my advice, I can but candidly give it. I think that it is not safe; and therefore, do not attempt it until it is, for you know the consequences. You would doubtless be imprisoned and possibly might not be released so soon again. You had better go to your relatives in Tennessee, and there remain until you can go with safety. God bless you.

Truly your friend,
T. J. Jackson

The date on Jackson's letter must have been a mistake on his part because on January 29, 1862, Belle was in Front Royal, Virginia. She arrived at Front Royal from her family's home in Martinsburg by the beginning of 1862. General Jackson could have intended the date to have been 1863 instead of 1862, or he made an error in the month, writing January instead of November, which is most likely. In January 1863, Jackson's headquarters was near Fredericksburg, Virginia, on a plantation known as Moss Neck, which the Corbin family owned. He spent the winter at Moss Neck catching up on writing official reports. He was not at or near Culpeper Court House. Also, Belle arrived in Tennessee before the end of 1862, so the letter had to have been sent to Belle sometime between November 29, 1862, when General Lee sent for Jackson's command to come to Fredericksburg, and the middle of and no later than the third week of December 1862.

* * * *

After receiving Jackson's letter, Belle did not hesitate to leave Virginia and traveled to Tennessee. For about six weeks, Belle visited with her family and soon became restless, wanting to be "on the go" once more, but it was then that the widow of her relative, Judge Samuel B. Boyd, Belle's first cousin who had left Martinsburg when she was seven, and who was also a former mayor of Knoxville, prevailed on Belle to spend the winter and spring in their home. Mrs. Boyd had a large family of boys and girls, some of who were Belle's age. The Boyd family lived in the Blount Mansion on Hill Avenue, and the mansion was formerly the home of William Blount, the first territorial governor of Tennessee.

On February 12, 1863, Belle arrived in Knoxville and began her extended stay with her family at Blount Mansion, but not until she was first a guest and visited with General J. News quickly spread of Belle Boyd's arrival in Knoxville. According to Belle, she wrote, "The second night after my arrival I was serenaded by the band, and the people congregated in vast numbers to get a glimpse of the 'rebel spy'; for I had accepted the sobriquet given me by the Yankees, and I was known throughout the North and South by the same cognomen." After the band played one or two songs, the people in the street called for her appearance on the balcony.

There was an article published by the *New York Times*, dated February 23, 1862: "Confederate spy Belle Boyd is serenaded in Knoxville by the Florida Brass Band. When the crowds outside her home demands her presence, she appears in a window and thanked them for the compliment."

Belle liked the notoriety but dreaded speaking to a large crowd. She begged General J. to be her substitute, and he should thank them for her. General J. did as ask. But the crowd was relentless and continued their demands. She begged but knew they would not be satisfied until she appeared for them. She agreed and complied with their wishes. Belle steeled her nerves and stepped forth from the window. The crowds cheered louder as she appeared on the balcony before them. Uncharacteristic of her, Belle did not have a formal speech for them or appropriate words to express her gratitude, and what Belle said to the crowd did not personally please her. She was "morally convinced" that she would break down if she attempted anything like an oration. Shortly, the crowd became silent, and Belle told her kind-hearted audience the following words: "Like General Joe Johnston, 'I can fight, but I cannot make speeches.' But, my good friends, I no less feel and appreciate the kind compliment you have paid me this night."

Belle felt relieved when she finished speaking; the Florida Brass Band began playing the Southern air *Dixie* and another selection, *Good Night*.

Who was General J.? General J. was General Joseph Johnston. Johnston was in Tennessee by order of the Confederate War Department investigating claims of General Braxton Bragg's unfitness to lead the Army of Tennessee after their defeat at Stone River, south of Nashville, on the last day of December 1862 and the first day of January 1863. Belle knew Johnston from her brief stay at Mrs. Wynn's boarding house after her release in August 1862 from the Old Capitol Prison.

Most believed Belle spoke to her audience and was serenaded with music from the balcony of Blount Mansion. Belle was specific in her memoirs that she walked onto a balcony. The problem is, the Blount Mansion had porches, but the house never had a balcony. No windows large enough at Blount Mansion opened where she could have walked out onto a balcony. Where General Johnston resided at the Lamar House on Gay Street, the structure had large windows that she could walk through and where she could walk out onto a balcony. This is where Belle gave her speech and was serenaded with music because she wrote the next day, she "now became the guest of my relative, Judge Samuel Boyd; and pleasant indeed was my visit to Knoxville." To suggest even further that this event occurred at the Lamar House, Belle, in her own words, had not even begun her visit with her Boyd kinfolk.

Belle was very happy with her reception to Knoxville. An article appeared the next day in the *Daily Register*:

The fair and fearless Virginia heroine whose daring defense of her father's house when Charlestown, {Martinsburg} Va. was first invaded by the Yankees, and whose invaluable service in conveying information to our lines in spite of the espionage of the craven foe, have won for her from the Northern press the title of the most courageous and dangerous of rebel female spies, is now sojourning in this city at the residence of her cousins, Samuel B. Boyd, Esq. She was serenaded last night by the Florida Brass Band, and on being loudly called for by the crowd appeared at the window.

The Memphis *Daily Appeal* published an article on Belle confirming General Johnston's appearance in Knoxville, dated February 24, 1863: "The *Register* boast of the distinguished personages in Knoxville, on the 17th. Among them it enumerates General Joe Johnston, Gen. Price (Old Pap), Belle Boyd and many other hero and heroines."

While Belle stayed in Knoxville, she became very close to her cousin, Sue; they were the same age. Eighty-eight years later, on March 11, 1932, Sue still remembered in a letter to Mary Nelson that Belle was "gracious, a witty and brilliant talker" and had a "perfect form." In her letter, Sue recalled her life experiences with Belle by remembering that she was a fearless and magnificent rider of horses, that they attended parties, balls, and kept company with young officers and gentlemen of social standing. Belle became very popular with the officers, even showing off her Confederate officer's uniform.

Belle also described her time in Knoxville as "gay and animated beyond description. Party succeeded party, ball followed ball, concert came upon concert," and she "took no thought of time." The rigors and hardships of war, prison life, her Old Capitol romance with Lieutenant McVay, and all she had experienced previously had faded.

In the spring of 1863, Belle wrote, "I made up my mind to make a tour through the South, and then return to Virginia." Her cousin, Sue, remembered Belle was "restless" and wanted "new fields to conquer."

Before Belle departed Knoxville, she freely conversed with three Union officers on their way to Libby Prison in Richmond, Virginia. The officers were Captain Warren P. Edgarton, 1st Ohio Artillery, who had been captured at the fight at Murfreesboro, Tennessee, Lieutenant M. L. Paddock, an adjutant of a reserve artillery unit,

160

Department of the Cumberland, and Lieutenant T. J. Spencer, Assistant Ordnance Chief of General William Rosecrans's staff. While Lieutenants Spencer and Paddock were traveling on a passenger train nine miles from Nashville, Texas Rangers of General Joe Wheeler's cavalry of the Army of Tennessee captured them. The officers were paroled but recaptured again by Wheeler's cavalry and taken to the commanding officer, who informed them their "parole was illegal." They finally ended up at General Braxton Bragg's headquarters in Tullahoma, Tennessee. They were all placed on a train and sent to Libby Prison in Richmond, Virginia. They were on the train destined for Knoxville and stayed the night in the city. That evening they quartered at the Lamar House at their own expense, where they "were allowed considerable liberty" and "received kind treatment." According to an article published May 12, 1863, in the *Cleveland Morning Leader*, they "met Belle Boyd, the famous rebel spy at Knoxville, however, and were permitted to converse freely with her." According to the article, several Union ladies came to the parlor with her and made the acquaintance with the prisoners. The prisoners, on learning they were leaving, were allowed to "bid the ladies good-bye in the presence of the Chief of Police and a guard."

According to Lieutenants Spencer and Paddock, they were captured on April 10, 1863, which means that Belle was still in Knoxville during the first three weeks of April and had not yet traveled to Alabama.

As Belle traveled further through the South, she was received with joy and found the people were warm-hearted, sensitive, and receptive to her. When her arrival was anticipated at the towns she passed, invitations of the most hospitable were extended. Many offered her assistance, and regards of affection were innumerable. Belle accepted as many invitations as time permitted, visiting productive cotton plantations in Alabama, and witnessing first-hand what life was like on a vast estate. She visited Montgomery, the first Confederate capital, during the early months of 1861, where she "attended a ball held there, and was the belle." While in Montgomery, "she stopped a duel between two Frenchmen who were going to fight in the garden attached to the hotel." After visiting Montgomery, she continued too Mobile. She wrote that it was like "one long ovation." Indeed, the

Southerners did love her, especially the young women who idolized her and thought of her as their hero. As many of the young Southern ladies looked at and listened to Belle, they too wished they could have played the same part she had experienced in the war and received the same glory now being bestowed upon her. They treated her quite differently than the young ladies from Virginia.

Before arriving at Mobile, Belle received a telegram that Stonewall Jackson had been wounded at Chancellorsville, Virginia. She wrote the rumor she heard was that the wound was "trifling, so slight, indeed, as to be of no consequences." Confederate soldiers of the 18th North Carolina regiment, Jim Lane's brigade, accidentally wounded Jackson on the evening of May 2 while he was on reconnaissance beyond Confederate lines. As a result, Jackson was wounded in his left arm, was recovering from having his left arm amputated, pneumonia set in, and died on May 10, 1863.

Belle was at the Battle House Hotel when she received a telegram that Jackson had died. The telegram said:

Battle House, Mobile, Alabama

Miss Belle Boyd,

General Jackson now lies in state at the Governor's mansion.

T. Bassett French,
A.D.C. to the Governor

Belle felt the shock and later wrote her feelings in her memoirs: "These few words were the funeral oration of a man who, for a rare combination of the best and the greatest qualities, has seldom or never been surpassed" Belle continued, "It is not for me to trace the career and paint the virtues of Stonewall Jackson: that task is reserved for an abler pen, but I may be permitted to record my poignant grief for the loss of him who had condescended to be my friend." She believed the sorrow of the South was absolute and unquenchable. Even the soldiers felt the sting of Jackson's death. John O. Casler of the 33rd Virginia Infantry of Jackson's old brigade best summed it up for the soldiers

162

who served under him when years later, after the war, he still felt the sting of his general's death, "We all wept like babies. We believed that the star of the Confederacy had faded, and now our cause was doomed." Belle never did mention in her memoirs or any other publication after the war whether she ever visited the grave of Stonewall Jackson at Lexington, Virginia. Still, he always had a special place in her heart and mind.

Belle departed Mobile wearing a black crape band on her left arm, an outward sign of inward mourning for Stonewall Jackson and proceeded to Charleston, South Carolina. While at Charleston, she went aboard a Confederate gunboat and, through a spyglass, observed the Union Navy's blockade of the South Carolina coast. In the evening, she had dinner with General Beauregard, who commanded the army defending the Charleston area, and his staff. After dinner, an officer, who had received a basket of fruit from one of the blockade runners, gave it to her. One note of interest, she was given a parrot bird that she taught to speak "Miss Belle" and "Stonewall." After her short stay in Charleston, Belle returned to Richmond.

Belle's tour of the South had concluded. Besides Jackson's untimely death, it had been a very successful trip and a happy occasion in her young life. She would never forget it, but it would also be the last time she received such undying gratitude and devotion and given such celebrity status during the war. Now Belle returned to Virginia where another chapter in her life awaited, one that would not be too pleasant and would begin to diminish her role as a Civil War spy.

Footnote: Nellie Grey was used as a pseudonym by Myrta Lockett Avary when she wrote about Nellie's war experiences. Nellie Grey's real name is Margaret Bowden; she had married Major Joseph Van Holt Nash, 13th Virginia Cavalry.

Source: *Author's Collection*

Lamar House

Chapter 18

Belle's Return to The Valley

Belle must have returned to Richmond, Virginia, sometime during the first several days of June 1863 because she immediately headed for home using the route to Charlottesville into the Shenandoah Valley. She wrote, "I learned on the best authority that the Confederate troops were making a second advance down the valley, their objective being the recapture of Winchester," and "she was now very anxious to get home." The *Rockingham Register* in Harrisonburg, Virginia, published on Friday, June 5, 1863, places Belle in that city: "Miss Belle Boyd, the Confederate heroine, and the victim of Yankee persecutions has been in Harrisonburg for a few days' past. She is stopping at the American Hotel and is probably en route for her home in Martinsburg." The newspaper article places Belle in the Shenandoah Valley ahead of the Confederate army because the Battle at Brandy Station was not fought until June 9, four days later. According to Private John O. Casler of the 33rd Virginia Infantry, of General Edward "Allegheny" Johnson's division wrote in his memoirs that they began marching up the Richmond Turnpike on Wednesday, June 10, toward Chester's Gap in the Blue Ridge Mountain overlooking Front Royal. This newspaper article confirms that she must have traveled a different route than General Richard Ewell's Second Corps. {Ewell was Jackson's successor} because if Belle had traveled the same route as the army, she would have paused long enough to visit her cousin, Alice, at the Fishback Hotel in Front Royal. It had been a year since she had seen her cousin.

A written incident involving Belle occurred in the Shenandoah Valley before General Ewell's Second Corps entered the Shenandoah Valley at Chester's Gap along the Blue Ridge Mountain. After Belle left Harrisonburg, she traveled north through the Shenandoah Valley to Woodstock. She met up with an old acquaintance, Major Harry Gilmor, who had served under Turner Ashby and now whose cavalrymen were cooperating with Brigadier-General Albert Jenkins's Confederate cavalry brigade. Gilmor's orders were to scout the Yankees' position around Winchester. When Belle learned of Gilmor's mission, she wanted to go along on the expedition. Major Gilmor refused her request, but Belle was persistent; therefore, he informed her that she must obtain General Jenkins's permission. She agreed. Gilmor wrote a vivid account of his experience with Belle in his book, *Four Years in The Saddle*:

She rode with me to the quarters of General Jenkins, to whom I had to report before passing out through our lines. We found him sitting before his tent, and after dispatching my business, Miss Belle presented her request. I fixed myself rather behind her, that I might give a signal to the general not to consent. The fact is, I did not care to be accompanied by a woman on so perilous an enterprise; for, though she was a splendid and reckless rider, of unflinching courage, and her whole soul bound up in the Southern cause yet she was a little, mark you, only a little headstrong and willful, and I thought it best, both for her sake and mine, that she should not go. I hope Miss Belle will forgive this little ruse. The general, of course refused, which made her furious, but he was firm, and I rode off without her.

If Belle had gone with Major Gilmor, she would have made it to Martinsburg because, according to what he wrote in *Four Years in The Saddle*, his scouting mission was very successful, writing, "The enemy's picket line being only a mile out of Winchester, I made easily the entire circuit of that town as well as Martinsburg, in which I learned the exact position of every stationary force, large and small, in the lower valley, with an accurate account of their numbers. A courier was sent immediately to General Ewell with the information I had gained. He was then marching through Chester's Gap, near Front Royal."

Major Gilmor's courier carrying the information for General Ewell must have reached the general sometime on June 12. According to Lucy Buck, the advance of Ewell's corps marched into Front Royal.

166

On that day, Ewell must have been delighted at Gilmor's message about the position of the Union forces in and around Winchester because John O. Casler wrote that "he was in a hurry to get to Winchester still with the element of surprise, which he had enjoyed thus far."

Belle would have been captured if she had gone with Gilmor as far as Martinsburg. According to his written account, the Yankees still occupied Martinsburg; therefore, intentionally, the wisest decision was made by Gilmor not to take her with him. Instead of allowing her anxiety to overrule logical reasoning on her part to be with her family, it proved to be the best decision on Gilmor's part until the town was occupied once more by Confederate troops, allowing her time to spend with them. Belle never wrote about this incident with Major Gilmor in her memoirs.

Major-General Robert Milroy was from Indiana and the commanding officer of the 8,000 Union soldiers who made up the Eighth Corps at Winchester, Virginia. At the beginning of the war, Milroy was colonel of the 9th Indiana Infantry during the 1861 Western Virginia Campaign. He was promoted to brigade general in September 1861, commanded a brigade in General John Pope's Army of Virginia, and was promoted again to major general in November 1862. Milroy arrived in Winchester on January 1, 1863. Over six months, he had oppressed the civilians at Winchester, banishing some and sending them south through the Shenandoah Valley because they had refused to take the oath of allegiance.

As two of General Ewell's three divisions of the Second Corps approached Winchester on June 13 and began the fight for the city and its surrounding fortifications, Belle was "close upon the rear" of the Confederate army. When the attack began, she wrote she was four miles from the scene of the action. Since Belle had been in Harrisonburg and Woodstock, she followed the Valley Turnpike, which brought her to the Kernstown area, three miles south of Winchester, an area already controlled by Confederate General Jubal Early's division.

When the battle opened, and the Union artillery began to boom away at Winchester, it reminded Belle of the fight at Front Royal, which she had been involved in thirteen months earlier. Very early,

Belle decided she would only be a spectator for this battle at Winchester and not get involved, but that was about to change. Belle met up with a wounded officer, who rode with her to a hill, which gave them an unimpeded view of the fight. Belle was mounted on a white horse, making a good target for Union artillery about three-quarters of a mile away. Belle wrote, "A foolish report had been circulated through their army that in battle I rode a white horse, and was invariably at General Jackson's side." Because of this mistaken idea, Belle believed the Union artillery battery trained its guns on her.

By this time, Belle and the Confederate officer had been joined by several civilians attracted to the fight around Winchester. They were mounted on horses and mules, which the Union soldiers had overlooked. When an artillery shell exploded nearby, the animals stampeded, and Belle and the others quickly left the hill, but it was an incident she would never forget.

On June 15, Milroy's Union force could not hold Winchester and retreated hastily up the Valley Turnpike toward Martinsburg and the Potomac River. It was a one-sided victory for the Confederate army, and other than the surrender at Harpers Ferry the previous year; it was next to the most significant capture of weapons for the Confederate army during America's Civil War.

The Confederates captured twenty-three pieces of artillery, primarily rifled guns, 300 loaded wagons, 300 horses, a large supply of commissary and quartermaster supplies, and 4,000 Union soldiers. The Confederates also captured many small arms, ammunition, food, clothes, and medical supplies.

General Milroy made good his escape to Harpers Ferry with about 1,200 men from his corps, and Winchester had been a disaster for the Union army.

The Confederate forces under Ewell pressed the pursuit up the Valley Turnpike until the remaining Union force, including those at Martinsburg, crossed the Potomac River into Maryland. Belle believed Milroy's "skedaddle" was more disgraceful than General Banks's retreat in May of 1862.

After the fight at Winchester, Belle temporarily stayed behind to help care for the wounded. After the fight at Winchester June 13-15, many citizens' homes were turned into hospitals. Once more, Belle nursed the wounded. A Confederate officer in Harry Gilmor's Maryland battalion, a prisoner on a train from Washington to Fort Delaware in January 1865, recalled to another prisoner his experience at Winchester in 1863 involving his interaction with Belle Boyd. He asked the other comrade beside him if he had heard of Belle Boyd. The other prisoner cautiously answered his friend that her name was not unfamiliar. The Confederate officer said, "Well, there isn't a Southerner who would not lay down his life for her. When I was at the battle of Winchester, I was wounded, and she came into the hospital where I was and inquired if there were any Maryland boys there. Amongst other delicacies, she gave me some nice peach brandy. She and Mrs. G were in the fort, if I err not, cheering us on when we made a charge and drove the Yankees back." The other prisoner, the Maryland Confederate officer, was speaking to was Belle's first husband, who I will write about in another chapter. Mrs. G. was most likely Mary Greenhow, a Winchester resident and loyalist to the Southern Confederacy.

Now that General Ewell's Second Corps was moving north to Martinsburg; the way was clear for Belle to return unhindered to her family and home.

Chapter 19

Martinsburg 1863

Late on June 15, General Ewell's Second Corps began to cross the Potomac River opposite Williamsport, Maryland. As they moved north toward Hagerstown, Maryland, and into Pennsylvania, many in the south believed a significant victory in the north would end the war because of the continual peace movement among many Northern citizens. Many Southerners also continued to hold out hope that there would be acceptance and intervention by England and France or at least one of the two European countries. Belle wrote, "The hearts of the sympathizers with the South beat high with hope."

When Belle returned home, her father Benjamin, who was now forty-six years old and in poor health from the hardships of campaigning, was home on leave from the army. He did not return to serve in the Confederate army. It was a joyful reunion for the Boyd family that would not last long because General Lee and the Army of Northern Virginia were badly defeated by the Union Army of the Potomac and its new commanding officer, Major-General George Gordon Meade, on July 1-3, at a little town in Adams County, Pennsylvania, called Gettysburg. The Battle of Gettysburg had been the costliest battle of America's Civil War, with an estimated 46,286 casualties in the Union and Confederate armies for the three-day fight and an estimated 60,000 from both armies from June 3 until July 24.

Many citizens living in the South were dismayed and in awe over the staggering numbers of casualties. Many contemporary historians consider the campaign pivotal to America's Civil War. Confederate Captain William Bright, an aide to Major-General George Pickett, best put the Southern feelings into context when years later, he wrote, "Virginia bled again at every pore. There would be few firesides in her midst where the voice of mourning would not be heard when the

170

black-lettered list of losses would be published." Not only did the Southern army lose in Pennsylvania, but Union Major-General Ulysses S. Grant won a long, hard-fought campaign to capture Vicksburg, Mississippi, and its 25,000-man Confederate army, thus securing the Union army's control of the vital Mississippi River and splitting the Southern Confederacy in two. Many in the South were depressed and disheartened over these two major Union victories.

Belle, a year later, recorded her feeling about the Battle of Gettysburg when she wrote, "How many of those brave and noble fellows who went forward proudly to the front, eager to avenge the wrongs the South had suffered, who had left the beautiful shores of Virginia to defend their native soil, found a soldier's grave! Or, perchance, they were not even buried, their bodies lying upon the battlefield where they fell, with no covering save the blue canopy of heaven, their bones left to bleach in the sunlight or gleaming ghastly white in the moon's pale beams."

After Gettysburg, one local historian wrote, "Martinsburg became one general hospital. Many of the churches were occupied in this way; in many instances their interiors were completely destroyed. The citizens were as loyal as any situated near the border, and Union soldiers were kindly treated, and as faithfully nursed, when wounded, sick, and suffering, as many of them could have been in their own homes, and the same kindness was shown to those of the Confederate army."

A war correspondent for the *Richmond Enquirer* wrote what he experienced and witnessed in Martinsburg after the fight at Gettysburg. His story was published on July 21, 1863:

"In reaching Martinsburg, you feel as if you had left Virginia and reached Yankee-doodle-dom. It is thoroughly Unionized, Commodore Benman of the Federal navy, has his family residing here. Miss Belle Boyd also lives here, as does the family of Col. C.J. Faulkner.

I learned that our soldiers are scowled at, and jeered as they pass through and that, per contra, the Yankee prisoners are always cheered, the women here calling them 'our soldiers,' and begging permission not infrequently to be permitted to serve them such delicacies as they have.

171

But with all this rottenness, there is still a trace of Virginia left in a few of those residing near here. For example, I last night made with quarters at the house of a true Southern man, whose board and side board would do no discredit to Virginia of other days. His girls are true Southern women, and regale us with true Southern airs."

Belle wrote about the aftermath of the fighting at Gettysburg and what it was like living in her community "Martinsburg soon became one vast hospital; for, as fast as they could be brought to the rear, the Confederate wounded of the great battle were sent southward. There was no established hospital in my native village, it being too near the border; so that churches and many of the public buildings were obligated to be used temporarily for that purpose." Belle's house was used as a place for the Confederate wounded. She constantly occupied her time attending to them.

Another article was written and published on July 21, 1863, in the *Richmond Enquirer* by the same war correspondent concerning the needs of the Confederate wounded being attended to by Belle and other ladies in Martinsburg. The newspaper published, "The true patriotic Southern women of this place, have been very attentive to our wounded. We have four hospitals here. Among those ladies most attentive, I have mentioned the names of the Miss Faulkner, daughter of Hon. C.J. Faulkner, Miss Summers, and Miss Belle Boyd."

While the Army of Northern Virginia passed through Martinsburg toward Winchester, Belle debated whether she should stay and help nurse the wounded or leave and return south beyond the Confederate lines of defense. Belle knew it would only be a matter of time before Union troops would once more occupy Martinsburg since only a division of Confederate cavalry under General Matthew Butler, who now commanded the division of the wounded General Wade Hampton of South Carolina. Belle's mother and father wanted her to stay behind with them. Belle hoped it might be possible by keeping quiet and staying out of sight. Belle's mother became ill when the last Confederate soldiers left Martinsburg. There was no longer any indecision about the right decision. Instead, she decided to remain behind and help her mother, who was pregnant with another child. For a while, all was quiet. Belle's mother gave birth to a baby girl who

172

they named Mary. On the third day after her little sister's birth, Belle's servant came running into the room to announce that Union troops were coming. Belle looked out the window and noticed they had halted in front of her home. Belle's freedom was in jeopardy.

Two Union officers knocked on the door of Belle's home. Her father answered the door and told Belle the officers wanted to see her. Belle immediately went into the drawing room, where her father introduced her to them. The highest-ranking officer was Major Nathan Goff of the 3rd West Virginia Infantry. The 3rd West Virginia Infantry's service record shows that between July 18 and 19, they were encamped "near Hedgesville," a small village about two to three miles west of Martinsburg and near the city.

Major Goff began the conversation, "Miss Boyd, General Kelly commanded me to call and see if you really had remained at home, such a report having reached headquarters; but he did not credit it, so I have come to ascertain the truth."

General Benjamin Kelly, to whom Major Goff referred, was the commanding officer of the Department of West Virginia. Martinsburg was no longer a city in Virginia but was now in the new state of West Virginia, established on June 20, 1863, the only state to be admitted to the Union during America's Civil War. Kelly had been informed through a spy living in the area or through newspapers that Belle had returned to Martinsburg with the Confederate army as they moved across the Potomac River. A newspaper article by the *Richmond Daily Dispatch* appeared on July 15, 1863, the day after General Lee and the Confederate army crossed the flooded Potomac River and the second fight at Falling Waters occurred. The correspondent wrote, "Martinsburg is the home of the vivacious and celebrated Belle Boyd, as obnoxious to the Yankees as she is enthusiastic in our cause. She has determined to have the presence of the enemy now liable to occupy Martinsburg at any day."

Now according to Major Goff, the nature of his visit was to verify for General Kelly that Belle had physically remained behind and not departed with the Confederate army.

Major Goff, who was only a year older than Belle, proved to be a good choice to confront Belle. After the war, Goff became a United States Congressman from West Virginia, Secretary of the Navy, and a United States Federal Judge. But he would share one thing in common with Belle Boyd, imprisonment. He was captured in June 1864 and spent months at Libby Prison in Richmond, Virginia.

Belle ignorantly answered; hopefully, the officer would see the innocence and justification of her staying with her family and caring for her sick mother. "Major Goff, what is there so peculiarly strange in my remaining in my own home with my parents?"

Major Goff seriously replied, "But do you not think it rather dangerous? Are you really not afraid of being arrested?"

Belle continued to play the cat-and-mouse game of innocence. Belle attempted to manipulate the officer into believing she was harmless, and she had good reason for staying home and not fleeing south, hoping to win his favor like other officers who she had manipulated in the past. "Oh no! For I don't know why they should do so. I am no criminal."

This time, Belle met an officer who would not allow her to control the playing field and allow himself to be vulnerable to her wiles, "Yes, true, but you are a rebel, and will do more harm to our cause than half the men could do."

"But there are other rebels besides me."

Yes," Major Goff replied, "but then not so dangerous as yourself."

When Major Goff departed from Belle's home, he had not allowed himself to be deceived by her nor did he sympathize with her such as other officers had done in the past, allowing for sympathy which led to manipulation.

Four days later, sometime around July 23, according to the records of the 123rd Ohio Infantry, thirty-five-year-old Major Horace Kellogg, and men from Company C of that regiment arrived at Belle's home and placed her under arrest. Her father, concerned for her safety and its effect on her sick mother, pleaded with Major Kellogg to allow her to stay at her home under house arrest, a request granted. According to Belle, nineteen-year-old Private John B. Fairchilds was assigned to guard her, although other sentries were placed around the house.

July was hot in Martinsburg. Between the oppressive weather, her mother's illness, and her confinement, Belle needed to get out of the house, but anyone leaving the house needed a pass. A pass is a

174

document entrusted to anyone who needs to move around, go about their business, or remain in a community, signed by the provost marshal of the occupying army. The pass was a common standard during the war.

One day Belle did receive permission to walk from the commanding officer, "Miss Belle Boyd has permission to walk for half an hour, at 5 o'clock this a.m., giving her word of honor that she will use nothing which she may see or hear to the disadvantage of the U. S. troops."

Belle walked out of her house and down a few blocks before she was "arrested and sent back, with a guard on each side, their muskets loaded." Within the hour, she received another message from the commanding officer that she was "not allowed to promenade freely in Martinsburg." There must have been some misinterpretation on Belle's behalf; concerning where she could walk, and in the original order by the commanding officer; he did not forbid Belle to walk from her house. Belle felt insulted over the apprehension, but she knew her troubles had not ended.

Many years later, while Belle gave a historical recital of her war experiences at Norwich, Ohio, several members from the 123rd Ohio Infantry regiment were in attendance as well as one of her former guards from the Old Capitol Prison. The former soldiers were Major Kellogg and Private Fairchilds from the Ohio regiment and Walter Perrin from the prison. Weeks later, Belle told a reporter from the *Toledo Commercial*:

It was at the conclusion of my entertainment, and a large number of the audience had remained to be introduced, an informal reception as it were. Among others, I was presented to Captain Kellogg of the 123rd Ohio, who arrested me at Martinsburg, Virginia {West Virginia} in 1863 after the Gettysburg fight. He in turn introduced Mr. John Fairchilds who he had detailed to stand over me until the arrival of secret service men from Washington. Just to make the chain complete, they introduced me to Mr. Walter Perrin, who belonged to the reserves and who stood guard over me at the Old Capitol Prison in Washington.

In Belle's newspaper interview and memoirs, she must have made a mistake regarding Horace Kellogg's rank, calling him captain instead of major. According to Kellogg's service record in the *Ohio Civil War Index*, he was promoted from captain to major on March 6, 1863, which meant at the time of Belle's arrest in July 1863, he had already attained the higher rank. On December 6, 1864, he was promoted to lieutenant colonel. His regiment had been practically annihilated at Winchester on June 15. Major Kellogg and a few survivors had escaped across the Potomac River only to return and do provost and picket duty around Martinsburg after the Gettysburg battle.

While remaining under arrest at her home, Belle requested that Colonel Andrew T. McReynolds, the 1st New York Lincoln Cavalry's commanding officer, visit her. Colonel McReynolds refused her request but instead sent Captain James H. Stevenson, Company C, in his place. According to the 1st New York historian, Lieutenant William H. Beach, Captain Stevenson was amazed when he first met Belle. She made quite an impression on him. Lieutenant Beach wrote in the regiment's history, "She entertained" Captain Stevenson "by appearing clad in a gold-bespangled uniform of a captain of Confederate cavalry, with a revolver in the belt." Since Belle was under arrest, Lieutenant Beach did not disclose in the regimental history if she was allowed to keep her revolver.

Belle remained under house arrest in Martinsburg for thirty days awaiting her fate. During that time, she was anxious and hoping soon she would again be at liberty to do as she pleased. Belle must have had hope that liberty was possible because an article appeared in the *Alexandria Gazette* on August 21, 1863: "Miss Belle Boyd is in Martinsburg, VA, paroled and will go south." But that did not happen, and her hopes were crushed.

Why did it take so long for Belle's fate to be determined by Union authorities? Once they had heard and confirmed through Major Goff that she was in Martinsburg and had not departed with the Confederate army, immediately, once more, she again became a threat to them because they knew she would continue her spying activities. They waited for four days before arresting her and to determine if they were going to place her back in prison or if they were going to escort her beyond the Union lines at Martinsburg with the warning that if she returned, they would send her back to prison. This last warning is one that they often carried out among disloyal Southern civilians who refused to take the oath of allegiance. But again, she could carry the intelligence to the nearest Confederate forces regarding the strength of the Union garrison at Martinsburg. Or she could return stealthily as some Northern newspapers had accused her of doing before, she went to Knoxville. But apparently, after future investigation, Secretary of War Stanton decided to bring her back to Washington and imprison her again, only this time it would be for a longer duration.

When Belle was freed from the Old Capitol Prison for the first time and went on her tour of the south at General Jackson's suggestion, Union authorities hoped she had learned her lesson and would stay south, but that all changed when they learned she was back in the Martinsburg area. Secretary Stanton believed it would be dangerous for her to be free in the area of operations for the Union Army, knowing it would only be a matter of time before Belle would be roaming at will among the Union camps looking for a young and vulnerable officer who she could extract information from and send that information to Confederate forces. She was too great of a liability and too dangerous to be given her liberty.

On August 27, the new provost marshal, Major Walker and one of Captain Johnson's detectives arrived at Belle's home to arrest her, and "that the Secretary of War, Mr. Stanton, had ordered it" and she was to take her "departure from home at eleven a.m. the next day."

Belle thought of escape but knew it was useless because of the heavy guard detail surrounding her home. Belle's mother continued her recovery from her sickness but grew worse after learning the news of her daughter's soon-to-be imprisonment. Belle's father became concerned for her safety and decided to accompany her to Washington.

The next day when the detective arrived, Belle said a "tearful adieu" to her "poor mother, brothers, and sister, who wept bitterly" as she departed.

It would be the last time during the war that Belle Boyd would see Martinsburg.

Source: *Wikipedia*

Nathan Goff

Chapter 20

Second Imprisonment

When Belle arrived at the Old Capitol Prison on August 28, 1863, she did not realize when she said farewell to her father, it would be the last time she would see or speak to him. Instead of Belle being placed within the confines of the Old Capitol, such as her imprisonment in 1862, Union authorities placed her in a room for "distinguished guests" in a large brick building adjoining the Old Capitol known as Carroll Prison. Carroll Prison was once a hotel owned by Mr. Duff Green, but since Belle's first incarceration, it had been converted into a receptacle for rebels, prisoners of state, hostages, blockade-runners, smugglers, desperadoes, spies, criminals under sentence of death, and lastly, many Union officers convicted of defrauding the U. S. Government. Many of the Union officers were quartermasters and army contractors.

The Washington *Evening Star* newspaper was quick to publish on August 29 under the heading: "The Notorious Belle Boyd" her imprisonment:

Among the commitments to the Old Capitol yesterday afternoon, we noticed the name of the notorious Belle Boyd. Belle, it will be remembered, was sent South some time ago, but her restless, roving disposition would not permit her to remain there, so she paid occasional visits by stealth to her friends inside our lines, gaining such information from them as they were able to impart, and hastening back with it to the South. Intelligence of her movements finally reached headquarters, and one of Capt. Johnson's detectives was dispatched to Martinsburg, where he was said to be, with full authority to arrest her and bring her to this city. The errand was successfully accomplished, and Belle Boyd is again a prisoner in the Old Capitol.

Belle's imprisonment was voiced in other publications. The *Alexandria Gazette* published on August 31, 1863, "Miss Belle Boyd has been arrested in Martinsburg, and again committed to the Old Capitol Prison." Even though both the *Alexandria Gazette* and the *Evening Star* reported she was confined at the Old Capitol as the previous year, it was Carroll Prison; William Wood was the superintendent of both facilities.

Even diarist Margaret Leech wrote, "Belle Boyd, back in Washington" and "she has been given one of the best rooms in Carroll Prison, the Old Capitol annex." Belle's arrival back in Washington was well publicized.

Belle's room in Carroll Prison had already been the temporary home for Miss Antonia Ford, a Confederate spy, and a lady who Belle identifies as Nannie T. Belle's first days of imprisonment were monotonous, long, and weary. She spent many hours standing and looking out of her barred windows. Occasionally, a friend or an acquaintance walked or rode by, pause, and nod at her in acknowledgment. These people were considered Southern sympathizers and quickly seized and made to dismount from their horses or step out of their carriages and "forced to enter the bureau of the prison, there to remain until such time as it should please their tormentors to let them depart." Even women who acknowledged Belle were not exempted from scrutiny by the guards. It was considered a serious violation of regulations by Union authorities, so much so that the provost marshal, William Doster, had published in the Washington *Evening Star*: "The officer of the guard at the 'Old Capitol Prison' will not allow signals to be made to the prisoners under his charge by men or women passing in front of his building. This practice has led to insubordination, and in one case to a fatal result. Any one, without respect to person, violating this order will be sent to the Central Guard House."

As on her previous visit to the Old Capitol, Belle heard the old familiar sound of someone grating against the wall. The sound came from a room adjoining hers. While Belle watched and listened, she noticed plaster being removed, and a knife blade was recognizable. With "unspeakable joy," she began to set to work from her side of the wall, and soon communications were opened with the next room through a hole large enough to pass tightly rolled notes. She soon learned the identity of her new neighbors as gentlemen by the names of Brookes, Warren, Stuart, and Williams. Belle learned they had been in prison for the past nine months because they attempted to go south to join the Confederate army. Her correspondence with the four male prisoners did not last long because someone she called Mr. Lockwood, whose first name is John, soon discovered what they were doing. He removed the men from their room, and had the the hole closed with plaster.

Several days after Belle's neighbors were removed, Miss Ida P., arrested for being a rebel mail carrier, was placed in the room next to Belle. Belle wanted to speak to her about Confederate mail routes, but soon workmen arrived to board up the door adjoining Belle's and Miss Ida's rooms. Belle watched how the workmen nailed up and placed the planking over the door, specifically the keyhole. She pointed it out to her new friend, and they attempted to dislodge it, but their efforts produced no effect. Belle thought of the sentry outside her door and bribed him with oranges and apples to allow her to use his bayonet. Belle wrote in her memoirs that "he unfixed it from his gun, then with the whispered injunction of 'be quick, miss'" handed it to her. Unknown to Belle when she wrote her memoirs, and maybe she never knew, the sentry was Lyons Wakeman, a woman who had disguised herself as a Union soldier with the 153rd New York Infantry. Her real name is Sarah Rosetta Wakeman. The service record for the 153rd New York Infantry shows that the regiment served on guard duty in Alexandria and Washington from October 1862 until February 1864.

According to Sarah Wakeman, there were three female prisoners at Carroll Prison when she served guard duty. She wrote, "Over to Carroll Prison they have got three women that is confined in their rooms. One of them is a Major in the union army and she went into battle with her men. When the Rebels bullets was acoming like hail storm she rode her horse, and gave orders to the men. Now she is in Prison for not doing according to the regulation of war. The other two is rebel Spies and they have catch them and put them in Prison. They are smart looking women and [have] good education."

In February 1864, the 153rd New York Infantry transferred to Louisiana and served with General Nathaniel Banks during the Red River Campaign. Towards the end of the campaign, Sarah Wakeman became sick and died from chronic diarrhea on June 19, 1864, in New Orleans, Louisiana.

The three women Sarah Wakeman wrote about were Annie Jones, Miss Ida P., and Belle Boyd.

After Belle received the soldier's bayonet, she could release the board and open the door. Shortly, Superintendent Wood came running up the stairway to Miss Ida's room. As he entered Miss Ida's room, Belle had only enough time to place the bayonet under a bed frame. She knew the guard would soon be relieved and would have to account for the missing bayonet; therefore, she suggested they all go to her room, which was the larger of the two, a request Superintendent Wood agreed. After entering Belle's room, she made up an excuse about leaving a pocket-handkerchief behind in Miss Ida's room. She quickly excused herself, returned to Miss Ida's room, removed the bayonet from under the bed frame and returned it to the sentry, all without Superintendent Wood's suspicion or knowledge.

Why was Belle allowed to visit another woman prisoner's room? During her first imprisonment, she had been forbidden to associate with other prisoners. The reason was that Union authorities hoped sometime during their conversations Belle and Miss Ida would share information that could be overheard about Confederate mail routes and Confederate covert activity that Belle and Miss Ida were willing to share. It did not work. Shortly, Miss Ida was released from Carroll Prison.

*   *   *   *

One evening at about 9:00, Belle sat in her room singing *Take Me Back to My Own Sunny South* when a large crowd gathered across the street from her room listening to her song. After they departed, she lowered her gaslight and placed her head sadly against the window of her cell room. Suddenly, she said, "I was soon startled from the reverie by hearing something whiz by my head into the room and strike the wall beyond." At first, she thought someone was trying to take her life. Once she regained her composure, she noticed an arrow had struck the wall of her room opposite her window. Fasten to the arrow was a note with the message:

"Poor girl! You have the deepest sympathy of all the best community in Washington City, and there are many who would lay down their lives for you, but they are powerless to act or aid you at present. You have many warm friends; and we daily watch the journals to see if there is any news of you. If you will listen attentively to the instructions that I give you, you will be able to correspond with and hear from your friends outside.

On Thursdays and Saturdays, in the evening, just after twilight, I will come into the square opposite the prison. When you hear, someone whistling 'Twas within a mile of Edinbro' town,' if alone and all is safe, lower the gas as a signal and leave the window. I will then shoot an arrow into your room, as I have done this evening, with a letter attached. Do not be alarmed, as I am a good shot.

The manner in which you will reply to these messages will be in this way; Procure a large india-rubber ball; open it, and place your communications within it, written on foreign paper; then sew it together. On Tuesdays, I shall come, and you will know of my presence by the same signal. Then throw the ball, with as much force as you can exert, across the street into the square, and trust to me I will get it.

Do not be afraid. I am really your friend." The note was signed C. H.

Naturally, Belle felt afraid and cautious Union authorities were entrapping her and that her imprisonment would be extended, possibly for the duration of the war. But Belle was adventurous and willing to take a risk and put her trust in a gentleman she did not know and who might be her enemy.

Without suspicion or regret, Belle quickly secured an India rubber ball and began corresponding with C. H. She learned that he was "without doubt, honorable and sincere in his profession of sympathy."

Through C. H., she became "possessed of much valuable information regarding the movements of the Federals" in this unique style. Through C. H., she received small Confederate flags made by the Southern ladies of Washington. The sentries guarding the outside or inside of the prison never knew of Belle's correspondence with C. H., or how she got the small Confederate flags that she willingly displayed.

Belle never revealed C. H.'s identity because she never knew his identity while in prison, nor did she mention his identity years after the war concluded. It would have been unwise for him to reveal himself to her because of the possibility that one of their correspondences might have been intercepted by Union guards, which would have led to his arrest and possibly the breakup of his intelligence circle of friends. Also, anyone with access to spying and covert activities would never use their real name or initials because it would have been too easy for a good detective to have tracked them down and expose them. Instead, many spies and individuals in covert activity used a pseudonym. We may never know C. H.'s real identity.

On several occasions, while Belle was at Carroll Prison, she attached one of the small Confederate flags onto a broom handle and placed it out the window to irritate one of the guards walking his post along A Street. She stepped back out of sight, and as they looked up at her room, they shouted various orders and threats. When not obeyed, they fired their muskets, sometimes musket balls striking her cell room ceiling, but while they reloaded, she walked over and looked out the window as though nothing had ever happened. For Belle, this was not only sport but also her way of showing her defiance of Union authority and loyalty to the Southern cause.

In September 1863, while Belle exchanged correspondences with her phantom messenger at Carroll Prison, she became ill. She secured help from a physician at the prison, but finally, an old Confederate physician, a prisoner, diagnosed her with typhoid fever. Typhoid fever is a bacterial disease that has an onset of thirty to sixty days before full manifestation and can be debilitating to a person. The common belief among physicians in the 1860s was that part of the patient's treatment should include lower temperatures and fresh air. Belle wrote, "the room in which I was confined was low and fearfully warm, and that the air was fetid and rank with the fumes of an ill-ventilated Bastile." Her room faced the canal where there was mosquito infestation, often-dead animals were found floating or submerged in its water, and the residents' human waste in the waters was a constant sanitary problem.

While she laid sick on a bed, friends and family petitioned Secretary Stanton to gain access to her, but all requests were denied. One application requested she be moved from the prison, but Secretary Stanton denied that one also with the admonishment, "No, she is a …rebel; let her die." When all else failed, she invited President Lincoln to visit her, but that did not happen.

After three weeks and the help of a nurse, Belle regained some of her strength and walked. Major-General John Martindale, the Military Governor of Washington permitted her to walk in the Capitol Square for thirty-five minutes each day, in the evening from 5-5:30, escorted by a guard. On September 15, The Washington *Evening Star* published, "The close confinement in which Belle Boyd charged with being a spy, has been held having been found to have an unfavorable effect upon her health, the rigor of her imprisonment has been somewhat migrated, and she is also allowed the privilege of walking half an hour each day under guard on the grass plot opposite the prison."

When the Southern citizens knew Belle was walking in front of the prison each day, many of them appeared to get a glance of the *Rebel Spy*. One day while she walked, several young girls passed and dropped a piece of Bristol board near her with a Confederate battle flag, and her name engraved on the board. The corporal of the guard took quick notice and picked up the board before Belle had the opportunity to gather it. The guard was going to arrest the girls, but through Belle's pleading intervention, he relented and instead reprimanded them and released them from his custody. After Belle promised not to say anything about the affair, she bribed the guard with five dollars. The guard allowed Belle to keep the flags. Unfortunately for Belle, Secretary Stanton soon revoked her walking privileges in the square once he learned about the incident in the newspapers.

Margaret Leech a Washington resident also wrote, "After an attack of typhoid fever, Belle obtained permission from General Martindale to walk in the park for a half-hour each evening, under guard. So many ladies and gentlemen congregated to watch her, uttering pitying expressions as she passed, that the permission was revoked by Mr. Stanton."

On September 15, 1863, an article was published in the Washington *Daily Republican*. The correspondent wrote about Belle's health, notoriety, patriotism to the Southern cause, and virtues. Interestingly, the correspondent wrote about a Belle Boyd imposter in Philadelphia, who the young copperhead gentlemen praised. The article said:

A chapter about Belle Boyd...It is well known that this woman is now imprisoned in the Old Capitol, having been arrested at her home, in Martinsburg Va., soon after the retreat of Lee through and from that place. The reason for her arrest is that she violated the conditions of her parole by being within the Federal lines. She was obligated to leave her home with the rebels, when the rebel army left it; but this she failed to do, and to now justify suffering for the violation of her parole. The reports recently sent forth by Washington correspondents that her health was seriously impaired by her imprisonment, we learn, is wholly without foundation. From her peculiar temperament, it would seem that there are few persons who are more largely gifted with the power of keeping themselves company.

Perhaps there is no Southern woman more notorious during this war than Belle Boyd. Traitors and sympathizers with traitors have surrounded her name with a romantic heroism almost equal to that of Joan of Arc. Mahoney was in the Old Capitol at the time of her first imprisonment, his villainous book (Prisoner of State) he denounces the Government for visiting what he terms indignities upon this 'charming' and 'heroic' lady, and says she was desperately loved by all the 'gallant,' and that after being sent South, she had adopted and married a dashing young officer. Of course, this was all false. She is still Miss Belle Boyd, Mahoney and his book to the contrary notwithstanding.

There is nothing especially prepossessing about the person of this young lady. She evidently courts notoriety...is dashing and would apparently rather appear fast than otherwise, though where she is best known, she is regarded as a virtuous young lady.

The statement sent to the New York papers sometime since that she had been an inmate of a house of ill repute in Philadelphia, we are assured, does her character great injustice. She has not been in that city, but was impersonated by a woman on Twelfth street, who assuming her name, and claiming to be a rebel spy, attracted a bevy of young copperheads around her, and illustrated through the old adage, 'fools and their money soon parted' The counterfeit Belle was a much better looking woman, lacking however, the intelligence and vivacity of the original. When Belle was in the Old Capitol before 'My Maryland' was her favorite song, but now she says it is 'played out.' She is an incessant singer of rebel songs, however, and is most implacable hater of the Government. Her past history proves that she lacks not the inclination, and to a large extent is possessed of the spirit, to dare almost anything to aid the rebellion.

Superintendent William Wood, like General Shields, always showed Belle favor even though he knew she was deadly in her activities and loyalty toward the Union cause and that she was sure to cause havoc wherever there was an opportunity, even at Carroll Prison. At the Old Capitol Prison and Carroll Prison, she was required to obey the rules and regulations of the prison. But she always maintained a certain flexibility over the other female prisoners, finding favor with Superintendent Wood. It was not because Belle was a female prisoner but because she was Belle Boyd, the young lady with charisma, a charismatic personality, and a warm and friendly conversationalist who knew the power of words. Later in his life, William Wood wrote his observations of Belle: "Belle Boyd, the rebel spy, was a resolute devil-may-care 'spirited maiden;' she had the advantage of a fair boarding school education and was well up in the winning ways of such establishments. Miss Boyd regarded a desperate venture as a part of all enjoyable fun. During her stay at Carroll Prison, she never appeared as a termagant or fault-finding scold, a common

187

distemper which I suppose to be contagious with the average female prisoner."

One day while Belle still recovered, Captain James Mix, 11th New York Infantry, informed her that a lady had arrived at the prison and was in a room at the far end of the hallway on the floor below her. A few days later, Belle came face to face with the new lady prisoner that Captain Mix had spoken of earlier, writing, "I saw our new inmate. Judge of my astonishment on recognizing in her my prisoner at Front Royal, who had requited my kindness to her when there by informing the general that I was a bitter enemy of the Yankees. She proved to be…alas! That I should have to write aught derogatory to one of my own sex…not what she had represented herself, the wife of a soldier, but a camp-follower, known as Miss Annie Jones."

The previous year twenty-year-old Annie Jones accused Belle of being a spy while at Front Royal. Now Annie Jones was a prisoner being accused by General Judson Kilpatrick of being a spy for the Confederacy. Annie Jones had previously accused many prominent Union officers of sexual affairs. The accusations had been so greatly voiced by her that President Lincoln had to become involved in the investigation. President Lincoln interviewed Annie and she admitted spending time with Union officers, most notably General Kilpatrick as a "guest of different officers who kept her supplied with her own tent, horses, orderlies, escorts, sentinels, and rations." She confessed to having an affair with John Lockwood at the prison who offered to pay her for sex. Superintendent Wood discharged Lockwood after the allegations, but in 1864, President Lincoln and Union authorities agreed that she should be released from prison on the condition she stay away from Washington and the Army of the Potomac.

Belle wrote that Annie was said "to have been insane; but how far this report is to be credited I know not." When Belle witnessed this event and later wrote this entry in her memoirs, she expected Annie would be sent to a "Lunatic Asylum." Even when Belle wrote her memoirs, she had believed, based on Captain Mix's report about Annie Jones, that this was to occur. Instead, Annie was released in July 1864, eventually moving to Vicksburg, Mississippi.

When Captain Mix informed Annie Jones of her fate, he also informed Belle she would be sent to Fitchburg jail in Massachusetts for the duration of the war. Fitchburg jail housed seventy prisoners and was used to imprison Southern female spies. When Belle received the news of her fate, she felt faint and collapsed and suffered a relapse of typhoid fever.

When Benjamin Boyd, who was still ill heard the news of Belle's sentence, he rushed to Washington to make every attempt to have her sentence commuted, but until then, Belle had more adventures.

Chapter 21

Imprisonment Adventures

In November while Belle was still in prison, The *Camden Confederacy* newspapers picked up an article that was first published in *The Washington Republican*, reporting on her activities, her state of mind, and her reputation at Carroll Prison. The article said: "The *Washington Republican* speaking of Miss Belle Boyd, now imprisoned in Washington, states that she still retains all her vivacity and sings rebel songs incessantly. The same newspaper says that all stories affecting her reputation either as a woman, or questioning her fidelity to the South, are false and slanderous."

One evening while Belle was recovering from her illness and looking out the cell room window, a significant cough attracted her attention. After noticing the sentry had his back turned, Belle looked to see the direction of the sound. When she did so, she noticed a "note, tightly rolled up, thrown towards" her. She read the note that was just signed "K." He was from Virginia, requesting aid and money to make an escape attempt with two other prisoners. Belle agreed to help in the escape. She gave him forty dollars, and with the help of her archer friend, C. H., she planned for their safety once they escaped.

Above K's room was a garret occupied by his two friends, who intended to escape with him. They planned that K would get in the garret with his two friends while everyone was returning from supper before the escape attempt. While returning from supper, K was on the garret staircase to carry out his scheme when a guard commanded him to halt. The guard insisted he did not belong there; Belle stood nearby in the doorway to her room. She called the sentry's attention and said, "Sentry, have you been so long here and don't know where the prisoners are quartered? Let him pass on to his room." K joined in and declared he knew where he was going. The sentry rescinded his order

190

and allowed K to proceed. Belle sent for Superintendent Wood and began to carry on a conversation in her cell room with him. She wanted to create a diversion. They heard the cry of "Murder! Murder!" nearby.

When Superintendent Wood heard the murderer cry, he raced to the room window, and noticed below some sentries waiting for their turn at guard duty. Wood immediately ordered them toward the sound of the cry. According to Belle, her friends made their escape by "removing in haste a portion of the roof, scrambled upon the eaves, descended by a lighting conductor into the street below, and made off sheltered by darkness." The following morning when K and his friends were not at roll call, Wood suspected Belle of having knowledge or assisting in the plan. However, her complicity in the scheme could not be proven, and she was not punished. Mr. K may have been an alias for a gentleman known as J. G. Thompson. The Washington *Evening Star* published on October 1: "Thompson was confined in the upper part of the prison and succeeded in getting upon the roof of the building, on the corner of Pennsylvania Avenue and First Street East, used a boarding house, and escaped down the lightning rod to the ground." Another article about Thompson was published several days later in the *Alexandria Gazette*: "A young man named J. G. Thompson, son of a restaurant keeper confined in Old Capitol prison, charged with being a rebel mail carrier succeeded in making his escape on Thursday night." The records of the War Department confirmed the escape took place. The two newspaper articles believed only one person was involved, J. G. Thompson, instead of three, as Belle was led to believe and wrote in her memoirs. Belle wrote she saw and communicated with Mr. K. She never mentioned the names or initials of the other two prisoners, but she did write, "when the roll was called, and the prisoners were mustered, Mr. K. and his companions were found to be missing." There must have been three names called because the War Department records verify the escape of three prisoners; therefore, Belle must have been correct.

As at Martinsburg in 1861, when the provost marshal read Belle the *Articles of War*, she again was threatened with execution. A journalist who interviewed Belle in 1893 wrote, "She was captured after Gettysburg and sentenced to be shot but on five Federal officers being held by President Davis as hostages to suffer similar penalty should sentence be executed upon her. President Lincoln commuted the death penalty with the provision that should she be found in the North again she should be shot."

Severe penalties for spying were not issued for women during America's Civil War. There were many female spies, most notably Rose Greenhow, but even though she had a relationship with a powerful United States Senator by the name of Henry Wilson and operated a significant spy ring in Washington, she was not executed for her covert activities, but banished to the South. Not until President Lincoln was assassinated was a conspirator woman named Mary Surratt executed. And even with the death penalty looming for her, many believed she would escape the hangman's noose. Threatening Belle with execution was no more than intimation at the time, and it was meant to try and neutralize her with fear that if she were captured again, they would carry out their threat.

Secretary of War Edwin Stanton soon agreed Belle was to be banished to the South and not able to return until after the war. This often happened during the war. For example, Union General Robert Milroy, who commanded 8,000 Union soldiers in Winchester, Virginia, from January 1863 to June of 1863, banished Southern sympathizers and residents beyond the Union lines, who refused to take the oath of allegiance to the United States Government. In 1862, citizens living in Harpers Ferry, Virginia lived under the same threat. When they were banished South some of their homes were confiscated by the United States Treasury Department and sold, with the money being used from the sale of the house to help fund the Union war effort. It was agreed Belle was to be released on December 1. Before Belle's scheduled departure, a Confederate colonel gave her letters of introduction to Confederate States Vice President Alexander Stephens, and Chief Auditor of the Southern Treasury Department, Bowling Baker. Belle wrote, "These letters he spoke of my untiring devotion to the Confederacy, of the zeal that I had shown to serve my country at all times, and of my kindness, as far as lay in my power, to my fellow-prisoners." Belle intended to smuggle them South on her person. The letters were considered contraband, and if they had been discovered, her parole could have been withdrawn and she could have been sent to Fitchburg jail for the duration of the war as first intended by Union authorities.

Before Belle was released from Carroll Prison, Secretary Stanton had her photograph taken to distribute to all the Union armies and forces in the field, and the days of Belle roaming freely among Union encampments had ended.

Early on the morning of December 1, Belle, Captain Mix, and an orderly sergeant departed from the prison. Belle hoped to see her sick father who stayed with a niece in the city, but her request was denied. On December 2, the *New York Tribune* published that Captain Mix had left Washington "with the notorious Belle Boyd, who is to be delivered to rebel authorities at that place." Another article appeared that same day published by the *Alexandria Gazette*: "Miss Belle Boyd who has been confined at the Old Capitol Prison in Washington, for some time, is to be sent to Old Point and turned over to the commanding officer at that place, to be by him delivered at City Point for exchange." Unlike the first imprisonment in 1862, there were no correspondences or reports found in the *Official Records of the Union and Confederate Armies* concerning Belle's second imprisonment or her release.

Belle was now free, but what other adventures and risk awaited her?

Chapter 22

Belle & the Beast

The following day, Wednesday, December 2, around 9:00 in the morning, Belle arrived at Fortress Monroe. Immediately, Captain Mix went on shore and made the necessary arrangement for releasing Belle to the provost marshal, Captain John Cassels, 11th Pennsylvania Cavalry, who was Major-General Benjamin Butler's aide-de-camp. On November 2, 1863, Butler assumed command of the Department of Virginia and North Carolina. Belle was to remain at Fortress Monroe until the exchange boat was to leave for Richmond.

Shortly, Captain Cassels, whom Belle found pleasant, escorted Belle to General Butler's headquarters. Forty-five-year-old Benjamin Butler came from Lowell, Massachusetts. Before the war, he practiced law, was a democratic politician who opposed the war, and was an officer in the state militia. At the beginning of the war, he received an appointment as brigade general and was given credit for restoring order in Maryland during the early traumatic days of the war. Butler was one of the first officers to be appointed to the rank of major general. In May 1862, Butler and his Union force captured New Orleans, Louisiana. At New Orleans, he earned the reputation of "Butler, the Beast "because of his General Orders Number 28. The general orders came about because the ladies of New Orleans, in every conceivable way, displayed their contempt for Union officers and their soldiers. The orders were posted as follows: "As the officers and soldiers of the United States have been subject to repeated insults from the women (calling themselves ladies) of New Orleans in return for the most scrupulous non-interference and courtesy on our part, it is ordered that hereafter when any female shall by word, gesture or movement, insult or show contempt for any officer or soldier of the

United States, she shall be regarded and held liable to be treated as a woman of the town plying her avocation."

General Orders Number 28 did not concern General Butler, but the rest of the South felt disturbed. When the House of Parliament in England viewed his order unfavorably, Butler pointed out that he had borrowed it from the Ordinances of London.

When Belle was escorted to General Butler's headquarters, she was aware of his reputation and General Orders Number 28.

General Butler began the conversation, "Ah! So, this is Miss Boyd, the famous rebel spy. Pray be seated."

Belle displayed her first act of defiance, "Thank you, General Butler, but I prefer to stand."

"Pray be seated," General Butler asked, "But why do you tremble so? Are you frightened?"

"No; ah! This is, yes General Butler; I must acknowledge that I do feel frightened in the presence of a man of such world-wide reputation as yourself."

According to Belle, her feeling fearful and intimidated appeared to play into his masculinity and pleased him.

Belle wrote he rubbed his hands together and smiled benignly saying, "Oh pray do be seated, Miss Boyd. But what do you mean when you say that I am widely known?"

"I mean, General Butler," Belle answered, "that you are a man whose atrocious conduct and brutality, especially to Southern ladies, is so infamous that even the English Parliament commented upon it. I naturally feel alarmed at being in your presence."

According to Belle, General Butler expected praise and gratitude for his courtesy and attitude and proper etiquette, but instead he became visibly angry by her answer. If it were not that Belle was being exchanged for General Nathan Goff Jr. of Rhode Island he may have had her confined. Whether Belle knew the soldier that she was being exchanged for when this conversation took place she did not include in her memoirs.

General Butler was a well-known military figure and a powerful political one. Belle still feared she could be sent back to the Old Capitol or Carroll Prison, writing, "For General Butler was all-powerful in the North about this period."

Belle remained held in custody with three other ladies. They were Julie and Ann Lomax, both sisters of General Lunsford Lomax of Jeb Stuart's cavalry, and Miss Euphemia Goldsborough. The two Lomax sisters were detained because of their connection to General Lomax, but on December 6, they were released and returned to Baltimore. It was a different situation for Miss Goldsborough. Euphemia Goldsborough had previously smuggled necessities into Southern hospitals and Northern prisons. On occasions, she had helped prisoners escape captivity. Euphemia Goldsborough was arrested in Baltimore. While in custody with Belle, Goldsborough smuggled dispatches on her person to take to Richmond, where she lived for the war's duration. The *Richmond Examiner* published she had been in "correspondence with the rebels and sentenced to banishment."

About Belle's punishment, the *New York Herald* published on December 4, "Miss Belle Boyd arrived this morning from Washington, in the charge of a lieutenant {Captain}. She is to be sent over the lines, to remain during the war." Belle shared the same fate as Euphemia Goldsborough, banishment to the South, but only Belle would not cease her covert activity.

That same Wednesday evening, December 2, the provost marshal sent Belle and Euphemia Goldsborough to report to headquarters and be ready to depart for Richmond. When Belle and Euphemia arrived, two detectives, one a man and the other a woman, went through their luggage. Belle tried to reassure them she had just come from prison and carried nothing of value, but that did not deter the two detectives. While going through Belle's two trunks, they discovered two suits of private clothes, a uniform for a Confederate officer, and a dozen linen shirts. Also, she had in her possession several pairs of army gauntlets, felt hats, and something that she cherished the most, "field-glasses which had formerly belonged to Stonewall Jackson." According to Belle, these items made it into Carroll Prison "by means of an underground railway, of which Superintendent Wood" did not know. Belle pleaded with the two detectives to allow her to keep Stonewall Jackson's field glasses, but they refused, instead turning them over to General Butler. Belle was interrogated but did not surrender to their pressure and gave them no information about the underground railway.

The detectives also informed Belle that she would have to undergo a personal search. When the female detective searched Belle, the detective discovered $20,000 in Confederate notes, $5,000 in Federal greenbacks, and $1,000 in gold. All the money was considered contraband and confiscated, but it did not stop there. Captain Cassels informed Belle that if she had no letters or papers on her person and took the oath of allegiance to the United States Government, she would not have to undergo a further personal search. However, Belle still had in her possession the letters of introduction to Vice President Alexander Stephens and Bowling Baker. Rather than be personally inspected by strangers and what she considered humiliation, she wrote, "I told him I could not make such a declaration, handing him my letters at the same time." He then asked Belle if she had anything else, and Belle handed him about $3,000 in Confederate money, which he returned, declaring it worthless.

After Belle, had finished being inspected, she departed with Euphemia Goldsborough to the wharf and was placed on a tug and sent out to the Union exchange boat, *City of New York*. On the *City of New York,* Major John Elmer Mulford received the two women. Major Mulford was the assistant agent of exchange, who would take Belle and Miss Goldsborough up the James River to Aiken's Landing.

Around 7:00 the following morning, Belle's ship got underway but shortly ran aground. It was around 8:00 in the morning when they got underway once more. As the *City of New York* gathered full steam, Belle noticed a tugboat fast approaching. She became fearful General Butler had decided to arrest her after learning of all the contraband that had been confiscated. Her fears were not unfounded, writing, "When General Butler, smarting with the remembrance of my farewell sarcasm, had beheld the letters that Captain Cassels had taken from me, he commanded that I should be followed, and, if recaptured, should be sent at once to Fort Warren, in Massachusetts Bay. As he issued the order, he remarked to those who surrounded him that he would take 'a leading character in Beauty and the Beast.'" Major Mulford had been angry over the delay after running aground and ignored the pursuing tugboat; thus, the steamer Belle rode on easily outran the smaller vessel. When the tugboat returned to Fortress Monroe, and Belle was not captured, Belle wrote, "He" {General

Butler} was almost beside himself with rage at being thwarted in his revenge." Belle did not say by whom, but she later wrote she got her information from good authority.

Late on Friday evening, December 4, the *City of New York* arrived at City Point where Belle and Miss Goldsborough were transferred to a Southern flag of truce vessel. It was a slow trip because the vessel had to maneuver through the maze of sunken ships at Chapin's and Drury's Bluffs. After arriving at Drury's Bluff, Belle and Miss Goldsborough spent the night because the Confederate truce boat had not arrived.

The following morning the Confederate truce boat arrived to receive Belle and Miss Goldsborough. When they boarded the Confederate vessel, Captain W. H. Hatch, the Confederate assistant agent of exchange introduced himself to the two ladies. Once they departed for Richmond the journey took a considerable amount of time because they had to proceed slowly through the military obstructions at Drury's Bluff. Even though the tugboat traveled cautiously, it became entangled with some of the obstruction. Belle and Miss Goldsborough had to transfer to a tugboat that took them the rest of the journey to Richmond. Belle arrived at the Spotswood Hotel at 8:00 in the evening.

Again, Southern newspapers announced Belle's arrival in the South. The *Richmond Daily Dispatch* was the first to announced Belle's arrival in their publication: "A flag of truce boat arrived at City Point yesterday afternoon. Among the passengers was Miss Belle Boyd," followed on December 8 by the Memphis, Tennessee *Daily Appeal* newspaper, "Among the passengers, say the *Richmond Sentinel*, of the 5th, who arrived at City Point on Friday in a flag of truce boat, was Miss Belle Boyd.

"When she {Belle} reached Richmond, she was met with a most enthusiastic reception," said the Yorkville, South Carolina *Enquirer*.

The following week, Belle attended a dinner party, feeling "joyous and light-hearted" little dreaming of the news that would overwhelm her with sadness.

*   *   *   *

On Monday morning, December 14, Captain Hatch sent a note to Belle's room informing her that he was the bearer of sad news. He also informed her he and the hotel proprietor's wife would visit her. She was perplexed at the note's meaning and "could not imagine what he meant." When Belle was ready, she sent for them. When Captain Hatch first saw Belle, he asked her if she knew her father had been ill. Immediately, she knew the meaning of Captain Hatch's visit, saying as she fell to the floor, "My God! Is he dead?"

Benjamin Boyd had died. Under its heading of "Deaths," The *Richmond Daily Dispatch* had published that very morning Benjamin Boyd's death. The newspaper wrote, "In Georgetown D.C., on the 6th inst., Benjamin Boyd, of Martinsburg, Va., (father of Miss Belle Boyd, now in this city) in the 47th year of his age."

Benjamin Boyd's death was also published in Northern newspapers as far away as Dayton, Ohio. There was an article published in the *Dayton Dailey Empire* on December 14: "Mr. Benjamin R. Boyd, father of Miss Belle Boyd, who was recently sent a second time across the lines, died at Georgetown, District of Columbia, on Sunday night, while on a visit at that place. Mr. Boyd previous to the war, was a merchant at Martinsburg, but retired from the business."

Belle became ill and felt lonely. She wanted to return home to her family. Several Confederate politicians intervened on her behalf and even Belle sent letters to President Lincoln and Secretary Stanton, but her most urgent plead was communicated to her family's friend Ward Hill Lemon, who was now the United States Marshal of the District of Columbia, "Relieve my grief. My father's dead. My Mother, nearly wild with grief & I am exile" and she continued, "I pray you will listen to my entreaties." Her request was denied. Belle tried to write her mother, but all efforts failed, writing, "My letters to and from my mother in Martinsburg were intercepted; and from December, the 16th, until I arrived in London, and then not until the following October, did I receive one line from her, though she had written repeatedly."

It was a long time before Belle did finally receive a letter from her mother informing her that once her father learned of her fate, he had grown worse and had died the day after she arrived in Richmond. But

Belle was consoled when she learned that her mother and siblings had been sent for and were able to see Benjamin before his death.

While Belle was sick in Richmond, many friends cared for her and attempted to nurse her back to health. Sometime in February 1864, Belle traveled to Mobile, Alabama, and the home of Mrs. Ann Elizabeth Semmes. Mrs. Ann Elizabeth Semmes was the wife of Captain and later Admiral Raphael Semmes of the Confederate Navy. Admiral Semmes was the cousin of Brigadier General Paul Semmes, who was wounded during the second day's fight at Gettysburg and shortly after died from his wound.

Belle wrote about her visit and experience with Ann Semmes: "Mrs. Semmes treated me with as much attention as though I had been her own daughter, and invited me to visit them at their home in Mobile. I had always been termed 'the child of the Confederacy,' or 'the child of the army;' and, no matter where I went, I was welcomed both by the gentry and the people.

After Belle left Mobile, she passed through Atlanta, Augusta, and other cites on her return to Richmond. The *Richmond Dailey Dispatch* published an article on February 5, 1864: "Miss Belle Boyd is in Atlanta, and, the *Intelligencer* says, will soon leave for Europe."

Several years after Belle's second trip to the Deep South, she had an encounter on the train between Chester and Columbia, South Carolina, with an individual. Whether the individual was male or female, they did not disclose their identity in the newspaper article. The unknown author of the article submitted a first-hand account that was first published in the *New York Watchman* and later the Yorkville, South Carolina *Enquirer* of their experience with Belle. According to the story's author, once they boarded the train, they could not find a seat and had to stand for a while before they found a seat with Belle and her escort, a major in the Confederate army.

After the author of this story and Belle began to speak, Belle said, "Perhaps you have heard of me; I am Belle Boyd."

The author answered, "Yes; you are one of our heroines."

"Thank you," Belle softly replied.

The unknown author wrote:

We did not tell her how, in our Northern home, where fate had placed us the first two years of the war. She had been to us a peculiar object of sympathy and solicitude. How we daily scanned the papers from some record of her daring...how we had mourned over her imprisonment, and thought with horror of what might be her ultimate punishment. Now we were in our own sunny South, quietly sitting, talking with her, after a second captivity of many long and tedious months. She had just been released from prison, and her mind seemed full of horrors she had endured.

Belle spoke at length with the unknown author about her second imprisonment at Carroll Prison. "She was completely shattered in mind and body; the typhoid fever, from which she had just recovered, had left her with a violent cough, and in a miserable state of health."

The unknown author wrote that Belle "never mentioned the service rendered to her country; her mind only reverted to the fearful horrors of her prison life" and another fearful encounter. Belle revealed the most mortifying circumstances of her career as a spy was when she was escorted to General Butler's headquarters at Fortress Monroe through a file of "Negro soldiers."

Belle also revealed she dreaded the idea of being taken captive if the blockade runner that she would be traveling on to England were captured. If captured, Belle said, "I will throw myself into the sea sooner than again fall into the hands of the Yankees."

The Confederate major who escorted Belle took the unknown author to the side and said, "She was the bravest person under fire ever seen; and had done more to advance the cause of the South than some of the generals, that she was the only regularly commissioned female officer in the Southern army, and well deserved the compliment."

Shortly after Belle began to sing, Home Again, many Confederate soldiers traveling in the passenger car drew near to listen to her sing. When finished, they complimented Belle and thanked her for the song.

Even though Belle still suffering physically and emotionally, she was still full of spirit and ready to carry out any plan or operation to further the Southern Cause. Her loyalty to her home state of Virginia and the Southern Cause was unquestionable.

Source: *Civil War Women*

Euphemia M. Goldsborough

Chapter 23

Captured Again

In March, Belle returned to Richmond, still feeling the effects of her sickness. Belle knew she could not return to Martinsburg because the city remained behind Union lines. Belle felt "restless and unhappy at the death of her father." Belle determined to go abroad and visit Europe as soon as she could arrange her affairs. When she discussed her plans with President Jefferson Davis, he whole-heartily agreed. It must have been discussed between Belle and Davis that Belle would carry dispatches because Davis gave orders to Confederate Secretary of State Judah Benjamin. Belle planned to travel to England on a blockade runner with $500 in gold for expenses, and she was to report to Henry Hotze, a Confederate agent.

Blockade-runners were used to carry goods away from the Union navy's stranglehold on the Confederate seaports along the Atlantic east coast and the Gulf of Mexico southern ports. Many blockade-runners were privately owned but also in partnership with the Southern Confederacy. They generally displayed the Confederate flag when not in danger, but when near the Union Navy, they displayed the British flag, the Union Jack. The ships did not have passenger accommodations and were used only for transporting, smuggling, and outracing the Union fleet.

Belle was supposed to leave Richmond on March 25 but could not do so because of her lingering illness, and instead, she departed on March 29 for Wilmington, North Carolina. Wilmington was a central depot for blockade runners during America's Civil War, and this would be the type of ship used to escape to England.

Unfortunately, A train accident caused Belle to miss the first blockade-runner, but she caught the next one, the C. S. S. *Greyhound*, which arrived two weeks later. An officer commanded the *Greyhound* she called in her memoirs, "Captain Henry," but, his name was George Henry Bier. Bier held the rank of lieutenant, but since he was the highest-ranking officer on the *Greyhound* it was only natural, she referred to him as captain. Bier was from Maryland and just a little older than Belle. He had attended the United States Naval Academy, but resigned his lieutenant's commission from the navy in April 1861.

Belle was acquainted with Lieutenant Bier's family and gladly accepted his offer to take passage on his ship.

According to another *Greyhound* passenger, Lieutenant Bier was "a splendid fellow he was: a graceful dash of manner, which yet beamed with intelligence, an exuberant hospitality, a kindness that when it did a grateful thing so gracefully waived all expressions of obligation. He had been all over the world; was familiar with great capitals of Europe; bored the marks of a wound obtained in the campaign of Stonewall Jackson."

Lieutenant Bier's new 201-foot ship, the *Greyhound*, was a three-masted, single-propeller known as a "fast sailor" with a 372-ton iron hull with a red streak blended into its light color. The light hull helped to obscure their profile against the daytime horizon. Kirkpatrick McIntyre and Company of Greenock, Scotland, had recently constructed it in 1863 and delivered it to the Confederacy on January 5, 1864. Blockade-runners were built for speed, invisibility, and handiness with a certain amount of storage, essential for a successful operation. When the *Greyhound* departed from Wilmington with Belle to Bermuda, it carried 820 bales of cotton, 135 tons of tobacco, and 25 casks of turpentine.

On May 8, 1864, Belle said farewell to her friends and boarded the *Greyhound*. Belle realized the dangers and was anxious, writing, "I knew that the venture was a desperate one; but I felt sustained by the greatness of my cause; for I had borne a part, however, insignificant, in one of the greatest dramas ever yet enacted upon the stage of the world."

There were several passengers with Belle and her two servants, "an Irish girl and a Negro" on the *Greyhound*. They were Mr. Edward Pollard, the *Richmond Examiner's* co-editor, who became one of the ablest writers for the Southern Confederacy and the Lost Cause. Pollard used the alias E. A. Parkinson; another gentleman on board was Mr. Newell. The two gentlemen knew Belle as Mrs. Lewis, the alias she used for the journey. According to Pollard, "three fugitive conscript stowaways" were also discovered at Wilmington; one was a liquor dealer who was taken ashore.

When the *Greyhound* departed down the Cape Fear River, Lieutenant Bier decided not to go far before dropping anchor. Lieutenant Bier's reason for dropping anchor was because the moon was shining, which would help the Union navy to detect them, so they waited until the moon disappeared, and it would be more difficult for the Union navy to detect them. According to Edward Pollard, the *Greyhound* neared the Confederate garrison, Fort Fisher, because he noticed "the signalmen blinking at each other with their lights in sliding boxes." According to Pollard, "it was necessary to get a dispensation from the fort for the *Greyhound* to pass out to sea."

Lieutenant Bier, or as Belle called him, "Captain Henry," had the advantage over his Union adversaries when running the blockade of Union ships. He could choose his time of departure; he could get his steam up; he could choose his area, weather, and circumstances. His vessel also used smokeless anthracite coal for fuel. The Union Navy was disadvantaged because they never knew when the blockade runner was coming.

On Belle's twentieth birthday, the *Greyhound's* crew took up her anchor, and steam rapidly raised, and she shoved off, passing the sunken Confederate ironclad, *Raleigh*. As the lookouts took their place on the boat, no more pleasantries were exchanged, and no more conversation was carried on, but instead, everyone felt anxious, knowing they would soon be in the location of the Union fleet. Most blockade-runners, when they departed, hugged the shoreline slipping by the last vessel of the Union Navy. The blockade runners were usually invisible even on a clear night, and with little water depth, they could easily pass well inside the blockaders. Finally, after two hours, the *Greyhound* passed the Union blockade near Fort Fisher.

It was a hazy day around noon on May 10 when a sailor sounded the first warning aft at the masthead. A Union ship was spotted about five to six miles behind them. According to Edward Pollard, the aft lookout shouted to Lieutenant Bier, "He is a side-wheel steamer, and is bearing directly for us."

Lieutenant Bier shouted, "Give her her way," and there was a tumultuous rush by the crew to the engine room. Shortly black smoke curled above the smoke stack and white foam revealed the startled *Greyhound* was making desperate speed."

Immediately with the increase of extra steam, the race was on to outrun the approaching Union navy cruiser. The chase continued for about an hour, but it appeared useless because the Union navy cruiser was, with every passing moment, getting closer to the *Greyhound*. At about this time, Lieutenant Bier faced mutiny when some of the crewmembers became unruly. Still, with a revolver in his hand, the Confederate captain declared, "he was master of the vessel yet."

Shortly Lieutenant Bier warned Belle, "unless some unforeseen accident should favor us, such as temporary derangement of the Federal steamer's steering apparatus, or breaking of some important portion of her machinery, we might look to New York instead of Bermuda as our destination."

Belle believed that unless "Providence interposed directly," she would be captured and have nothing to look forward to than a third imprisonment.

When the Union cruiser closed within firing range, they fired some shots at the *Greyhound*. Belle recalled, "A thin, white curl of smoke rose high in the air as the enemy luffed up and presented her formidable broadside. Almost simultaneously with the hissing sound the shell, as it buried itself in the sea within a few yards of us, came the smothered report of its explosion under water."

The Union guns followed in rapid succession, exploding close while others were well off range, and still, others bursting in the air. According to an article first published in the *Boston Post* and republished later by the *Cleveland Morning Leader*, the correspondent wrote, "During the attack upon the *Greyhound* Miss B, came on deck, took a seat upon a bale of cotton, and quietly sat fanning herself, watching the explosion of shells. "

Lieutenant Bier continued to order more steam, but finally, he turned and said, "Miss Belle, I declare to you that, but for your presence on board, I would burn her to the water's edge rather than those infernal scoundrels should reap the benefit of a single bale of our cargo."

Belle replied he should act without reference to her and to do his duty because she was not afraid.

While Belle and Lieutenant Bier spoke, the Union ship continued to fire on the *Greyhound*, with shells exploding all around, but fortunately for Belle and the crew of the vessel, they were not struck.

The Union warship fired what Belle described as a "hundred-pound bolt" that passed between where she was standing on the deck and Lieutenant Bier standing on the bridge a little above her.

Lieutenant Bier was concerned the Union warship's captain was not going to give them mercy. When the Union warship neared, they commanded Lieutenant Bier to haul down his flag, or they were going to fire on them again. Lieutenant Bier complied with the request, and the British flag was lowered, but before the Union navy boarded the ship, the crew dumped overboard twenty to thirty thousand dollars, the "equivalent in value to about six thousand pounds sterling." Belle quickly raced off to the lower deck and disposed of the letters and dispatches, tossing them into the furnace before returning to the upper deck.

As much as possible, all the *Greyhound's* cargo was tossed overboard. Edward Pollard wrote, "papers, memoranda, packages of Confederate bonds, were ruthlessly tossed into the purser's bag to be consumed by the flames in the engine room; the contents of trunks were wildly scattered over the deck."

*   *   *   *

At 1:40 on May 10, the Executive Officer, Lieutenant Louis Kempff and some crewmembers of the U.S.S. *Connecticut* boarded the *Greyhound*. Immediately Lieutenant Kempff asked Lieutenant Bier for his papers, which the rebel captain answered he had no papers in his possession.

Lieutenant Kempff informed Lieutenant Bier he would have to accompany him onto the U. S. S. *Connecticut* to be interviewed by Captain John J. Almy. Lieutenant Bier did not resist, and departed with Lieutenant Kempff to the Union vessel.

A Navy ensign named William Swasey was left on board with a crew to detain Belle and the rest of the crew of the *Greyhound*. Belle did not care for Swasey and writes that he is an "officer as unfit for authority as any who has ever trodden the deck of a man of war. His subordinates were, I imagine, well acquainted with his character and abilities at all events, they treated his orders with not respect, but ridicule."

While Belle was being held in her cabin, many Union sailors on the *Greyhound* helped themselves to the wines. A Union sailor told Belle that he had been the one who fired the cannon shot that passed her head.

When Belle heard what another Union ensign by the name of John M. Reveille said she replied, "That man, whoever he may be, is an errant coward to fire on a defenseless ship after her surrender."

Belle remembered many years later the capture of the *Greyhound* and that she had been blamed for its demise by one of the passengers, "The day before the blockade-runner '*Minnie*' was captured, and her people told their captors that I was to sail the next day. I had two servants, an Irish girl, and a Negro. Edward Pollard of the *Richmond Examiner* was also on board. Well, we were captured by the United States steamer *Connecticut*, which was watching for us. Pollard was so unkind as to remark that 'if it hadn't been for that nuisance'...myself...' the *Greyhound* would have got through.'" Belle never forgot the accusation made by Edward Pollard.

Belle was correct in what she told the reporter concerning the C. S. S. *Minnie*. According to the United States Naval War Records, The U.S.S. *Connecticut* captured the *Minnie* on May 9. In the *Official Reports*, The U.S.S. *Connecticut* chased the *Minnie* for four hours off Cape Fear while steering toward Bermuda, also flying the British flag. When captured, it carried the same cargo as the *Greyhound* and a Confederate navy officer as its only passenger. The crew of the *Minnie* disposed of $10,000 in gold and $17,500 in government currency the same way the *Greyhound* crew disposed of their monies.

The Navy's war records revealed the capture of the *Greyhound* the next day. The coordinates when the *Greyhound* was captured were at latitude 330, 3 N and longitude 750, 55 W, 109 miles east of Cape Fear, the exact coordinates where the *Minnie* was captured the previous day. In his report to Rear Admiral S. P. Lee, Captain Almay wrote, "I have placed a prize crew on board the *Greyhound* and ordered her to Hampton Roads to report to you. Acting Ensign Samuel Hardinge Jr. is in charge."

An article appeared in the Washington *Evening Star* newspaper published May 14, 1864 verifying the report, which said, "The noted Belle Boyd was on the blockade-runner *Greyhound*, and is now in Hampton Roads."

How did Belle know later in life that she and the crew of the *Greyhound* had the *Connecticut* on the watch for them once they departed from Wilmington? According to Captain Almy, he had eighty prisoners on board the *Connecticut* that he needed to take to port at Hampton Roads, some of them from the crew of the *Minnie*. Belle did not leave the *Greyhound* after its capture to board the *Connecticut*. She never had any association or conversation with the *Minnie's* crew and could not have learned from them about information of her passage on the *Greyhound*. Could Belle have learned her information from Ensigns William Swasey or John Reveille? If she did, she did not write about it in her memoirs. It was not until later, in an interview in 1893 while in Boston, that Belle first revealed her knowledge that the crew of the *Connecticut* was watching for them. She must have had a source who revealed to her the mystery behind the capture of the *Greyhound*; that source could only have been her future husband, Ensign Samuel Hardinge. Like many Union officers at Front Royal and Martinsburg, Hardinge was willing to accommodate Belle to win her heart and loyalty. But, as one reporter recalled, he had nothing short of the "gift of gab."

Another question was, how did the U.S.S. *Connecticut* gain speed so fast on the *Greyhound*, which was built light and for speed to outrun the Union fleet? The U.S.S. *Connecticut* was listed in the Navy's registry as a second-class paddle wheeler with eleven guns assigned to the North Atlantic Squadron. One reason is that during the last two years of the war, the captains and the crews of the Union navy became more seasoned and wiser to different tactics used by the Confederate navy. If any escaped, they were usually the blockade-runners, but again it was not the case with the *Greyhound*.

After the capture of the *Minnie* and knowledge that the *Greyhound* was due to leave Wilmington the following day, the information gave Captain Almy an advantage over his adversary to be on the watch and knowing that the *Greyhound* would take pretty much the same route as earlier mentioned with the exact latitude and longitude coordinates near Cape Fear. Another problem is that the *Greyhound* did not have its steam up because, by the time the watchman looking aft from the ship spotted the *Connecticut*, they were already gaining on them. It can only be that the *Connecticut* was expected and spotted the *Greyhound* long before the watchman aft at the *Greyhound's* masthead spotted the Union vessel. It also takes time to get up steam for any size vessel, and Lieutenant George Henry, as Captain Almy referred to him in his *Official Report*, was surprised by the sudden appearance of the *Connecticut*. It was due to Lieutenant Bier's error and misjudgment and the surprising appearance of the *Connecticut* that he lost his ship, cargo, and crew because had the *Greyhound* been traveling with more steam, she would have done what she was built to do, and that was to outrun the U. S. S. *Connecticut*.

Source: *Author's Collection*

Blockade-Runner

Source: *United States Navy*

U. S. S. *Connecticut*

Chapter 24

Reprieve

Once Captain Almy decided to take the *Greyhound* to Hampton Roads, Virginia, he placed a Navy prize crew and a prize master on board the blockade runner. A prize master is an officer who oversees a prize crew of the prize it is handling, in this case, the *Greyhound*.

Captain Almy wrote in his report about the capture of the *Greyhound* dated May 10, 1864:

At 12:10 discovered a strange sail bearing N.W. from us. Immediately gave chase and saw that she was a three-masked propeller burning black smoke, with all sails set...Steamer throwing cotton overboard...Fired a shot from the No. 2 pivot gun at her and one from the No. 1 broadside gun, upon which she rounded to and hauled down the English ensign...boarded her, and she proved to be the Anglo rebel steamer Greyhound, having run the blockade last night from Wilmington, N.C.... loaded with cotton, tobacco, and turpentine, and having among her passengers the famous rebel lady, Miss Belle Boyd, and her servant...sent a prize crew on board the Greyhound, Acting Ensign Samuel Hardinge., in charge.

The U.S.S. *Connecticut's* prize master was Lieutenant Samuel Wylde Hardinge. In all other United States Government documents, they refer to Samuel W. Hardinge as holding the rank of lieutenant and not as an ensign.

Belle wrote about the first time she met Lieutenant Samuel Wylde Hardinge Jr., writing, "I saw at a glance he was made of other stuff than his comrades, who preceded him; and I confess my attention was riveted by the presence of a gentleman."

Who is Samuel Wylde Hardinge Jr.? Samuel was born on November 11, 1842, to Samuel Sr. and Sarah Harding in Portsmouth, New Hampshire. Unlike his father, who spelled his last name Harding, Samuel and his youngest brother, William, used their surname, Hardinge.

Belle's description of Samuel Hardinge was that "his dark-brown hair hung down on his shoulders; his eyes were large and bright. Those who judge of beauty by regularity of feature only, could not have pronounced him strictly handsome." Belle also judged him as a "refined gentleman" and her "Southern proclivities, strong as they were, yielded for a moment to the impulses of my heart."

When Samuel Hardinge first boarded the *Greyhound*, he ignored Belle. Instead of introducing himself to Belle, he sent the officers and crew of the *Greyhound* along with Mr. Pollard and Mr. Newell to the *Connecticut*, keeping only Lieutenant Bier or "Captain Henry," the steward, cabin boy, cook, Belle, and her servants on board. Hardinge then made sure the *Connecticut's* marines secured the ship. The prize crew immediately changed their mischief conduct. Hardinge was a strict disciplinarian while on duty but was very well respected by his men, who would follow him anywhere.

When ready, Lieutenant Hardinge went aft of the ship, and seeing Belle, he requested permission to enter her cabin. Belle granted his request, and then she acknowledged she was a prisoner.

Lieutenant Hardinge reassured Belle he was in command of the *Greyhound* and she was not to consider herself a prisoner but a passenger. Belle felt relieved.

At 8:00 in the evening, the *Connecticut* got underway, proceeding north with the *Greyhound* riding astern. It was a sleepless night for Belle because all she could think about was the thought of another imprisonment, only this time at the Fitchburg jail for the duration of the war as she was previously promised when at Carroll Prison five months ago.

The next day, Belle learned their destination was Hampton Roads and the *Connecticut* would be towing the *Greyhound* into port.

The following evening Belle again was her usual self, sitting with Lieutenants Bier and Hardinge. When Lieutenant Bier departed, Samuel Hardinge took advantage of his time with Belle and began to

214

quote passages from Byron and Shakespeare. Samuel Hardinge did not waste time but asked Belle that evening to marry him. When Samuel Hardinge proposed marriage to Belle, she later wrote that he might be "useful" to the Confederacy in the future, but she preferred that he would give her time to consider his proposal. Although Belle had received previous offers of matrimony from other soldiers of the blue and gray, Hardinge's proposal was seriously considered because even though she knew little about him, she was attracted to him.

The following morning as the *Connecticut* and *Greyhound* were entering Hampton Roads, all Belle could think about was whether General Benjamin Butler was still in command of the Union forces at Fortress Monroe and what would be her fate once he knew she was among the captured of the *Greyhound*. Her worst fears were assured when she learned from Samuel Hardinge that Butler was still at Fortress Monroe.

While Belle thought about her possible fate with General Butler, the *Connecticut* broke off from the *Greyhound* and proceeded in the direction where Union Admiral S. P. Lee was located. The *Greyhound* continued toward and moored beside the steamer, the U.S.S. *Baltimore*. Lieutenant Hardinge departed and went to the flagship U.S.S. *Minnesota* to report. He was gone for two hours before returning and once more got the *Greyhound* underway to join the *Connecticut*. After about three-quarters of an hour, the *Greyhound* came alongside the Union ironclad the U.S.S. *Roanoke*, where Commodore Guerte Gansevoort, acting commanding officer in Admiral Lee's absence, had his headquarters. Admiral Lee had departed up the James River.

Commodore Guerte Gansevoort was a fifty-two-year-old Dutch American from New York and a veteran of the War with Mexico. Gansevoort had spent his whole life in the service of the United States Navy. At the time of Belle's capture, he was helping to fit out ships acquired for blockade duty.

When Belle first noticed Commodore Gansevoort, she described him as being "Not over-polite, and, upon reaching the deck, swore soundly and lustily, d----right and left, and was evidently as wild a mannered man as ever scuttled ship or cut-throat." Belle perceived from his actions that he had been drinking liquor.

Commodore Gansevoort had already been informed about Mrs. Lewis's real identity, saying, "This is Miss Belle Boyd, is it?"

Before Belle responded, Lieutenant Bier, entered and said, "What! By----! George, old fel---"

Commodore Gansevoorte remembered his social status with Lieutenant Bier and cut the conversation short, but his hesitancy against the Confederate officer did not last long because after champagne was brought to the cabin, Commodore Gansevoorte wrote out a parole for Lieutenant Bier that it would extend as far as Boston. When Lieutenant Hardinge requested a copy of the document after signing it, Commodore Gansevoote stated that his verbal orders were sufficient and denied his request.

Commodore Gansevoort turned to Belle and said, "You, Miss, when you arrive at New York, can go on shore, provided Mr. Hardinge accompanies you," adding, "I will not enforce a written parole with you but will take a verbal promise. Don't be at all alarmed, you shan't go to prison."

Before Commodore Gansvoorte departed from the *Greyhound*, he ordered the English flag be removed. Lieutenant Hardinge reacted and informed Commodore Gansvoorte that this was a violation of law respecting a natural vessel captured in time of war. Angrily, Commodore Gansvoorte told Lieutenant Hardinge that he did not want any "sea-lawyer arguments."

After a series of contradictory orders, the *Greyhound* set sail, but because of strong gale winds blowing, Captain Almy of the *Connecticut* ordered the vessel to wait for better conditions, which delayed their departure until the following day.

The following morning, a tug arrived from Fortress Monroe and went alongside the *Connecticut*, and soon, all the prisoners from the *Greyhound* and *Minnie*, except Mr. Pollard, were transferred to the tug and taken ashore. Mr. Pollard returned to the *Greyhound*.

Belle did not feel disturbed. Although Captain Almy knew Belle's real identity, he allowed her to remain on the *Greyhound* and leave for New York and Boston. General Butler had no authority over Belle because she had been captured outside of the territorial boundaries of the United States. Belle was in naval custody, and Secretary of the Navy, Gideon Wells, would eventually decide her fate.

Chapter 25

Escape of Captain Henry

The *Greyhound* was off to New York, where it would take on coal before proceeding to Boston. When the *Greyhound* neared New York, a health officer boarded the ship and asked the passengers a few questions before allowing the vessel to proceed further up the East River. Once Lieutenant Hardinge departed the *Greyhound* to report his arrival, the vessel continued and tied up at the Navy yard to take on coal.

Many spectators had arrived to get a glimpse of Belle since she had been so publicized in the New York newspapers but were disappointed because a tugboat came alongside the *Greyhound* and took Belle and Lieutenant Bier off the *Greyhound*. Belle wrote, "When Mr. Hardinge returned in the afternoon, the dock was filled with gazers, who, excited by that morbid curiosity exhibited by the world in general, had come to witness, as they supposed, my debarkation. In this they were somewhat disappointed, for everything had been arranged so nicely that not one of the many there assembled knew when I went on shore."

Once Belle and Lieutenants Hardinge and Bier arrived at Canal Street in the city, they obtained a carriage and rode to the home of a friend that Belle was acquainted with while living in the city. At her friend's house, she removed the money she had concealed that belonged to her and Lieutenant Bier and was not, "as the Yankee papers averred, part of the ship's money" that had been thrown overboard previously to the capture of the *Greyhound*. Lieutenant Bier placed the money in a bank.

How did Belle and Lieutenant Bier place money in a bank without Lieutenant Hardinge's knowledge? Was Hardinge still with Belle and the Confederate naval officer at the time? Did the Confederate naval

217

officer go off on his own under some pre-condition? Or had Hardinge already determined to play along with the scheme because he had already asked for Belle's hand in marriage and wanted to win her heart? Even though she does not reveal to her readers how this scheme was pulled off in her memoirs, Hardinge had already allowed himself to be pulled into their plans directly or indirectly.

Belle and Lieutenants Hardinge and Bier went to a performance of *Bel Demonio* at the Niblo's Theater. The story was a romantic drama of John Brougham, in which the noted lyric artiste Mademoiselle Vestivali appeared. Belle later remembered that day when she wrote about her war experiences and Virginians who were suffering at home: "What a contrast did the gay, wealthy city of New York afford at this period to my own sorrow-stricken land! Here there was no sign of want or poverty. No woe-begone faces could I see in that assemblage; all was life and animation."

Lieutenant Hardinge called for Belle the following morning, and they returned to the *Greyhound*. Lieutenant Bier and Mr. Pollard, who had also been paroled for the day, had already returned to the vessel. Over the next four hours, Belle and the others were allowed to receive visitors; several military and naval officers were among them.

At 4:00 in the afternoon, the *Greyhound* departed from New York. After the *Greyhound* got underway, Lieutenant Hardinge reaffirmed his marriage proposal to Belle. Belle wrote, "So generous and noble was he in everything that I could not but acknowledge that my heart was his. I firmly believe that God intended us to meet and love, and, to make the story short, I told him that I would be his wife." Although Belle and Samuel Hardinge were on different sides of the war and had different social views, she believed that a woman can sometimes work wonders. She hoped to convince him to change his loyalties to the South. But before Belle accepted his proposal, she tested him concerning his steadfast loyalty to her. In an interview in 1893 about Hardinge's marriage proposal, Belle said, "I would if he would agree to give me his signal book covering every flag of the U. S. Naval code, leave the navy, enter the service of the Confederacy and help the captain of the *Greyhound* escape. My hand was the barter, and he accepted."

*   *   *   *

On the way north to Boston, it had been hoped that the crew of the *Greyhound* could recapture the vessel, but the idea was abandoned because Captain Almy had refused to allow the chief engineer and first officer to make the journey. Any attempt to recapture the vessel without these two officers faded.

On May 19, the *Greyhound* entered Boston harbor, and Belle noticed in the distance Fort Warren, which was used as a prisoner of war facility. Belle began to wonder if the fort would be her new home for the duration of the war. For Edward Pollard, it was a different case. As they passed Fort Warren, Pollard had Union sailors reminding him of his fate.

On May 20, 1864, the *Boston Post* published the first article about Belle and Mr. Pollard's arrival: "The steamer…had on board as passengers and somewhat famous rebel spy, Miss Belle Boyd, and Mr. Pollard of Richmond, author of a Southern history of the Rebellion. Miss Boyd came on board the steamer at Wilmington as Miss Lewis, and her deportment on shipboard is described by the officers as very lady-like." The *New York Herald* followed with an article on the same day, announcing: "The prize steamer Greyhound captured off Wilmington arrived here this afternoon. The famous rebel spy Belle Boyd is a passenger." And yet another article in the *Alexandria Gazette* was published the following day, May 21, 1864, about Belle and Edward Pollard's arrival in Boston: "A dispatch from Boston announces that Mr. Edward A. Pollard, one of the editors of the *Richmond Examiner*, and Miss Belle Boyd, were passengers on board the *Greyhound* when that vessel was captured."

Belle, and Lieutenants Bier and Hardinge had come up with a plan for the Confederate naval officer's escape from the *Greyhound*. As the *Greyhound* came to port, Lieutenant Hardinge went forward to give orders to his men while Belle, Mr. Pollard, and Lieutenant Bier were seated in a cabin in the aft part of the vessel. While Belle offered a couple of water channel pilots some wine, Lieutenant Bier casually walked up onto the deck and stood there briefly until a harbor boat arrived alongside the *Greyhound* to take Hardinge to shore.

Shortly, Lieutenant Hardinge appeared, and after realizing he had mislaid the papers he needed when going ashore, he went below to look for them. At this time, Lieutenant Bier stepped into the small vessel and, with the help of the tide, quickly disappeared.

When Lieutenant Hardinge reappeared, and discovered the small boat was gone, he concluded that the waterman had grown tired of waiting and had departed. Lieutenant Hardinge called for another boat and left for shore to report to forty-three-year-old John Sheppard Keyes, the United States Marshal for the District of Massachusetts. Keyes later wrote when he first saw Hardinge that, he was "a boyish young middy."

Immediately, Marshal Keyes and some friends at his office accompanied Lieutenant Hardinge back to the *Greyhound*.

When Lieutenant Hardinge, Marshal Keyes, and Keyes's friends arrived on the *Greyhound*, Edward Pollard drew his first impressions of Keyes by later writing, he "was a little Yankee with gimlet eyes, and who with the fondness of his nation wore official insignia, had dove himself with immense metal buttons marked U.S."

Marshal Keyes remembered first meeting Belle and Edward Pollard after boarding the *Greyhound*. He later wrote, "I found a middle-aged and rather young lady with a black servant and a rather truculent looking Southerner as passengers. To the ladies, I was introduced by the midshipman who had brought home the prize, they passing under the names of Lewis and to the man as Mr. Pollard."

Lieutenant Hardinge misrepresented Belle as Mrs. Lewis to Marshal Keyes, knowing she was *Belle Boyd: The Rebel Spy*. But Hardinge did not know that Marshal Keyes already knew Belle's identity. Instead, Keyes had already received the information from Washington.

There was one piece of cargo neither Belle nor anyone else mentioned in their writings about the trip north on the *Greyhound*: the vessel carried a stallion. According to Marshal Keyes, he found "a blazed stallion on board in a sort of pen made by cotton bales, and game calk. This last I found had been the cause of the condition of the cabin, as every mirror on board had been used up in his fights with the reflection of himself in it for the amusement of the ladies."

Marshal Keyes asked where Lieutenant Bier was and Belle answered she believed he was on the deck, to which Lieutenant Hardinge departed to seek out the Confederate naval officer.

While Lieutenant Hardinge was gone, Marshal Keyes and Belle began a conversation. Marshal Keyes must have been probing for information from Belle since he knew who she was, but Belle claimed she did not give the marshal any information and continued her alias of Mrs. Lewis. Shortly, Lieutenant Hardinge entered the cabin and "coolly" announced that Lieutenant Bier had escaped. Belle acted surprised and implied Lieutenant Bier had just been with her in the cabin but, all along, laughing inwardly.

An article confirming Lieutenant Bier's escape was published May 24, 1864, in the *Washington National Intelligencer*: "The captain of the blockade runner *Greyhound*, which reached Boston on Thursday noon, escape during the excitement incident to her arrival. The ship was surrounded by boats from the shore, and there being little or no lookout kept, the captured captain availed himself of the neglect and got ashore, dodging his captors."

Belle wrote, "Again, I have got the best of the Yankees."

Chapter 26

Boston & Canada

Marshal Keyes immediately sent out detectives throughout Boston looking for Lieutenant Bier and his recapture. Through the medium of a friend Belle knew, she soon found he was seeking shelter away from the authorities.

Once all the formalities and conversation concluded, Marshal Keyes escorted Belle to the Tremont House in downtown Boston where he had "procured a suite of rooms." Belle later told a correspondent she had been allotted three rooms, and her meals were served. She remained at the Tremont House until Union authorities decided her fate in Washington.

The Tremont House, built in 1829, was a plush four-story luxurious hotel at the corner of Tremont and Beacon Street. The hotel included indoor plumbing for toilets, hot baths, bellhops, and guest-locked rooms. Charles Dickens and Davy Crockett were among its famous guests who lodged at the Tremont House.

After Marshal Keyes arrived at the Tremont House with Belle, he informed her he would have either the "supreme pleasure" of taking her to Canada or the "unpleasant task" of delivering her to the "tender mercies of the commandant of Fort Warren." After telegramming Secretary of the Navy Gideon Wells for instructions, Marshal Keyes interviewed Belle and informed her that he knew she was Belle Boyd, not Mrs. Lewis. Marshal Keyes later wrote he informed her she was "the famous rebel spy who had bamboozled so many Union officers."

According to Marshal Keyes, Belle finally admitted her real identity but "denied for many reasons to pass under her assumed name." After further examination of her baggage, Marshal Keyes "found that she was the Belle who had played such tricks" on the "soldiers as had been reported in the newspapers, and caused her to be sent out of harm's way." Belle admitted to Marshal Keyes that "she had seen a hard winter and spring and was on the way to Europe to recruit her health." According to Marshal Keyes, Belle "had lost much of her beauty but still had a grace of manner and some fascination that she had exercised with great effect on young Hardinge."

Later that evening, after Lieutenant Bier escaped the *Greyhound*, Keyes told Belle they had arrested him in Portland, Maine. Belle wrote, "I knew that there was some mistake and could hardly restrain my laughter; for all this time Captain "Henry" was lying *perdu* in Boston, under an assumed name. I was well aware of the captain's residence." Belle was correct about this bit of information because she revealed many years later how she helped "Captain Henry" Lieutenant Bier escape to Canada via New York, writing:

"I hadn't been at the Tremont House a great while, however, before I discovered my Captain as a guest of the hotel, having a room directly over my suite."

We had to be awfully careful, and it was great fun playing possum with the detectives who came to the house. We got a barber, and changed the Captain from a blonde to a brunette. One night he left for Canada taking the signal book with him."

Lieutenant Bier used "the name of Howe" after his escape.

Once the Boston newspapers learned Belle was at the Tremont House, their correspondents wanted interviews to see the notorious rebel spy. Belle wrote, "The public journals were indefatigable in noticing all my movements," and the "week-day new-sheets gave notice," writing "she converses freely and well, and is evidently a female of intelligence and quick understanding."

By now during the war, Ulysses S. Grant had been promoted to the rank of lieutenant general and given command of all United States armies. General Grant took the advice of his good friend, Major-General William T. Sherman and kept his headquarters in the field away from Washington politicians. Instead, Grant stayed with Major-General George Meade and the Army of the Potomac where the fighting occurred.

The May campaign in Virginia in 1864 had seen some of the heaviest and bloodiest fighting of America's Civil War. Battles had been fought with great vigor at the Wilderness and Spotsylvania with enormous casualties to both armies; Belle was aware of the entire fighting in Virginia and freely gave her views on the war. One Boston newspaper wrote an article on Belle's stay in Boston. The *Cleveland Morning Leader* republished the article: "She entertains and expresses strong admiration of, sympathy with the South, but not in offensive terms. She thinks the pending contest between Lee and Grant will terminate the war in favor of the victor. These Generals she considers the two ablest officers in the country."

Belle knew the war was in all probability lost to the Southern Confederacy because General Grant was not like his predecessors, who retreated and reorganized after a campaign of heavy fighting and defeat; instead, he was like a bulldog and kept fighting and looking for an advantage over his foe. And the morale and momentum among the fighting men in the Army of the Potomac were still strong, especially after the fight at Gettysburg and the fall of Vicksburg, Mississippi. Even though she did not comment on it, Belle most likely knew the war would not continue, and that is why she said that whoever would be the victor would win the war. She proved to be correct.

While in Boston, Belle took advantage of her freedom and went shopping, and many citizens watched her every move. Marshal Keyes recalled the days of Belle's visit to Boston, and how infatuated some of the city's citizens were with her, writing, "when she had got over her sea trip, she started out shopping, and my office was soon filled with startling reports of her presence in stores and her gold coins with which she paid for her purchases. She was a troublesome customer as she was overrun with curiosity seekers and had no discretion herself."

Why didn't Marshal Keyes ask about the gold coins that Belle carried and used for purchases in Boston? Why didn't he confiscate the coins considering the money "contraband?" If she had been operating where the armies were located, the money would have most likely been confiscated, but since Boston was not touched by the war physically, such as Virginia and other Southern and border states, the only conclusion is that Marshal Keyes showed leniency toward her

224

believing her request to go abroad would be granted just so the Union authorities could be rid of her. She would need some of the money for expenses.

While in Boston, Belle's mother wanted to come and see her. She was about thirty-six hours away by train, but Marshal Keyes denied the request. Belle felt greatly disappointed because she was denied the visit, and her mother was not allowed to send her letters; Union authorities intercepted those she attempted.

Belle claims that "many Boston ladies and gentlemen visited" her "despite the Government spies who hovered about" her quarters. Belle never wrote or disclosed their names or how they eluded those detectives watching her room nor did she disclose whether they were loyal to the Confederacy. Marshal Keyes's detectives later might have questioned those citizens to determine their loyalties and what might have been discussed with Belle to gain information that she might have revealed to her guests. But Belle was too smart to make a blunder.

Three weeks had passed, and Belle had not received any news about her fate. Belle remained anxious to know what Union authorities would do with her, whether they would send her back to prison. Belle took the initiative and sent a letter to Secretary of the Navy Gideon Wells through Marshal Keyes informing him she "really was Belle Boyd, and wished to go to Canada" so she "might communicate with her mother." The *Washington National Republic* published an article on May 25, 1864:

A letter was received in this city to-day from the notorious female spy, 'Belle Boyd,' forward to the Secretary of the Navy by United States Marshal Keyes, of Boston, at Belle's request. She is the 'Mrs. Davis' {Lewis} captured on the Greyhound. She says she was allowed to leave the South for a foreign land to recover her health, which had been much impaired by former imprisonment; that she was on board a British ship {the Greyhound} when captured and was intending to go to Canada to settle until 'the cruel war is over,' in order to be near her mother, who lives somewhere in the vicinity, as soon as possible. She said she assumed the name of Davis {Lewis} 'in order to escape notoriety.' This declaration is positive evidence of insanity, upon which Belle's earnest plea to be released from imprisonment will undoubtedly receive favorable consideration.

Although Belle liked the notoriety in the newspaper, she did not care to be construed as "insane."

*　　*　　*　　*

Lieutenant Samuel Hardinge went to Washington to plea for Belle's release. Once he did all he could do for Belle at the United States Navy Department in Washington, he returned north by train to New York City on Monday, May 26. On the train, Hardinge displayed his feelings of disgust to another passenger seated next to him. He was upset over Belle's detention and possible imprisonment. According to the United States Navy Department records, Lieutenant Samuel Hardinge was in uniform while traveling to Washington. He became quite conspicuous in his words expressing his anger and disgust concerning Belle's detention. Hardinge appeared disloyal, indignant, and "boasted that he would have her released" and carried her silver-mounted revolver. Also, there was another reason why he was going to Washington besides trying to secure her release. He wanted to apply for a furlough, which he hoped would be granted, and he could marry Belle if her request were granted and sent to Canada. This could cause problems for his career in the United States Navy and his new wife, a known Confederate agent. The Navy knew through sources that Samuel Hardinge and Belle were romantically involved with each other and planned to enter marriage possibly. This information Marshal Keyes already possessed as well as an "old salt," who had informed the marshal that he was used as a "sailing pilot." According to Marshal Keyes, the pilot said there were "many incidents of the voyage, that made it as sensational as the stories of pirates and buccaneers." He also said Belle had some "fascination that she exercised with great effect on young Hardinge."

Lieutenant Samuel Hardinge was unsuccessful in securing Belle's release from detainment, nor did he successfully obtain a thirty-day furlough from the Navy. Instead, Admiral Silas Horton Stringham at the Boston Navy Yard sent for him. The Admiral had other plans for

Hardinge. Samuel Hardinge was arrested and detained at the Navy yard along with other officers who served under him on the *Greyhound*. Neglect charges were brought against him for being negligent in allowing Lieutenant Bier's" escape from the *Greyhound*. After his arrest, he was detained on the U.S.S. *Ohio*. Samuel sent Belle a letter:

"My dear Miss Belle:

It is all up with me. Mr. Hall, the engineers and myself, are prisoners charged with complicity in the escape of Captain H. The Admiral says that it looks bad for us; so I have adopted a very good motto, viz: 'Face the music!' and, come what may, the officers under me shall be spared. I have asked permission of the Admiral to come and bid you goodbye. I hope that his answer will be in the affirmative."

Within two weeks after sending her letter to Secretary of the Navy Gideon Wells, Marshal Keyes received an answer by telegram that Belle was to be sent to Canada. If captured again within the boundaries of the United States, she would be shot. Why did the Union authorities in Washington allow Belle to escape imprisonment, knowing she did not want to go to Canada to recruit her health? It was not that they believed that a third imprisonment would do any good to keep her confined, it was not that they could allow her to return to Martinsburg to live behind Union lines where she could continue spying, it was not that they believed that she had had enough of the war, but Belle gives the answer to the question. Later in life, she said, "There was quite a dispute over myself because I was under sentence of death, if again found in the North, but it was finally agreed that I had been captured on the high seas, and was not, therefore, justly amenable. Accordingly, it was decreed that I be banished from the country."

Union authorities could not agree on what to do with her, but let her go free and continue her journey with the warning that she would be shot if captured again within the United States. Belle did not take the warning seriously because the government had never previously

227

executed a woman. It was mere intimidation. Although shooting her could be considered foolish on their part, they mostly wanted to be rid of her, considering her at this point in the war more of a nuisance than a threat since the two major armies were no longer operating in Northern Virginia and the Shenandoah Valley where she had operated, but further south near Richmond.

Of course, Belle's banishment from the country and sent North to Canada all played into her plans because she did not destroy the essential papers on the *Greyhound* just before its capture and as she wrote in her memoirs. But as she said in an interview many years after the war, "I delivered my dispatches." Not only did Belle want to go to Canada, but she also wanted to continue to England to deliver the most critical dispatches verbally and those she still possessed on her person.

Belle was glad to be going to Canada, but Edward Pollard's fate was far more severe. Pollard was sent to Forts Warren and Monroe where he spent the next eight months before being released. He was one of the greatest writers to pen the history of the Southern Confederacy.

When Belle and her servant were ready to leave Boston by train, Samuel Hardinge received a parole for the evening and had the opportunity to say his farewell to Belle. Belle wrote, "With a sad heart I had bidden good-by to Mr. Hardinge, although I trusted that he would soon rejoin me."

Marshal Keyes escorted Belle. He traveled with Belle to Rouse's Point, New York, and then across the Canadian border, where he placed her on the train, informing the "conductor who they were, and got his promise to see them through." After his adventures with Belle, he finally said, "Glad to be so well rid of her."

According to Belle she arrived at Montreal where she "met many Southern families, refugees, and Confederate sympathizers." The British provinces had become a haven for exiles. The *Montreal Gazette* published an article on June 4, 1864, announcing Belle's arrival in Canada: "Among the arrivals yesterday at the St. Lawrence Hotel was Miss Belle Boyd of the Confederate States of America. The name of the lady is familiar to our readers through the telegraphic reports from the South in which her exploits as a secret agent of the Confederates have frequently been related." On June 8, the

Washington *Evening Star* carried Belle's arrival in Canada by publishing, "Belle Boyd has gone to Montreal probably to create sympathy and a sensation."

While in Montreal, Belle was hailed as a celebrity. As she experienced in Knoxville, Tennessee the previous year, she was once more, according to the *Montreal Dailey Transcript* newspaper, serenaded: "The Royal Artillery 'swells' in Montreal, young men who do a heavy standing-around business serenaded Belle Boyd." Belle dressed and made the artillerymen a little speech and invited a chosen few to a bottle of wine in the front parlor.

While in Montreal, Lieutenant Bier contacted Belle; he was with his wife at Niagara along the Canadian side of Niagara Falls. Belle wrote that Lieutenant Bier had a great reward for his capture and that "spies were stationed on the bridge to watch, and, if possible, to entrap us, should we by chance be foolish enough to venture within their power."

About a week after Belle arrived at Niagara, she was with Lieutenant Bier at a table at the Clifton House when she noticed two poorly dressed men with waxed mustaches who appeared to take great interest in her party. After watching them closely, Belle and Lieutenant Bier were sure they were detectives sent to watch them and with who they made contact while in Canada. In addition, a Confederate spy network and espionage agents worked from Canada into the northern region of the United States.

The two detectives boarded a train that took Belle, Lieutenant Bier, and his wife to Toronto. When Belle and Lieutenant Bier and his wife arrived at Montreal, they determined once, and for all the two men were detectives, so Belle took lodging at the St. Lawrence Hotel. Lieutenant Bier and his wife took lodging at the Donegana Hotel. Within a few hours, Belle learned that one of the detectives was lodging at her hotel and the other at Lieutenant Bier. Belle and Lieutenant Bier were convinced the two men had been assigned to observe and shadow them. When Belle, Lieutenant Bier, and his wife arrived at Quebec, the Confederate naval officer escaped to Halifax. According to Belle, Lieutenant Bier "managed, by way of Bermuda to get that book through to Charleston."

Belle stayed behind in Quebec for some time, but soon arranged to take a steamer to Bermuda with the detective still shadowing her, but Canadian authorities intervened and denied the detective passage on their ship.

Belle remained in Bermuda long enough to secure passage on another ship that took her to Liverpool, England. She was finally free of Union authority and their spies hovering about, but she remained concerned for Samuel Hardinge, who was still detained in Boston to "face the music."

Footnote: Lt. Bier eventually returned to Baltimore, Maryland, where in 1869, he became the Adjutant of Maryland. He was married three times and eventually moved to Key West, Florida, where he died in 1905.

Source: *Author's Collection*

Tremont House Hotel

Chapter 27

Marriage

Lieutenant Samuel Hardinge was held as a prisoner on board the U.S.S. *Ohio* until July 8, 1864, when the United States Navy dismissed him on the charge of negligence of duty for allowing the escape of the *Greyhound's* captain. According to the *New York Herald*, the correspondent wrote, "Hardinge reported that he {Captain Henry} made his escape in the confusion attending getting the steamer to the wharf unnoticed." The alibi must have been Hardinge's defense in the matter, but it was to no avail. The Navy's investigation and reason for dismissing Lieutenant Hardinge from the Navy were as follows: "For your neglect of duty, in permitting the Captain of the prize steamer *Greyhound* under your charge to escape, you are hereby dismissed from the Navy of the United States as an Acting Ensign on temporary service."

Hardinge could have been court-martialed and sentenced to imprisonment for allowing Lieutenant Bier's escape directly or indirectly, but that did not occur. Why not? Union authorities knew the relationship between Belle and Hardinge. Years after the war, John Keyes wrote his biography about why he believed Hardinge was not court-martialed from the United States Navy. Keyes wrote, "He was discharged from the Navy, and only escaped a court martial by his youth and inexperience counting in his favor."

Following Samuel Hardinge's dismissal from the United States Navy, an article appeared shortly afterward in the Washington *Daily National Republican*: "The Government having knowledge only of the negligence of Lieut. Hardinge promptly dismissed him from the service. This produced at the time quite a consternation in New York, where he is a member of the 'Ship Masters Association,' also, in Boston, where he belongs and where his family resides."

232

The sting of an undesirable dismissal from the navy greatly angered Hardinge. He had been humiliated not only by the United States Naval authorities but was also remembered not so kindly in later years by his superior officers. Later in life, Captain and now Rear Admiral Almy later recalled his experience and relationship with Samuel Hardinge and Belle Boyd during the *Greyhound* incident: "The prize master of the *Greyhound* was a young volunteer officer with the rank of master in the United States Navy, rather a good-looking fellow. It seems while on board the *Greyhound* together he and Belle Boyd became greatly interested in each other, which ripened into affectionate friendship." Admiral Almy continued to write, "She fascinated the prize master to that degree that he turned traitor."

Immediately after his dismissal from the Navy, Samuel Hardinge caught a steamer from Boston to Liverpool to join Belle. On the trans-Atlantic journey, he made the acquaintance of a Boston merchant, who remembered how "thoroughly traitorous" Belle had made him. Hardinge constantly quarreled with the Boston merchant on politics and the war. The quarreling became so heated that Hardinge challenged the Boston merchant to a duel, but that did not occur. The Boston merchant believed Hardinge's conduct on the journey across the Atlantic was "scandalous."

Samuel Hardinge's steamer arrived in Liverpool, England before Belle's steamer arrived from Bermuda. Hardinge left a letter with Mr. Henry Holtz before departing for London and then onto Paris looking for Belle.

When Belle arrived at Liverpool and reported to Mr. Holtz with letters of introduction from the Confederate Secretary of State, Holtz gave Belle the letter from Hardinge. After completing her business in Liverpool, she sent a letter to Hardinge where he could locate her in London.

After eventually reuniting, Belle Boyd and Samuel Hardinge were married on Thursday morning, August 25, 1864, at St. James Church in Piccadilly in London, England. Reverend Paul performed the marriage ceremony for the couple. The Reverend Frederick K. Hartford gave Belle away while Mrs. Edward Robinson Harvey attended the bride at the altar. Mr. Henry Howard Barber was

Samuel's best man for the ceremony. An article appeared in the London *Morning Post* announcing the occasion:

Miss Belle Boyd, whose name and fame are deservedly cherished in the Southern States, pledge her troth to Mr. Sam Wylde Hardinge, formally an officer in the Federal naval service. The wedding attracted to the church a considerable number of English and Southern sympathizers in the cause of the South, anxious to see the lady whose heroism has made her name so famous, and to witness the result of her last activity, the making captive of the Federal officer under whose guard she was being conveyed to prison.

There were some very notable people who attended Belle and Samuel's ceremony. The honorable General James Williams, former United States Minister to Constantinople, the Honorable John O'Sullivan, former Minister from Washington at Lisbon, Major Hughes and Captain Fern of the Confederate army, the Reverend Hartford, Mrs. Paul, Mr. Keen Richards of Kentucky, Mr. Henry Holtz, Mr. C. Warren Adams, Madam Carbelle, and Mr. Reay were all invited and in attendance at the ceremony.

It was a great honor for Belle to have Henry Holtz, James Williams, and John O'Sullivan attend her wedding. They were three of the Southern Confederacy's top men in England. They were there to give her special recognition for her service to the Southern cause. Henry Holtz was the chief Confederate propagandist in England. He was described as intellectually honest and possessed far more insight into public opinion than most individuals. James Williams, a former Minister to Turkey, helped through his newspaper articles to persuade the English upper- and middle-class citizens to rally around the Southern cause. John O'Sullivan held the position of Special Agent of the Confederate Government in London, much like an ambassador.

After the ceremony, Belle and her guests went to the Brunswick Hotel on Jermyn Street and enjoyed breakfast and according to the London *Morning Post*, "Many toast to The Queen and to President Davis and General Lee." Many other toasts took place before Samuel and Belle departed for Liverpool.

Years later, Belle said of her wedding, "We were married one day in the Church of St. James, Piccadilly. It was quite a swell occasion, and made much of at the time in the English papers." She continued, "Afterward I was presented in five different royal courts."

While Belle and Samuel were on their honeymoon, an incident occurred at the Washington Hotel in Liverpool that involved the same Boston merchant that Samuel Hardinge had challenged to a duel on the voyage across the Atlantic. The Boston merchant stayed at the hotel and met Belle. They must have been talking about Samuel because, according to the Boston merchant, Belle invited him to their room where he found Hardinge "dead drunk on the floor, and Belle pointing at him with scorn as the fool who had married her and wasted their ill-gotten money in drink."

This incident was just the beginning of Belle's troubles with Samuel in what would be a stormy relationship. In a letter Belle wrote home to her mother, she said, "I have received mark attention in London and on several occasions, been flattered in person by the Prince of Wales." This incident caused some problems for Belle and her husband because she wrote, "My husband shows his annoyance because I received the lion's share of attention from the nobility of England. He expressed his annoyance on more than one occasion by asserting that the Prince of Wales was not a proper person to bestow favors or flattery on an American lady. In short, my husband is jealous." Belle detested jealousy as the most "despicable malady of human weakness." On one occasion, she lost her self-control with her husband and declared, "I made a sad mistake in marrying an enemy of the South." Belle's declaration grieved Samuel Hardinge. He immediately declared his allegiance to the South. Belle reminded him of their agreement to marry and that he should "accept service with the Confederate States" at once. Belle informed her mother that her husband was taking the next steamer to New York and then to Richmond passing through Martinsburg. Belle wrote, "For my sake, I know you will treat him kindly." Belle wrote her mother that Samuel had asked her if there was anything he could do to help further the Southern cause. She told him to abduct Superintendent Wood alive, take him to Richmond, and present him to the Confederate authorities.

At about this time, an incident occurred in the United States pertaining to Samuel Hardinge. Marshal Keyes wrote about an interesting incident that occurred on a train from Springfield to Boston involving an unidentified young lady. Keyes wrote that he was looking for a seat after boarding the train when he noticed one empty beside a young lady. After receiving her permission, he sat beside her and began reading the *New York Herald* newspaper. The newspaper published an article about Belle and Samuel's marriage on the front page in startling headlines. According to Marshal Keyes, "I soon saw that the lady was greatly excited and interested in the paper." Marshal Keyes handed the newspaper to the young woman, who appeared to be greatly agitated. Marshal Keyes continued to write, "on reading the paragraph and her inquiry if I was in the Navy and if this account could be true! The gilt buttons of my uniform led to the first question, and in answer to the second, I told her who I was and what knowledge I had in the matter." The young lady became greatly distressed and nearly fainted, sobbed and cried, and was only partially soothed by all that Marshal Keyes could do or say to her. According to Marshal Keyes, "she was the lady to whom he {Samuel Hardinge} was engaged to be married, and to his circumstance, he owed his selection as prize officer to bring in that prize to enable him to fulfill his engagement."

On Samuel's arrival in Boston after capturing the *Greyhound*, Hardinge, he had written the young lady, his bride-to-be, a letter informing her he would soon visit her in New Haven, Connecticut, where she lived. The letter was the last correspondence she had heard from him or knew of his whereabouts. When she received no more mail from him, and he failed to come to New Haven, she set out to Boston to try and locate him, but it was on the train that she met Marshal Keyes and discovered what finally happened to Samuel Hardinge.

After listening to the young lady Marshal Keyes had a low opinion of Samuel Hardinge and thought of him as a "worthless scamp."

Hardinge was supposed to leave England and return to the United States with the intention of visiting Belle's family in Martinsburg, but

236

for some reason he did not leave until sometime in November 1864, and then he did not go directly South.

Chapter 28

Samuel Hardinge

Sometime in late November, Samuel Hardinge arrived in Boston. Marshal John Keyes wrote, "Hardinge was in Boston on his way to Va {Virginia} to get some money from the estate of Belle's father." The young lady Hardinge had previously been engaged to and who Marshal Keyes had met on the train to Boston also was in the city, and she called upon him desiring to know if he had located Hardinge. Marshal Keyes informed her "that if she called again in a little while," he "would probably present him to her in person." The young lady returned, but Marshal Keyes informed her that Hardinge had escaped his deputy by a few minutes. According to Keyes, he sent a telegram to Washington informing the authorities that Samuel Hardinge had been in Boston. Why Samuel Hardinge returned to Boston instead of a port further South is unknown. Hardinge could have had unfinished business in Boston, or he believed that since it had been published in the English newspapers that he intended to return to the United States, Hardinge decided to enter at a port where he would least be expected and possibly arrested.

From Boston, Hardinge traveled to New York and checked into a hotel before visiting his parents in Brooklyn. After Hardinge arrived at his parent's home, he spent most of the night "conversing on many topics" including his wife and future prospects. Hardinge did not return to his room at the New York hotel but instead went to his younger brother's room in his parent's home, where he began to compose a letter to Belle.

Around 9:00 the following morning, he awakened and went downstairs to have breakfast, but it was not a pleasant affair for Hardinge. He wrote, "There was very little said, a monosyllabic breakfast, one of those dismal feats where Death seems to reign supreme." It was a sad affair because his mother and father were upset over his marriage to Belle and the details, he had disclosed to them about his prospective future. That night he caught a train to Baltimore and then to Martinsburg.

After some delay, Samuel Hardinge arrived at Martinsburg. Like all the other passengers on the train, he was subjected to a strict examination of his traveling pass and baggage, and after about a fifteen-minute delay, he proceeded on his way.

When he arrived at Belle's mother's home, he was confronted by "one of the girls." He did not disclose to Isabelle his identity, but she shortly returned and asked if he was "Miss Belle's husband?" When he reassured her that he was Belle's husband, she disappeared and returned with "the whole sable household," who crowded around him and gave him a hearty welcome, especially Belle's Grandmother Glenn, who treated him like a son. The only family members who were not home were Belle's mother and one of her sisters, who were visiting Kearneysville, about seven miles east of Martinsburg.

Samuel Hardinge spent the evening conversing with the family. When he retired for the evening, he was allowed to use Belle's room, where he discovered it was untouched and had not been used since her last visit home the previous year. Hardinge wrote, "This was your room; here you had been held a prisoner and had suffered the torture of an agonizing doubt as to your fate. Here lay your books just as you had left them. Writings, quotations, everything to remind me of you." While he looked around the room, the servant appeared and informed him that no one had used the room during Belle's absences.

The followingt day, Hardinge departed from Martinsburg with the intention of returning to Baltimore, but when the train arrived at Monacocy station near Frederick, Maryland, he was arrested and charged as a deserter. According to the *Wheeling Dailey Intelligencer:* "S. Hardinge, who married in Europe Belle Boyd, the somewhat rebel spy, was captured in Martinsburg on Saturday." The paper errs in the location of Hardinge's capture. It was Monacocy station, according to Hardinge's memoirs. When arrested, Hardinge gave the reason for going to Martinsburg that he wanted to take his sister-in-law, Manie Boyd, north to educate her. His statements were discredited, and military authorities believed Belle lurked somewhere in the vicinity where Hardinge was captured.

When Hardinge was arrested, he bragged about his wealth, but when he searched, he had $14.00. The Wheeling newspaper described Hardinge as being a medium size man with dark hair, dark hazel eyes, and thin smooth face. He dressed tastefully in broadcloth, and wore a tall beaver hat and carried a cane when captured. The *Wheeling Dailey Intelligencer* wrote, "He cannot be called handsome, but his actions indicate that he thinks a great deal of himself, and he appears to have the gift of the 'gab' in abundance."

The following day at Hardinge's request, he was sent to Point of Rocks, Maryland, about five miles west of Frederick, where he claims he was "treated more like a dog than a human being." His stay at Point of Rocks was short because he was sent ten miles west to Harpers Ferry. At Harpers Ferry, Brigadier-General John Stevenson, the garrison's commanding officer, interviewed Hardinge

On December 2, General Stevenson accused Hardinge of spying for the Confederacy. Stevenson informed Hardinge that he was "the husband of Miss Belle Boyd" and that "he should be hung." Stevenson continued by commenting to Hardinge and his adjutant, Lieutenant Adams, "By-the-way, we hung one to-day; didn't we, Adjutant?" General Stevenson was serious about Hardinge and the hanging of a person that same day. A deserter from the 61st New York Infantry named William "French Bill" Loge had stepped across the Potomac River one day and joined a force of bushwhackers under the command of John Mobley. Mobley and his men operated in nearby Loudoun County, Virginia, and committed atrocities against Union soldiers and the civilian population. Loge was captured, convicted, and hung on the same day that Samuel Hardinge arrived in Harpers Ferry and on the fifth anniversary of John Brown's execution.

Samuel Hardinge asked General Stevenson what he planned on doing with him. Stevenson informed him that he would hang him if he could not prove his innocence or would send him to Washington, but that would not be the general's call; Hardinge was sent to Washington, where Union authorities confined him in Forrest Hall Prison located in the suburbs of Washington D.C.

Before America's Civil War, Forrest Hall Prison was used for entertainment for grand balls and banquets. The building was a large square room with four large windows facing the street that reached from the top almost to the bottom with iron bars. Hardinge wrote, "In a space little less than seventy-five feet square were crowded together over five hundred dirty, ragged, and filthy wretches, of all conditions and color, who had been here for many months." The prisoners lived and slept on{the}dirt floor. The walls were defaced with vulgar writings and pictures, punctured plaster, and since it was winter, there was little heat. The prisoners lived under constant threat of being shot. No one was permitted to look out the windows because if they did, they were instantly fired upon, and if others invaded the "neutral ground," they were "coolly and deliberately" shot down "like a dog." Four other windows looked out onto the Promenade, which was a small enclosure where the prisoners were allowed to walk and exercise each day for thirty minutes. One feature of the yard was what was known as the "hose." The "hose" was a method of torture and discipline, which was applied by fastening the prisoner in an immoveable position beneath a faucet that permitted drips of water to escape, which always fell in one spot on the prisoner's forehead, driving the prisoner to insanity or the guards would take the prisoner and bound him securely to a pole, while a steady stream of water, whose force was thirty pounds to a square inch would be played upon the individual's backside. In most cases, the prisoner could not endure the torture and would confess guilt to their crime whether they were guilty or not guilty. Afterward, they were led off to be executed or sentenced to life at another prison. Other prisoners did not surrender so easily to the torture but continued to endure it until they either fainted or until a medical attendant said, "enough."

Samuel Hardinge's stay at Forrest Hill Prison lasted overnight. The following day, guards escorted him to the provost marshal's office in Washington. Finally, they took him to the Old Capitol Prison and then to Carroll Prison, where he shared a room with a spy and a blockade runner.

On the second day of his arrival at Carroll Prison, he met Superintendent Wood, who said, "Ho, ho, here we are! So, you're the husband of the famous Belle Boyd, are you? Well, we haven't got her, but we've got her husband, that's next to it." Belle must have had conversations with Hardinge about her experiences with Superintendent Wood and her life at both the Old Capitol and Carroll Prisons. Now Samuel Hardinge had met Superintendent Wood and did not know how long he would be held a prisoner, but he decided to begin the process of trying to state his case and win his freedom.

With what little money he had left, he purchased some paper from a sutler and wrote a letter to Secretary Stanton pleading his case and innocence. When completed, his letter went first to Judge Turner, who was from the Judge Advocate Department and the individual who attended to all the prisoner's cases.

While at Carroll Prison, living conditions were more acceptable than during his short stay at Forrest Hill Prison. Hardinge could occasionally walk in the prison yard, purchase from sutlers, and receive mail. Few other prisoners were confined in his room, but he was denied all access to visitors. On December 24, he received a letter from Belle's mother that she had been denied permission to visit him. Belle's mother wrote, "What have I done, a weak, defenseless woman, weighed down with sorrow and care, that they will not permit me to come on to Washington, and see you?"

On the same day Hardinge received the letter from Belle's mother, he had an interview with Judge Turner about the letter he had sent Secretary Stanton. At the beginning of the meeting, Hardinge felt anxious to know when he would be released and if any charges had been filed against him.

Judge Turner answered Hardinge that he did not know when he would be released and informed him there had been no charges placed against him at the present.

When Hardinge asked why he was being held, Judge Turner informed him that it pleased the government.

Hardinge became angry and was warned by Judge Turner not to say anything that would get him into more trouble. When Hardinge appeared composed, Judge Turner said, "You are held here because it pleases Mr. Stanton; besides, your wife won't destroy any more of our army than she has done."

Samuel Hardinge was being held by Secretary Stanton and the United States Government in what amounted to a hostage situation so that Belle would be intimidated and not attempt or commit any covert activity or anything that might jeopardize the Union cause and keep her abroad. Hardinge believed his fate was sealed until the war concluded.

On December 30, Hardinge's parents obtained written permission to visit him in prison. While they were visiting and speaking on various topics, their conversation was interrupted. Then Hardinge was informed that he was being transferred to the prison installation at Fort Delaware. Although his life at Carroll Prison had greatly improved over his short stay at Forrest Hill, it was about to get a lot worse and more severe with the hardships he would endure at Fort Delaware.

Chapter 29

Hardinge at Fort Delaware

Fort Delaware was located on 288 acres of Pea Patch Island in the Delaware River near Delaware City, Delaware. The fort was built in 1817 to be used as a harbor defense but later converted into a military prison during the Civil War. The prison did not only house Confederate prisoners of war but also political prisoners, federal convicts, and privateer officers. When Washington authorities decided that Fort Delaware was going to be used as a military prison, there were wooden barracks constructed, or as Private Henry Berkeley called them, "wooden sheds," constructed to house the Confederate prisoners.

By August 1863, enough wooden barracks were constructed at Fort Delaware to house 11,000 prisoners and a 600-bed hospital facility. Also, there was an L shape barracks that had been constructed for the prison's Union guards. General Albin Francisco commanded the Union garrison and prisoners of war at Fort Delaware.

When Samuel Hardinge arrived at Fort Delaware around 10:00 in the evening on December 31, he registered and was imprisoned with the Virginia division. When Hardinge and other prisoners from Virginia entered their barracks, they were greeted on every side by shouts of "Fresh fish! Fresh fish!" and then afterward, they were asked where they came from, what command they served in, and many other questions.

When Hardinge had his first initial meal at Fort Delaware, he wrote that it consisted of a "piece of flinty bread and the smallest morsel of yellow pork with age." Most prisoners at Fort Delaware complained about the living conditions and the food. According to Private Henry Berkeley, they were given "two light meals per day consisting of three hardtack, a small piece of meat, three bites, and a pint tin cup of soup." Captain Robert Parke, 12th Alabama Infantry, wrote, "The fare consists of a slice of baker's bread, very often stale, with weak coffee, for breakfast, and a slice of bread and a piece of salt pork or salt beef, sometimes alternating with boiled fresh beef and bean soup for dinner. The beef is often tough and hard to masticate." The meals were served at 9:00 in the morning and again at 3:00 in the afternoon.

From his short stay at Fort Delaware, Samuel Hardinge felt physically and emotionally exhausted. On January 8, he received a letter from a friend smuggled through the underground route that gave him some hope. The letter said:

"THE HUSBAND of BELLE BOYD----The husband of Belle Boyd, the famous Rebel Spy, took refreshments in the guard-house of the Citizens' Volunteer Hospital on Friday afternoon, on his way to Fort Delaware. Dr. Kenderdine was careful to provide secure quarters for this noted individual."

But unfortunately, comfort did not come Samuel Hardinge's way. He suffered severe hardships like all other prisoners at Fort Delaware.

On January 2, Hardinge wrote in his memoirs that he complained of depression and his feet were so swollen that he could not put on his boots. Hardinge wrote about the poor living conditions and called the wooden barrack "pens." Hardinge wrote, "These habitations, boarded and roughly put together, remind one very forcibly old-fashioned farmhouse barns, where, in old times, your poor horse shivered the night through, standing uneasily in his stall, whilst his master slept comfortably within the chimney-corner." There were about 1,800 officers and political prisoners in the Officers' Barracks. In the Privates' Barracks, 9,000 to 10,000 Confederate prisoners of war were miserably crowded together in small spaces. Many of the soldiers were half-clad and suffered terribly from the Northern winter. According to Hardinge, many were from some of the wealthiest and most notable families of the South, many who were insulted and suffered starvation, and without "murmuring patriots whose names will yet live to be handed down to posterity as noblest among the noble." Lastly was the Galvanized Barracks. This barracks was occupied by Confederate soldiers who had taken the *Oath of Allegiance to the United States* after being imprisoned at Fort Delaware. The prisoners in this barracks stayed at Fort Delaware for up to one year and worked to prove their allegiance to the United States Government. They were allowed to draw their food supply daily and to live as the Union garrison, receiving boxes from home and family containing clothes and all types of luxuries.

Hardinge described the barracks he was lodged in as a "range in length from eighty to one hundred feet, and in breadth measured about thirty feet. They are separated from one thin partition of boarding, so that really, they are quite connected, as conversations carried on in one can be distinctly heard in the other. On each side of these places, wide structures of wood are built, two stories in height, which are by means of wooden chats nailed to the supports. Upon these elevated platforms, each prisoner is apportioned off so much space for his sleeping and cooking purposes."

Escape from Fort Delaware during the warm summer months were not infrequent, but during the cold winter months, escape was almost never attempted. Hardinge did not record in his memoirs that he ever attempted or knew of an escape attempt.

Samuel Hardinge was treated no differently than any other Confederate prisoner at Fort Delaware. He suffered the lack of food, clothing, the winter elements, and hardships like many of the other Confederate prisoners at Fort Delaware and was treated no different because he was the husband of Belle Boyd. If he had attempted to have escaped from the prison, he would have been just as quickly shot as any other prisoner. His emotional depression had undoubtedly taken a toll on him physically, which some Belle Boyd biographers have written must have led to his early death. But that would not be the case, as I will write about in another chapter. Samuel Hardinge's only crime was that he was the husband of the famous *Belle Boyd: The Rebel Spy.*

Chapter 30

A Changing World

While Samuel Hardinge was at Carroll Prison in Washington, Belle remained in London and began to experience financial hardships because of her lack of income. She was penniless, selling off her jewelry and most of her wedding gifts to survive financially. Belle decided to proceed with her original idea of writing about her life, experiences, and adventures as a Confederate spy operating in the Shenandoah Valley.

After Belle hastily finished her memoirs, she approached a thirty-six-year-old British Confederate sympathizer by the name of George Augustus Sala. Sala was a very influential journalist who came from a theatrical family where he had been introduced to some of the most respected authors and artists of his time. Sala began writing in 1856, drawing the attention of Charles Dickens. Dickens liked Sala so well that he began to publish his articles in his publication, *Household Words*. Sala's fame and notoriety increased among the British public. During America's Civil War, Sala began writing articles that were very critical of President Abraham Lincoln and the Union cause for *The Illustrated London News*. Sala was just the person for Belle to approach with her memoirs because he maintained what we know today as celebrity status, and he was the person who could help market her book to a particular audience.

When George Sala met Belle at her hotel on Jermyn Street, he found her to be in great distress of mind and body, writing, "She was sick, without money, driven almost to distraction by the cruel news that her husband was suffering the 'tender mercies' of a Federal prison." The newspapers had reported that Hardinge was in irons and was prohibited from receiving food and clothing. Additionally, Union authorities had been intercepting all the letters that had been mailed

247

to her from the United States to England. Belle believed some of those letters contained money intended for her. In an article published by the *New York World* and later in the *Clearfield Republican*: "Within the past few months her agent in the United States has sent her bills of exchange on London bankers to the amount of eight hundred pounds sterling, or nearly ten thousand dollars in greenbacks. She has never received a sum of this money. Her letters have been opened here, and the drafts extracted before going to her, and this is the reason she is in distress." If the London papers and the *New York World* were correct, where was the money coming from? Her book had not been published. Was this money the same money that Belle and Captain Henry had deposited in the New York bank, and was this one of the reasons why Samuel Hardinge went to New York other than to visit with his family? Or was it money she believed was being sent to her by Southern sympathizers in the United States, who were trying to assist her in the impoverish state that she was experiencing? Or the money did not exist. Belle never revealed where or what source she expected to receive any funds, but the newspaper revealed: "that she had written a book and that any number of publishers were ready to advance a handsome sum for its publication."

Belle believed for the United States Government to withhold, her money was cruel and unjust, writing, "I think it is so cruel of the Yankees to intercept my letters and intercept my money, and I don't know why I am thus persecuted." An English newspaper added, "It is cruel and it is beneath the dignity of any government to stoop to such means of revenge, such things in the dark ages would be called un-chivalrous." Newspapers in London and then the United States began to carry articles about Belle's financial distress. The first article appeared in the *Liverpool Courier* on February 4, 1864. In an excerpt, the *Courier* wrote, "Mrs. Hardinge is now in London, almost in a state of destitution, all her supplies being cut off." Belle's distress and living conditions in England were echoed by newspapers in the United States. The *Clearfield Republican* published that she was "in poverty and want" and recommended her to the sympathy of the Southerners in England. Another newspaper, *Orleans Independent Standard* in Irasburg, Vermont, published that Belle was "so poor that public appeals are made for relief." Another publication printed that her "husband is now tasting the sweets of a Yankee prison, she sold her wedding gifts, and knew all the bitterness of poverty and exile after enduring for many a long and weary months the insults, sufferings, and persecutions of the old Capitol Prison."

When Belle placed her manuscript in George Sala's hand at the Brunswick Hotel, she said, "Take this; read it, revise it, rewrite it, publish it, or burn it, do what you will. It is the story of my adventures, misfortunes, imprisonments, and persecutions. I have written all from memory since I have been here in London, and perhaps, by putting me in the third person, you can make a book that will be not only acceptable to the public and profitable to myself but one that will do some good to the cause of my poor country, a cause which seems to be so little understood in England."

Although Belle was very well educated, she realized and understood her lack of ability as a writer and in placing the most crucial emphasis on words and her ability to write a story that would not only be truthful but hold the reader's interest and how to use a phrase that hopefully would stir up more Southern sympathy. Belle did not believe Sala would totally discard her manuscript, but instead, she knew that no matter how well or poorly it was written that she had a story to tell and it would interest an audience well beyond the British public. She also enjoyed the support of Confederate authorities in England, using it as propaganda.

Sala took Belle's manuscript and read it, making only a few suggestions, such as adding some footnotes, writing, "The work is entirely her own."

When news reached the United States that Belle had written a book and intended on publishing it, attempts were made to try and suppress its publication. The London news publications picked up the story, and it was later published in the *New York World*: "The intimation to Mrs. Hardinge that the publication of her work would endanger the life of her husband was not without foundation, as there are officials high in power at Washington of whom she knows more than is generally known, and who will be shown up in their true light and colors in her book. They fear the truth."

Belle did have a weapon to fight back against Union authorities in what she believed were atrocities against her and because Union authorities were holding her husband in prison in what amounted to using him as a hostage so she would suppress her book. Belle knew and was in possession of more information than she ever revealed in her book. While in Richmond in September 1862, she made the acquaintance of Rose O'Neal Greenhow, who was the Confederate spymaster in Washington during the early days of America's Civil War. Greenhow had married Robert Greenhow Jr. and lived among the most influential and highest-ranking politicians from both the North and South prior to the war. After her husband Robert died, she continued to maintain her relationships with her political friends in Washington and the city's elite. When war broke out, she maintained an adulteress affair with one of the most powerful men in the United States Senate, Henry Wilson from Massachusetts. Senator Wilson was the chairman of the powerful United States Senate Committee on Military Affairs. He had access to all plans that the Union armies were undertaking, and Rose used her relationship with him to obtain any helpful information that he knew of and was willing to share with her.

When Greenhow was finally arrested for spying on August 23, 1861, Union authorities placed her under house arrest before sending her to the Old Capitol Prison on January 1, 1862. After her release from the Old Capitol on May 31, 1862, they banished her to the South. Greenhow eventually resided at the Ballard House in Richmond, where Belle lodged after her release from the Old Capitol in September 1862. Belle and Rose often visited the Confederate hospitals and shared information pertaining to their covert activities. This information is how Belle learned of Henry Wilson and was potentially willing to expose him.

As for Rose, she died a tragic death of drowning off the North Carolina coast in 1864. Henry Wilson went on to become the 18th Vice President of the United States, serving under Ulysses S. Grant during his second presidential term. The affair between Wilson and Rose was never made known or revealed to the general public.

Belle took the Union authorities' threat seriously. In return, she decided to take her own threat to the top of the United States Government, offering President Lincoln what amounted to an ultimatum. On January 24, 1864, she wrote the following letter to Lincoln:

250

Brunswick Hotel
Jermyn Street
24th Jany. 1865

Honorable Abraham Lincoln
President of the U.S. America

I have heard from good authority that if I suppress the Book I have now ready for publication, you may be induced to consider leniently in the case of my husband, S. Wylde Hardinge, now a prisoner in Fort Delaware. I think it would be well for you & me to come to some definite understanding. My Book was not originally intended to be more than a personal narrative, but since my husband's unjust arrest, I intended making it political, & had introduced many atrocious circumstances respecting your government with which I am so well acquainted & which would open the eyes of Europe to many things of which the world on this side of the water little dreams. If you will release my husband & set him free, so that he may join me here in England by the beginning of March, I pledge you my word that my Book shall be suppressed. Should my husband not be with me by the 25th of March I shall at once place my Book in the hands of a publisher.

Trusting an immediate reply.

I am Sir, yr. obdt. Sevt.
Belle Boyd Hardinge

Belle was not the only individual interceding on Samuel Hardinge's release from prison. Samuel's mother, Sarah also sent President Lincoln a letter, most likely right after her return from Washington after visiting her son at the Old Capitol Prison. Sarah Hardinge wrote:

To his Excellency Abraham Lincoln:
Sir,

A sick and almost heartbroken mother again sentenced to make another appeal to you for the release of her son Samuel Hardinge Jr., who, through gross misrepresentation and exaggeration on the part of the enemies, was first confined in Carroll Prison; and afterward, without being allowed to vindicate his own innocence, transferred to Fort Delaware. In the only letters which I have received from him since he has been there, he thus writes: "Oh My God! How long am I to remain in this horrible place, full of rebels and secessionists? Oh, my parents! Do all you possibly can to get me out of here. My God! My poor wife in England! She tells me in a letter 'For God's sake to send her some money!' And I in prison! Why should they put me in here? Who have taken the oath of allegiance to the United States Government and who have never done anything against it. Oh, it is hard! And I pray God daily and nightly that President Lincoln may grant my release.

I transcribe his own words that you may see what his real feelings are. I told you. Sir, in my recent interview with you, that he might, so far as I know, have been guilty of some small utterances, smarting as he was under the unfair and cruel suspicions cast upon him in the affair of the "Greyhound"; but, guilty of a single act against the good of his country, never! You, sir, can judge for yourself whether or not this is the language of a foe to the Government. Oh, President Lincoln! I implore and entreat you to grant my son's release! My health is rapidly failing under this dreadful blow! I appeal to your kindly nature!...When you think of the magnificent glorious Christmas gift which General Sherman presented to you, will you not confer upon a poor heartbroken mother, the...to you, small..., New Years gift of the liberty of her dear son.

Sarah A.M. Hardinge
Brooklynn, New York
January 1865

Samuel Hardinge did not disclose any notations about taking the Oath of Allegiance to the United States Government in his diary. As I wrote earlier, he suffered great hardships and a severe winter, just the same as the other prisoners at Fort Delaware. It is apparent that her son's imprisonment and hardships took a toll on Sarah Hardinge's health, and this was not the first time she had interceded on her son's behalf. Whether or not it was from a mother's plea for help and mercy for her son or it was from Belle's attempt to expose scandal and corruption in the Lincoln government, or the conclusion that the war was winding down and would soon end, President Lincoln ordered Samuel Hardinge's release from imprisonment at Fort Delaware. The release order by Secretary of War Stanton arrived on February 3, 1865, to General Schoepf:

"The Secretary of War directs the release of S. Wilde Hardinge, a prisoner at Fort Delaware."

*   *   *   *

After Secretary Stanton's order was read to Samuel Hardinge, General Schoepf informed him that he was free to leave Fort Delaware. General Schoepf asked if he was leaving the island tonight and Hardinge informed him he was leaving immediately for New York and he would give the government no trouble by remaining any longer.

After his release from Fort Delaware, Samuel Hardinge rowed a boat to shore, and walked sixteen miles to Wilmington, Delaware in the cold and winter darkness. When he arrived in Wilmington, his "rag-encased feet" were swollen. Around 10:00 in the evening, he arrived at the railroad depot just in time to catch a train to New York.

When Hardinge arrived in New York, he went first to his brother's place of business before continuing to Brooklyn, where he bathed and got some new clothes at his parents' home. There he awaited his passage on a ship to London to rejoin Belle.

On February 8, 1865, Samuel Hardinge set sail on the ship *Cuba* to reunite with Belle, arriving on February 19 at Liverpool, England.

On February 27, 1865, the New York Herald newspaper published an article about Samuel Hardinge's release. The newspaper believed Hardinge had gotten off too easy and should have been made to suffer imprisonment for a longer duration: "We think that her {Belle's} husband, Mr. Hardinge, who left our navy to marry the fair rebel and serve Jeff Davis, escaped very cheaply with a few months' imprisonment. He ought to have been punished much more severely."

*　*　*　*

In February 1865, America's Civil War was concluding. Confederate President Jefferson Davis sent three commissioners, Vice President A. H. Stephens, R. M. T. Hunter, and John Campbell to meet with Union representatives at Fortress Monroe, but a peaceful settlement failed because the Lincoln administration would only recognize an end to the war if the eleven Southern states would unconditionally return to the Union.

When the spring campaign began in March 1865, a series of battles between General Lee's Army of Northern Virginia and General Grant's Army of the Potomac began around the Petersburg, Virginia, area. On April 2, 1865, Grant's army penetrated Lee's defenses with an all-out assault, causing the Confederate army to retreat from Petersburg. That same evening, Confederate President Jefferson Davis and his government abandoned Richmond and moved to Danville, Virginia, before proceeding further South. Over the next week, Grant's army consistently confronted Lee's army until they reached Appomattox Courthouse, where on April 9, 1865, Lee surrendered the Army of Northern Virginia to Grant.

The war had still not concluded. Further south in North Carolina, Union General William Sherman's army had fought a series of battles against Confederate General Joe Johnston's army, resulting in Johnston's surrender at Bennett Place on April 26, 1865. The following month Union cavalry captured President Jefferson Davis in Georgia, and in May, the last major Confederate army surrendered, west of the Mississippi River, thus ending America's Civil War.

The conclusion of America's Civil War did not end joyfully but on a sad note. On April 14, 1865, John Wilkes Booth assassinated President Abraham Lincoln at Ford's Theater in Washington. Booth carried out his plan along with eight other conspirators. Like many citizens living in the North and South, they believed Lincoln's assassination was part of a larger conspiracy than John Wilkes Booth and those conspirators who were captured. Belle also had her beliefs and who she felt was responsible for Lincoln's death. She implicated Senator Jim Lane of Kansas. Belle quoted Lane, "'The Constitution as it is,' said the notorious 'Senator Jim Lane,' of Kansas, 'is played out; and I am ready to see any man shot down who favors the Union as it was talked of by Mr. Lincoln.'" And on the evening of the very next day, after Mr. Lincoln had favored a conciliatory treatment towards the South, "he was shot down!" In an article published first in the *New York Commercial* newspaper and republished in the Columbia, South Carolina *Daily Phoenix*, the article said about Belle: "Not satisfied, however, with a recapitulation of her exploits, she proceeds to inform the English public that she knew all about the assassination conspiracy. It was concocted, she says, by Vice President Andrew Johnson, General Butler, and 'Jim Lane of Kansas.' They planned to make way with Mr. Lincoln, Grant, Seward, and Stanton, and then raise themselves into power." She added, "not only were they doomed, but so also were all those most in favor of conciliatory measures toward the South." Belle never changed her opinion.

* * * *

During the middle of May 1865, the two-volume book *Belle Boyd in Camp and Prison* was published by Saunders, Otley, and Company in London and later in August by Blelock and Company in New York. An article in a Norfolk, Virginia newspaper said, "Belle Boyd of Virginia notoriety, variously known as the 'Martinsburg beauty,' 'Rebel in Petticoats,' 'Confederate spy' and Mrs. Hardinge, has no idea of passing as yet from public notice. On the contrary, she was just published, in England, an autobiography, with an introduction by a friend of the South, wherein she recapitulates her Virginia experiences."

George Sala wrote the introduction for *Belle Boyd in Camp and Prison*, but later when he wrote his own autobiographical writings, he made no reference to Belle or her book. In later years, Sala denied having anything to do with the project. Even though Sala denied any association with Belle and her book, an article appeared on July 1, 1865, in the *Dallas Herald*: "It is said Mr. G. A. Sala will introduce to the English reader the noted 'Belle Boyd,' whose marriage and romantic adventures have already supplied paragraphs to newspapers.

255

The work to which Mr. Sala contributes an introduction, will bear the title of "Belle Boyd in Camp and Prison written by herself."

Belle's book is very well written, and any reader can conclude that it was written by someone of that time period who was very well educated. Belle gives her readers a good first-person dramatic account of her early life in and around Martinsburg, Virginia {West Virginia}, and her close relationship with her family. Belle covers her Civil War adventures, but most emphasis is placed on her covert spying activities in the Shenandoah Valley, her experience of shooting a federal soldier at Martinsburg while defending her family, her two imprisonments, and her seduction and marriage to Samuel Hardinge. The last chapters of the book were written by Samuel Hardinge and with the greatest emphasis on his imprisonment and time in the United States between November and February 1865.

In the *London Times*, Belle's books sold for twenty-one shillings, which would be worth in today's market about $7.00. The *London Saturday Gazette* wrote," *Belle Boyd in Camp and Prison* is one of those books which the whole soul and spirit of the writer have evidently passed which are too earnest for artistic construction too real and heart felt either for self-concealment or self-display. The darling of the entire South, Belle Boyd may be regarded as the female genius or impersonation of the Confederacy in which her name has been a household word from almost the beginning of the war."

On August 19, 1865, *The Illustrated London News* wrote a review of the book, which was unfavorable and critical to Belle and her prospective readers. The newspaper wrote:

Belle Boyd in Camp and Prison. (Saunders, Otley, and Co.) hard words fortunately break no bones, or the Federals would long since have been a nation of mummies. A better-abused party never carried a war to a successful issue, and no one have they been more roundly abused than by "Belle Boyd," and her husband, Mr. Hardinge's respective sufferings are recorded. The martyrs do not confine themselves to personal experience; hearsay evidence is by no means excluded. It is probable that when the reader discovers who "Belle Boyd" and Mr. Hardinge were, that the former, had it not been for her sex, would undoubtedly have been hanged early in the war as a spy, and that a latter was a renegade from the Federal cause, he will consider they were treated not too harshly by the authorities, whom it would be absurd to hold responsibility for occasional vulgar brutality on the part of the underlying. The book is eminently 'bad style,' and, with the assistance of the portrait upon the frontispiece, will to a great extent destroy those charming ideas which romance suggested of la belle rebelle.

Another London newspaper, the *Star* was also critical of Belle's book and did not give her raving reviews. The *Star* admitted Belle had obtained a reputation during the war as a Confederate spy and "a very interesting and exciting book might perhaps have been made out of Miss Boyd's adventures; but the book is uninteresting and unexciting." The reviewer also added that Belle attempted to "make out a terrible case of hardship against the federal authorities, but fails utterly."

I have read Belle's book several times. When she wrote her book, she wrote the manuscript in a romantic style like most Southern writers during the 1860s time period would have committed to paper. True, she does not disclose the identity of all the individuals she was associated with or interacted with during the war. I have already written earlier in this book that she did not reveal their identity because the war was still going on at the time, and she did not want to reveal sources of information of those of the Union cause that she had deceived while writing her book or those individuals who she was associated with loyal to the Southern cause. How much of her book is fabricated? No accurate and objective historian or writer can say for sure because it was written over 150 years ago, and one must compare what she committed to paper with other sources. Those sources are period newspapers, letters, and now-available diaries. They are available so we can objectively draw conclusions and make judgments and evaluations of the truth and the facts so that history is correct and told as perfectly as possible to future generations. The main emphasis of Belle's book, however, written, I have verified through the newspapers, letters, and first-person accounts of her experiences, who she was either associated with or had personal experiences with her during the war. I have concluded that the main emphasis she writes about in her book is confirmed as she wrote them.

When Belle's book was released by its publisher, she began attempting to market and sell her work like all authors today. News advertisements appeared in many U. S. newspapers. On November 14, 1865, one of those advertisements appeared in the *Alexandria Gazette*: "Belle Boyd, in camp and prison, written by herself, 1 vol. 12 mo., $2."

With America's Civil War concluded and now a changing world, Belle now began to embark on a new adventure in her life. It was one that she would still experience the hardships and difficulties of surviving in a changing world.

Chapter 31

After the War: 1865-1869

For a short time, Belle's book provided an income for her and Samuel. On June 21, 1865, Belle gave birth in Hampstead, the northern area of London, to her first child, Mary Grace Wentworth Fitzwilliam Belle Boyd Hardinge, or as she was called, Grace. There have been some questions as to where Grace was born, the United States or England. In an interview with Grace's younger step-sister, Marie Isabelle Hammond Michael, by Belle's first biographer, Louis A. Siguad, she was confident that Grace was born in England, proven to be confirmed by birth records viewed by this author. Even though the war was concluded, many Southern covert operatives, Confederate government officials, and high-ranking personnel were living abroad. They considered it unsafe for them to return home, especially after the assassination of President Lincoln and the United States Government placed former Confederate President Jefferson Davis in prison. Belle did not consider it safe for her to return to the United States, but hopefully, there would be a future for her in England.

The income from Belle's book was substantial, but unfortunately, the money was only a temporary resource, soon leaving her looking for other income and adventures to pursue. Belle began to use her fame and notoriety to her advantage after playing a role in America's Civil War as a spy and the release of her book, which had been advertised and distributed throughout the United States. It was either at the suggestion of some very influential friends in London or through her own determination that she used her notoriety and British connections to propel her to a theatrical career. One of those acquaintances was George Sala. Sala was acquainted with British actress Kate Bateman and her father, Colonel H. L. Bateman, who was a well-known theatrical producer. Shortly, due to her influential acquaintances, Belle was placed under the tutelage of Avonia Jones, an American actress working in England, and the celebrity British Shakespearean actor, Walter Montgomery. Avonia Jones was born in Richmond, Virginia in 1839 and spent most of her life in the theater. Jones had acted in the most notable theaters in the South, Midwest, Canada, Australia, and had arrived in London in 1861. She was considered the best dramatic theatrical actress by 1860, and by 1865, she had no superior in the business. Walter Montgomery became an eloquent interpreter of Shakespeare. He had attained distinction and had extensively toured England and the United States. Both Montgomery and Jones were highly qualified and capable mentors for Belle.

Rumor and news began to spread throughout London about Belle's theatrical undertaking. An article appeared first in the *London Herald* and then on September 10, 1865 was republished in the *New York Herald*. The publication said, "A report is circulating among the clubs that Mrs. Hardinge better known as Belle Boyd the Confederate heroine is about to try her fortune on the London stage." The newspaper continued its narrative by reminding its readers of Belle's recent hardships by the collapse of the Southern Confederacy; that her "spirit and characteristic determination to extricate from the difficulties with which she is surrounded will command universal sympathy." The article concluded that "her appearance on the stage will no doubt prove a distinguished success."

Samuel and Belle's marital problems privately continued but soon became public in the newspapers. A gentleman who was intimately acquainted with Belle had just recently visited her in England and had returned to the United States. The gentleman told a journalist that Belle was going on the stage where "she intended to support herself" and that she preferred the part of "Lady McBeth" over "Pauline." Belle informed the gentleman "she would like to see her husband five minutes before she went on stage, for the purpose of dressing him down and giving her blood a healthy circulation." She finished by adding it would "fire her soul and keep it in a blaze through the performance."

While Belle's future held promise as an actress on the London stage, Samuel Hardinge's life declined significantly deeper into poverty and despair. On October 3, 1865, a London newspaper reported his bankruptcy. And again, on December 18, because Belle had purchased too much stationery, Hardinge was being sent to prison because he could not pay the bill; fortunately, he was released shortly.

A gentleman, who knew of Belle in London stated in May 1866 that "she had sued for a divorce from her husband, ex-Lieutenant Hardinge of the United States Navy." The reason given for the divorce was "utter worthlessness and dissipation." An English newspaper first published and then it was later republished by the *Pulaski Citizen* that Samuel Hardinge was "also in London in very destitute circumstances."

Hardinge tried to obtain passage on a Cunard steamer to the United States under the pretense that he had lost his ticket, but was removed from the ship at Queenstown. Belle and Samuel's relationship must have become very bitter and disagreeable on its future and direction in life. Belle had already written her mother about Samuel's jealousy and that he was prone to the drinking of alcoholic beverages, and unable to support his family. These reasons are why she sought a divorce from him.

Belle feared and believed there was the possibility of physical violence from Samuel, so she sought protection from a fellow actor who trained her for the stage. That actor may or may not have been Walter Montgomery. But for some reason, Belle did not proceed with her divorce from Samuel Hardinge. No written reason is given for staying together, but it may have been because there was an infant child to consider and support, and they both felt an obligation. They made a recommitment to renew their marriage. However, their reunion was short-lived. Whether or not the brief reunion was due to marital issues on the horizon or through mutual consent, sometime in May of 1866, Samuel Hardinge returned to the United States to try and obtain employment in the theatrical industry.

In late 1866, Belle first appeared as an actress at the Theatre Royal in Manchester, England, in the five-act play romantic melodrama, *The Lady of Lyons*. In the theatrical production, she was given one of the leading roles as "Pauline." Acting on the stage in Manchester was only the beginning for Belle. Her debut was a success for someone appearing on stage before a live audience for the first time. A journalist with the *Mobile Advertiser*, who was in England, received the opportunity to witness Belle's performance. He wrote an article that was later republished in the Memphis *Daily Public Ledger*: "The play itself is one that I never greatly admired, and do not at present remember of ever having been particularly pleased with any representation of it, that it had been my fortune to witness it, but if the fine points in the character which Miss Boyd undertook last night were ever brought out, she did it."

Belle went on that year to appear on the stage at London, Liverpool, Glasgow, Limerick, and New Castle. In some of her theatrical performances, she appeared on the theater marquee as Emma Hardinge. In theatrical as well as the present entertainment industry it was no different back in Belle's time period for an actor or actress to use a pseudonym.

While the English newspapers "enthusiastically applauded" her performances, most newspapers in the United States ridiculed her performances as "badly" and that she had "failed."

In the early months of 1867, no longer fearing persecution from Union authorities, Belle returned to the United States. Samuel was still in the United States and New York because the Columbus, Ohio *Statesman* newspaper wrote that he had been in the country "about six months," meaning that he must have returned to the United States sometime in May of 1866. While in New York, Samuel "advertised for five-star engagements," but when Samuel was unsuccessful, Samuel decided to go to New Orleans and try to obtain employment there. Samuel was supposed to take passage on the steamer *Evening Star* for the journey to New Orleans, but although his name appeared on the passenger's list, he did not take the ship for some unknown reason. Unfortunately, after encountering a hurricane on October 3, 1866, the *Evening Star* sank about 180 miles off Tybee Island, Georgia. Out of 300 passengers onboard, 283 of them perished. The *Alexandria Gazette* published on October 20, 1866: "Belle Boyd's husband was among the lost by the *Evening Star*." The Columbus, Ohio, *Statesman* also acknowledged that he had perished on the ship. When the tragedy reached England, the *Newcastle Chronicle* published on November 3, 1866: "It is with regret we have to announce the loss, on board the ill-fated 'Evening Star' on her passage from New York to New Orleans, the husband of Miss Belle Boyd." When the Columbus, Ohio *Statesman* newspaper wrote about the *Evening Star* disaster, they described Hardinge as "a young man, about 30 years of age, rather slimly built, and of good appearance."

Belle was surprised after reading the articles about Samuel Hardinge's death aboard the *Evening Star*. Belle said, "And subsequently, from his name being on her passenger list, was supposed to have gone down in the ship *Evening Star*, foundered off Hatteras. I wore a widow's weed for a year." After a year's absence from each other, one day, Belle received the shock of her life. Years later, Belle recalled, "I was surprised one day by my husband's suddenly turning up alive. We had a very happy reunion." Belle and Samuel made another attempt to resurrect their marriage.

Samuel desired to be an entertainer like Belle, so he attempted to find employment in the business by placing an advertisement in the newspaper. On January 30, 1867, an advertisement appeared in the Brooklyn *Daily Eagle*: "Lieut. S. Wylde Hardinge, the husband of Belle Boyd, offers his services as a reader gratuitously to literary societies or other parties, giving entertainment for worthy objects. As a dramatic reader and elocutionist, Lieut. Hardinge has few equals." Unfortunately, by October 1, 1867, Belle and Samuel separated once more for reasons at that time were unknown to the public. The Portland *Morning Oregonian* published, "Belle Boyd, the rebel spy, has run away from her husband and gone to live in Chicago."

When Belle returned home in 1867, she returned to Martinsburg to see her mother. The last time Belle visited her mother and family was in July 1863. An article was published on March 2, 1867, in the *Alexandria Gazette*, "Belle Boyd, whose eventful and romantic career during the war and since has been a prolific theme of song and story, arrived in Martinsburg last week on a visit to her mother." And another article appeared in the Staunton, Virginia *Spectator* that was initially published in the Martinsburg *New Era*. The article said: "Belle Boyd...The Martinsburg "New Era" says this lady, who acquired a world-wide reputation during the late war, as the 'Confederate heroine,' who has been sojourning in our midst for the past few months, will leave shortly to fill a number of engagements in the theaters of the Eastern and Western cities." According to Belle's daughter Marie, Mary Boyd was against her daughter returning to the stage: "Grandmother Boyd did not like mother going on the stage very much. But everything my darling mother did grandmother Boyd thought it was all right." When Belle finished visiting her family, she went to St. Louis to begin a theatrical production.

Her first appearance was at Ben de Bar's Theater in St. Louis, Missouri. Ben de Bar was an English actor, theatrical producer, and manager who owned several theaters in the United States. After she finished in St. Louis, she began to appear in starring roles in other stock theaters in the South and Southwestern United States. She was managed by John Smith, a well-known business manager, and agent, representing the famous Artemus Ward, Barney Williams, and Clara Morris.

In 1867, Belle maintained a busy acting schedule at playhouses in Baltimore, Memphis, St. Louis, Charleston, SC, Nashville, and Norfolk. She received considerable attention and praise for her work as an actress, appearing in *The Honeymoon* and *Faint Heart Never Won Fair Lady*. The Memphis *Public Ledger* wrote, "Miss Boyd possesses real ability as an actress," the Charleston *Daily News* in Charleston, South Carolina, reported that Belle "met with a hearty reception" at the Norfolk Theater, and in Nashville, it was reported by the *Union Dispatch* that "the press are loud in their praises of this accomplished artiste."

The price for one of Belle's performances ranged from fifty cents for a gallery seat to one dollar and fifty cents for an orchestra chair.

One of her greatest successes for the 1867 year as an actress came in October when she appeared in Memphis, Tennessee, for a performance. Much to her surprise, when she had finished her performance, many of those who were in attendance wanted to give her a benefit to show their appreciation and gratitude for her service and gallantry as a Confederate spy in the Shenandoah Valley, her imprisonment, and her suffering during America's Civil War, and to celebrate her new career as an actress. The article, which was published in the Memphis *Public Ledger* on October 3, 1867, said:

To-morrow evening a complimentary benefit, tendered by the citizens, will be given Miss Boyd. This is as it should be. Were Miss Boyd even destitute of claims on historic grounds, there is that in her past career which entitles her to consideration from Southerners, and readers an effort of this character most appropriated.

The paper and citizens give a congratatory to Miss Belle Boyd! We have witnessed your impersonations with a great deal of pleasure, and desire to manifest the gratification we have experienced from the unmistakable evidence you have given of genius and study. Will you permit us to offer our congratulations on your rapid advancement in the profession you have adopted, and tender you a complimentary benefit (which we hope to make worthy of the object,) before you leave the city, on the night that you may designate.

Thirty-seven Confederate veterans signed the article, and the signature at the top of the list belonged to Lieutenant-General Nathan Bedford Forrest, who attended her performance.

Belle was lodging at the Worsham House in Memphis and humbled and gratified by the love and appreciation the Memphis citizens and veterans showed her. She sent her answer:

GENTLEMEN... Your kind note has just been received. Allow me to return my heartfelt thanks for the interest you have taken in my welfare, also for the many kindnesses I have received at the hands of the good people of Memphis. I respectfully name Friday evening, October 4, as the occasion for the benefit you offer.

Several of Belle Boyd's previous biographers and current Website bloggers believed and wrote that Samuel Hardinge had died in England because of the hardships he had endured in prison during America's Civil War, that he was deceased by the end of 1865 or the latest, early 1866. In 1893 Belle even said in an interview in the *Boston Journal*, "Both husband and child {Grace} were taken from me." It is not a valid statement.

After reading several other biographies on Belle Boyd, I believe Samuel Hardinge died in England. After my article was published for the *Civil War Historian* in 2008, where I wrote, "she was a widow with an infant daughter," in agreement with other biographers, a local historian from the Martinsburg, West Virginia area soon corrected me. He gave me conclusive proof, a newspaper article written in 1868, that Samuel Hardinge did not die in England after returning from imprisonment, nor did he die on the passenger ship *Evening Star* after sinking in the Atlantic Ocean, but he was still alive at the time and lived much longer.

When I began the process of writing *Belle Boyd: The Rebel Spy*, I committed myself to research and to discover all that was available about her. Some of the best accounts came through newspapers. In addition to the newspaper article the Martinsburg historian gave me, I have discovered numerous other newspaper articles that show conclusive proof that Hardinge was alive and did not die in England. The truth is that Belle sued and was granted a divorce from Samuel Harding on January 17, 1868 by the New York Supreme Court. The reason for the divorce was infidelity. When the divorce suit was initiated by Belle, evidence of the accusations against Samuel Hardinge was submitted to Nathan Gratz to determine if Belle had a viable case against her husband. Once reviewed, Gratz submitted his opinion and evidence to the court. Samuel did not appear for the court proceeding, he was represented by his father, but in a written statement, he admitted to the charge of infidelity with a lady known as Fannie Sinclair. Samuel did not contest the divorce. The one piece of damming evidence that was submitted in court was a written document that said, "My Dear Colonel, a friend of Hardinge's giving the real and fictitious name of 'his damsel,'" Fannie stated that she "had a card of his {Hardinge} sticking in her glass," which was also produced as evidence for Belle. Judge Cardozo agreed with Belle and granted her a divorce from Samuel with full custody of their daughter, Grace. The article stated, "Belle asks no alimony from her former husband, and was apparently anxious only to get rid of him." She also asked and was granted the right to legally retain her maiden name of, Boyd.

This article first appeared in the *New York Herald* and many other national publications such as the Charleston, South Carolina *Dailey News,* and the *New Orleans Republican*. It also appeared in the

266

smaller local newspapers around the Martinsburg area, such as the *Spirit of Jefferson* and the *Shepherdstown Register.*

Even though, Belle was now divorced from Samuel Hardinge, he would still make a reappearance in her life in the future.

In more than one interview and newspaper article Belle always referred to Samuel as dead such as an article that appeared in the *New Orleans Crescent*, which said, "She is now a widow with one child by her marriage, a very pretty little girl." Newspaper articles such as this could explain the misunderstanding of why Belle's previous biographers were misled. Why did Belle deny she had divorced Samuel Hardinge? Was Belle trying to mislead history? Was Belle trying to mislead the public? She might have been trying to mislead consciously or unconsciously the public because, during her time period, society did not accept divorce as easily as our present society. During Belle's time, it was frowned upon. Most couples contemplating divorce thought long and hard about the future of their marriage, especially if children were involved and if a divorce was the correct way to proceed. This was because of how their friends and society would judge them. Belle was considered a celebrity at this time in her life, and so was Hardinge, who the *New York Herald* wrote had "acquired some notoriety as an author and actor." They were both in the spotlight of the news media and public opinion.

But Belle telling newspapers and journals that Hardinge was dead did not stop there. She also referred to her oldest daughter, Grace, later in life as dead. In an 1893 interview, Belle told a journalist, "Both husband and child were taken from me."

Belle's actions could only have come from saying it so often that she believed it. Death is a permanent separation, and now that she had terminated her relationship with Samuel Hardinge, he was dead to her. Another reason can be that she felt guilty consciously or subconsciously and took the blame for the failure of her marriage upon herself. Samuel probably possessed greater feelings for Belle than she might have felt for him. As for why Belle referred to Grace as being dead, I will write about that later.

Belle continued her performances by appearing in New York in the theatrical production of *Honeymoon* and *Faint Heart Never Won Fair Lady*. The *New York Herald*, a newspaper that tried in every way during America's Civil War to demonize and destroy Belle's reputation as a woman and her character, was now willing to move on from the bitterness of the war and give her a good review. The newspaper said she had "a good musical voice; reads well; walks well." Later in the article, the correspondent wrote," The experiment of this young debutante was a temptation perhaps worth trying on the supposed historical reputation of Miss Belle Boyd. Still, history moves so rapidly in the days that many a lion and lioness of yesterday are forgotten to-day, or will be to-morrow. She obtained the approval of the audience."

Belle soon moved on and joined Miles & Bates Stock Company in Cincinnati, Ohio, under the stage name Nina Benjamin. Author Louis Sigaud wrote that the change in her identity had a sentimental significance. Her name was a combination of the Christian names of two persons who were very dear to her. One of those names was her father's.

Throughout 1868, Belle continued to appear in theatrical performances not only in Ohio but also in Texas. According to the *Dallas Herald*, in December at Galveston, she appeared on the stage with Miss Fannie Price, who was the daughter of General Sterling, but controversy was on the horizon.

When it appeared that Samuel Hardinge had finally moved on with his life there appeared another episode with him and Belle. According to the *New York Tribune*, Belle appeared before the clerk of the Copyright Department of the United States District Court, which represented the Southern District of New York to obtain a copyright for her book, *Belle Boyd in Camp and Prison*. Belle claimed that her ex-husband, Samuel Hardinge had obtained a copy of her manuscript and attempted to sell her work to another publisher without her authority or consent. She wanted the publisher to halt the publication and that she might attain money from copies already published and distributed. The *Tribune* wrote, "Belle's appearance created somewhat of a flutter and excitement among the occupants of the U. S. Court buildings. She is a dash, good-looking woman, elegantly attired, and wore a small string of bells around the neck." The *Tribune* does not reveal the publisher's identity or how many copies were purchased. Instead, Belle received her copyright and won her case against further publication of her book.

In December 1868, she arrived in Austin, Texas, to give a "dramatic reading during the session of the Democratic Convention. She was accompanied by her agent and business manager, Maj. Thomas P. Ochiltree."

Belle remembered Thomas Ochiltree later in life when she said, "I have such bright remembrances of Tom Ochiltree down in Texas that I feel a strong friendship for the newspaper man." She continued her evaluation of him, "He was one of the driest and merriest writers I have met, so refreshing in his bright keen wit."

Before America's Civil War, Thomas P. Ochiltree was a former Democratic state politician in Texas who served as a delegate at the 1860 Democratic Convention in Baltimore, Maryland. He served in the 1st Texas Infantry during the Civil War, attaining the rank of major. After the war, he continued in Democratic politics while the editor of the *Houston Daily Telegraph*. Later he represented Texas in the United States Congress. At the convention in Austin, he was instrumental in inviting Belle to appear, and he handled her business affairs for her appearance. But his biography does not indicate or reveal that he was her business agent or booking agent for other theatrical performances.

At the beginning of January 1869, Belle performed a series of engagements in Houston, Texas, with another actress, Maude St. Leon. During the opening night of the play, the performance did not come off as intended. This was the night that Belle instead decided to take up what we would call today a "labor dispute." First reported in the *New York Democrat* and later in the *Spirit of Jefferson,* the article said, "This is the way Belle Boyd acted recently in 'Rosedale' after an actress, whose cause Belle espoused for in attention to business." According to the newspaper report, when the curtain rose for the beginning of the performance, a male actor, Mr. Matthews, who played the part of Colonel Cavendish May, began the performance by walking across the stage. But when Belle came onto the stage as "Lady May," she did not perform her acting role; instead, she walked "down to the floodlights and addressed the audience, complaining of her treatment at the hands of the Greenwall Brothers." The company manager R. D. Ogden came onto the stage to make an apology. After his apology, he dismissed the audience with the promise that the show would be presented the following evening. Belle did not only sympathize with an incident that involved Miss St. Leon, but the working conditions in which they were expected to perform also had implications for her.

Belle wrote an article that was published first in the *Houston Telegraph* and republished in the *New Orleans Crescent* where Belle and Maude St. Leon were to appear in February. Like a prosecuting attorney, Belle laid out the foundation for her case for misconduct and deception. She wrote, "It is with reluctance that I intrude myself upon the public, but the false insinuations contained in the card of Mr. R. D. Ogden, which appeared in the (Houston) Telegraph of the 8th inst., and the long-continued outrage and injustice which I have suffered from him and Messrs. Greenwall, leave me no other resort than the means of exposing the perfidy, duplicity, and ruffian conduct of these men who are earnestly seeking patronage and support of the public."

Belle continued to lay out her case in the newspaper against the Greenwall brothers and Mr. Ogden starting at the beginning of her employment. In November 1868, while Belle performed in Cincinnati, Ohio, she received an offer from the Greenwall Brothers through their agent R. D. Ogden to come to Texas to perform in a series of theatrical engagements. After Belle agreed to the terms of her contract, she departed for Texas, arriving in Houston on December 4. However, her performance was postponed until December 7, and then she was informed she could continue her performance until the "close of the engagement." But Belle believed this was the beginning of a scheme against her to get rid of her, hoping to terminate her contract, writing, "Since then I have become fully satisfied that this was the basest duplicity, and that there was a fixed design to deceive me on the part of these gentlemen, 'so called.' I have irrefrangible proof that they have more than once expressed themselves as determined to get rid of the contract on any terms."

Belle believed that Ogden and the Greenwall Brothers had misrepresented themselves and had deceived her into working for a company that could not honor its part of the signed contract. Belle was correct in her allegations against them because she kept a copy of a letter written to her from Ogden, which he believed had been previously destroyed. Some of the letter's contents said: "As Belle Boyd is here, and demands her time and salary, etc., the best and quietest way will be to give her one or two nights in Galveston and the rest here. By that means you get two good first nights, sure, out of her, and a half benefit, and then let her go, or go into the stock at the salary agreed upon. This seems to be the thing."

Belle believed the Greenwall Brothers and Ogden were "deliberately determined and sought to repudiate their agreement both in letter and spirit," They "refused to pay her one dollar for the heavy outlay and loss of time" to which she had been subjected.

Regarding Maude St. Leon's grievances with Ogden and the Greenwall Brothers, they had been subjecting her to "frequent insults and abusive epithets applied to her by Mr. Ogden and the Messrs. Greenwall." Because Belle sympathized with Maude St. Leon, she believed they took offense against her, writing, "My alleged espoused of Miss St. Leon's cause was but the pretext which they used for insulting me and finally driving me from the fulfillment of my engagement."

Belle wanted to finish her engagement, but during the evening of January 7, and a short time before the opening of the theater, Morris Greenwall visited Belle's room and began to use the "most abusing and insulting character" and attempted to physically strike Belle a blow before she made a determined defense for herself by pulling and threatening him with a dagger knife that she carried in her possession. Greenwall informed Belle to quit the rest of the engagements.

Like an attorney delivers their summation to a jury before they hand down their verdict, Belle committed her grievance to the public when she wrote: "I may have committed wrongs, but I have also suffered many wrongs; and, as a defenseless woman, I can only appeal to the public for protection and vindication from the ruffian outrages of those whom every spark of manhood seems to have fled." Belle concluded her letter to the newspaper: "One wrong, however, I have never sought to oppress the weak and defenseless; nor have I betrayed a cause which I espoused. To this, the cause of my land, the dear sunny South. I have been true, and I shall remain so with my life." Afterward, as she always did, she signed her name Belle Boyd.

Belle knew the news media was a powerful weapon and she knew how to use it to her advantage. As Belle concluded her letter to the newspaper, she sounded like a woman who was still just as defiant as when she was confronted by Union soldiers and Union authorities during the war. Belle still had a lot of fire left over from the war in her spirit for the issues and causes she believed were worth fighting for.

On February 11, Belle arrived in New Orleans to perform dramatic readings with Maude St. Leon at the National Theater, scheduled for the 17th and 18th. After the incident in Houston, she received a great review from a New Orleans theatrical critic. Of Belle's performance, the reviewer wrote, "Miss Belle Boyd found in the reading of Poe's 'Raven' a test of her ability as an elocutionist, and infused into it a feeling, a vivid reality which must have revealed the mind's eye of the listener the same gloomy vision which had haunted the poet's chamber. Her action, her play of countenance, her intonations were thrilling at times, and when retiring, she murmured in low measured tones, 'Never, never, never, more it was only to be followed by a storm of applause.'" The reviewer continued, "Both young ladies acquitted themselves creditably, and at times admirably. This is more-worthy of mention from the fact that it is necessarily no light undertaking for two readers to vary their dresses and character so frequently and rapidly, and unaided to keep up the interest of an audience for the space of three hours."

The same evening of Belle's show, a salesman by the name of John Swainston Hammond attended the National Theater and witnessed her performance. He was so fascinated by her beauty and personality that he arranged a meeting with her through a mutual acquaintance and began to pursue a romantic interest in her.

Forty-one-year-old John Swainston Hammond was born on June 3, 1828 in Liverpool, Lancashire, England to Thomas and Mary Hammond. According to John's children, he was educated at Oxford University and served as a distinguished officer in the British army during the Crimean War. When he came to the United States, he enlisted in the 17th Massachusetts Infantry as a first lieutenant in Company H. The men of Company H were known as the "British Volunteers" and were composed of mostly all young men of English birth, who were living in the Boston area before the war. According to John Hammond's service record, he enlisted with the 17th Massachusetts Infantry on August 21, 1861, and resigned his commission on May 15, 1862. After he left the army, he became a very successful tea and coffee sales representative, who traveled across the United States.

Not much is written or revealed about Belle and John's romance, but the *New Orleans Crescent* published on March 7, 1869, "It is rumored that she {Belle} is to be married sometime this summer to a young merchant of New York." Their relationship moved a lot quicker because Belle and John were married ten days later after the publication of this article: March 17, 1869. They were married by Dr. Leacock, the pastor of Christ Church in New Orleans, Louisiana.

Shortly after Belle and John's marriage, papers in the Shenandoah Valley in Virginia received the news and began to publish it. The *Staunton Spectator* wrote, "Mrs. Belle Boyd, the famous 'Rebel Spy,' has again entered upon the married existence. She took this important step in New Orleans on the 17th instant, a Mr. John Hammond being the lucky recipient of her 'true hearts best live.'"

Belle retired from the stage for the next sixteen years and gave up professional theatrical performances.

After Belle retired from her theatrical career and married John Hammond, Belle's health became troublesome; they moved to California, where she attempted to recover her health. The Washington *Evening Star* was one of the first newspapers in the east to pick up the story by announcing, "Belle Boyd is sick in San Francisco."

While Belle tried to recover from her illness, Samuel Hardinge visited her. Hardinge, now a resident of San Francisco, had made an impression on the well-known author Charles Warren Stoddard. Stoddard used Hardinge's character as a model for one of his stories. Since Belle and he had divorced, Hardinge had been living in San Francisco off the generosity of others. He tried his hand at acting but failed, and for a short time, became a ward politician for the Democratic party. The *Shepherdstown Register* published the meeting between Belle and Samuel on July 17, 1869:

"Belle Boyd, now Mrs. Hammond, is in San Francisco is very ill. Her ex-husband, Wylde Hardinge, is also, a resident of the same city. He is not inclined to quarrel with the present husband."

While Belle struggled with illness, she and John were expecting the birth of their first child. For some medical reason, which I will not speculate on, sometime around late October, or early November, Belle began to experience mental issues of depression and anxiety. She was temporarily admitted for insanity to a state "Insane Asylum" in Stockton, California. The national newspapers picked up the story quickly and published it. An article appeared on December 25, 1869, in the Baton Rouge *Sugar Planter*: "Belle Boyd the famous Confederate spy, a woman who raised a reputation, life, everything in the cause has gone mad. Her husband, Mr. Hammond has done everything in his power to resort her reason." Even the smaller local Martinsburg area newspapers picked up the story. On November 6, 1869, The *Shepherdstown Register* published, "Belle Boyd, late of Virginia, and well-known during the war from her connection with the confederate secret service, has been sent to the State Insane Asylum, in California." Dr. Shurtleff attended Belle and was sure she would soon be restored to regular mental health.

In late October or early November 1869, while Belle remained at the state institution, she gave birth to a son named Arthur Davis Lee Jackson. Belle named her son after her war heroes. After Arthur's birth, Belle felt restored mentally, but unfortunately, Arthur died in infancy and was buried in 1869 at Lone Mountain in San Francisco, California.

Throughout 1865 to 1869, Belle Boyd and her life was still the center of media attention and in some way, good or bad, she still attracted national attention.

*See Appendix A at the back of the book about Samuel Hardinge.

Chapter 32

1870-1879

Sometime in February 1870, John and Belle moved east for a short time to Baltimore, where according to the *Baltimore America* her mother resided, and had been residing in that city "for over a year." Again, by the middle of April, Belle had a relapse of mental issues and was confined for a short time at the Mount Hope Asylum in Baltimore. Could Belle's mental issues be a result of or related to the Typhoid fever, which she suffered from during the war? It can reoccur. Or did she suffer from what combat veterans refer to as Post Traumatic Stress Disorder {PTSD}? After all, many soldiers and civilians living and experiencing the horrors of war were emotionally disturbed by its horrors.

After Baltimore, Belle and John moved to Utica, New York, where they lived a quiet life and were active socially in their community. It was in Utica that Belle and John's second child, Mary Byrd Swainston Hammond or as Belle called her, "Byrdie" was born on February 26, 1874.

In December 1874, Belle arrived in Charlestown, Virginia {West Virginia} to visit with her sister, Mary, now the wife of Oregon Wentworth Rowland. After leaving Charlestown, Belle and her family traveled to Alexandria, Virginia where she visited "the house of a friend" with her husband and family.

Since Belle was no longer acting and pretty much out of national attention, ladies attempted to impersonate her as *Belle Boyd: The Rebel Spy*. One imposter, whose identity is unknown, traveled throughout the Deep South impersonating Belle, attempting to live off her notoriety and fame from the days of America's Civil War. An incident occurred in Atlanta, Georgia, sometime in November 1874 between the Belle Boyd imposter and the editor, Mr. St. Clair Abrams of the *Atlanta News* newspaper, who knew the real Belle Boyd. Abrams said that the real Belle Boyd "was tall, blue eyes, and light hair." Abrams described the imposter as "short, black hair, dark eyes, and about fifteen years older" than the real Belle Boyd. When Abrams published his suspicions about the imposter's character and person, she became angry, entered his office, and demanded an immediate retraction of the newspaper story. Abrams refused. When she made a motion, such as going for a weapon, Abrams apprehended her and turned her over to the police. The police discovered a derringer and a "Wesson seven shooter" in her possession. When another newspaper published the story about the Belle Boyd imposter-Abrams incident, they wrote she was "defiant and attractive."

First published in the *Savannah Advertiser* and republished on November 28, 1874 in the *New Orleans Crescent*, the paper wrote, "Belle Boyd: There are so many claimants to the name of this heroine of the war that is hard to place her, but we are informed by a gentleman, who assures the correctness of his statement, that the original Belle Boyd lives in Utica, New York, where she is leading a quiet ostentatious life as a wife of Col. Hammond." The articles continued to say that Belle was giving "readings, recitations, exhibitions on the piano" and that she was much respected and "loved for her amiable disposition and retiring deportment."

The incident in Atlanta with St. Clair Abram did not hinder the Belle Boyd imposter from doing engagements because she continued to appear in the Carolinas, Georgia, Alabama, and Florida. In Yorkville, South Carolina, she deceived the audience. The *Yorkville Enquirer* wrote on July 1, 1875, about the Belle Boyd imposter: "The story of the boldness and daring that characterized her movements was listened {to} with attention. The hair-breath escapes that crowned her adventures verged on the marvelous and were thrilling as a romance of the middle age."

In 1875 a young South Carolina lady, whose father operated an entertainment hall in Columbia heard from a friend, who saw "Miss Belle Boyd today on a train enroute to Spartanburg." The witness did not believe she was "handsome," but "passable." The young lady's friend hoped to hear her sometime in the future. The Belle Boyd the young lady's friend witnessed was certainly the Belle Boyd imposter because Belle lived in Baltimore and did very few lectures. She did one that was recorded in Hamilton, Ontario, Canada, a charity event, and another in Winchester, Virginia, both in 1878. The Belle Boyd imposter's best years were between 1874 and 1876.

The Belle Boyd imposter had obviously read Belle's book and studied newspapers about incidents she had been involved in during and after the war. And to do a good portrayal, she would have had to witness Belle in person in one of her theatrical productions to replicate her moves, expressions, and manner of speech. Was her speech slow or fast? Did she walk with grace, slow or fast? The Belle Boyd imposter would have had to have had some idea of who she was portraying to deceive the public and pull off a grand performance as was written in the Yorkville, South Carolina *Enquirer*.

By October 1875, suspicion of the real identity of the Belle Boyd imposter circulated in newspapers throughout the United States. First published in the Albany, New York *Register* and later republished in the *New York Herald*: "Belle Boyd whom many persons have said is not Belle Boyd continues to lecture in the South." But these newspaper articles that cast suspicion on the Belle Boyd imposter did not deter her from continuing to pose as the real Belle Boyd.

The days of the Belle Boyd imposter playing off the sympathy and charity of former Confederate soldiers and Masonic fellowship members were ending. An article that was first published in the *St. Louis Republican* and then again in the Jefferson City, Missouri *State Journal* said, "The woman who was once known far and wide as Belle Boyd and some of whose exploits have found an enduring place in history, has for some years led the quiet life of a respectable matron in the city of St. Louis. No consideration, apparently can induce her to lay aside this quiet domestic life to appear again before the public."

For quite some time, Belle did not intervene or try to prevent her imposter from using her name or capitalizing on her notoriety and fame. However, many individuals were becoming increasingly aware that the lady who claimed to be Belle was really an imposter posing as the real thing. The *St. Louis Republican* newspaper continued, "perhaps the fact that the celebrated Belle Boyd is now a respectable matron, residing in this city, would never have been revealed to the public had not her father been a member of the Masonic fraternity."

The Belle Boyd imposter knew all about Belle's family and early life and had been calling on the brotherhood for advice and sympathy, which amounts to charitable contributions—from the imposter's description in the article written by St. Clair Abrams in the *Atlanta News*, and that same description read by members of the Martinsburg, Virginia {West Virginia} Masonic lodge, who personally knew Benjamin Boyd and Belle, published their own description of Belle. According to the *State Journal* newspaper, they knew the real Belle as a "bright-faced, blue-eyed, light-haired maiden," and they knew the Belle Boyd imposter's description was false and did not fit that of the real Belle Boyd.

Around January 22, the Martinsburg Masonic Lodge prepared its own circular letter addressed to the Masonic lodges throughout the United States to beware of the Belle Boyd imposter and denouncing her falsehood. The Martinsburg Masonic brotherhood also stated: "The real Belle Boyd is now married, and living in St. Louis, Mo., with her husband and her mother, and two brothers reside in Baltimore." The letter was signed by Alexander Parks Jr., W. M., and B. Hugh from Martinsburg.

In the same article published in the Jefferson City *State Journal,* which included the *St. Louis Republican's* correspondent's observations of the real Belle Boyd: "On a bright Sunday morning, a trio consisting of an aged woman, a hale, well-looking man of middle age, a rather tall, thin lady of middle age, with deep blue eyes, light hair, and sharp Roman features, may be entering a certain church in this city. The old lady is Belle Boyd's mother, the gentleman her husband and the middle-aged lady is the veritable Belle Boyd of war-time."

The story was republished nationally in such newspapers as the *Memphis Daily Ledger*, the Andersonville, South Carolina *Intelligencer*, the Tarborough, North Carolina *Southerner,* the Jackson, Tennessee *Whig and Tribune*, and the Alexandria, Virginia *Gazette*. But it still did not end until Belle responded.

The story about the Belle Boyd imposter and the intervention by the Martinsburg Masonic Lodge, denouncing the deceivable tactics, led Belle to respond by reputing the imposter in the *Baltimorean* and republished in the Charles Town, Virginia {West Virginia} *Spirit of*

Jefferson: "I have forborne taking any notice of this matter, as I wish no notoriety. With me the past is the eternal past, and I have no wish to drag it from the grave in which it lies buried; but duty to myself, family and friends compels me to remove from the vile imposter to whom I have referred or has any claims to the name of Belle Boyd."

After the article was published nationwide, the Belle Boyd imposter shortly disappeared.

By autumn 1878, Belle and her husband lived in Baltimore, Maryland; a baby girl named Marie Isabelle Boyd Hammond, or as Belle called her, "Belle Jr., was born on October 31.

Chapter 33

1880-1889

The year 1880 was a sad and challenging year for Belle Boyd. On May 3, 1880, her mother, now living in Charles Town, West Virginia, with her daughter Mary died from suspected stomach cancer at age fifty-four. Belle attended the funeral, and ensured her mother was buried beside her husband, Benjamin, at Greenhill Cemetery in Martinsburg. It was the first time in many years that Belle had returned to the city, where she had many fond memories of her adolescent years.

While Belle lived in Philadelphia, Pennsylvania, in August 1881, a correspondent for the *Philadelphia Record* newspaper noticed Belle "sitting last evening on the porch of a comfortable residence in the extreme northwestern section of the city, (1914 North 12th Street) with a sweet little miss of three and another of seven summers, playing hide and seek around her chair." The correspondent continued there was "a lady who a score of years ago bore international reputation. Few, if any, of those who knew her once would now recognize in the handsome, well-preserved woman of commanding presence and high-bred bearing, with a complexion like a rose and lily combined, a wealth of sunny, chestnut brown hair, sparkling eyes, a sweet mobile mouth, and a face capable of varying expression, the vivacious, daring girl who in war times had but one name and that 'Belle Boyd, the Confederate spy.'"

The correspondent for the *Philadelphia Record* revealed that during her stay at the Old Capitol Prison in 1862, she became acquainted with President Abraham Lincoln by beginning a friendly correspondence with him. On one occasion, when Belle wrote a letter to the president, her letter paper was adorned with the Confederate motto, a snake entwined around a Confederate flag, and the inscription: "Don't tread on us, or we will bite." When President Lincoln replied to the missive, he sent back the motto with 'bite' erased and the word 'bust' as a substitute.

While in Philadelphia, Belle was content and happy with her role as a mother and wife. Her husband, John, provided a good income for the family, and they appeared to prosper. Even though Belle was a wife and mother, she did not wholly disappear from the public domain but became involved in writing for a paper called the *Quiz.* She said, "I was for a time assistant editor of the *Quiz,* a little paper published in Philadelphia of which Mary Heygate Howell was the editoress and upon which I wrote a great deal over the signature Mary Isabel Hammond."

Another happy addition to her family while living in Philadelphia was a son, John Edmund Swainston Hammond, born on October 31, 1881. Belle called him "Eddie."

Even though Belle lived a domesticated life in Philadelphia, more ladies appeared as Belle Boyd imposters throughout the country, attempting to profit off her wartime notoriety. Others used her name to apply for credit and then attempted to defraud the proprietor. One incident occurred in Philadelphia when a woman identifying as Mrs. John S. Hammond purchased $150 worth of furniture from Mr. Averill Barlow. Shortly again, the imposter entered the store and purchased another $155 worth of furniture. When Mr. Averill learned that the real Belle Boyd was leaving town, he tried to have the goods seized by the court.

In many ways, Belle continued to be the subject of newspaper stories by imposters posing as *Belle Boyd: The Rebel Spy.* Ladies were devising fraud scams to obtain merchandise or by correspondents writing war stories that involved her role as a spy or imprisonments.

In 1882, Belle wrote to former Confederate President Jefferson Davis, who lived at "Beauvoir" on the Gulf of Mexico near Biloxi, Mississippi. Like many other veterans or individuals who played some part in the war, Belle relived the horrors of the war and their association with comrades or persons who they knew had suffered in some way. Belle later recalled, "Do you know, it seems to me, I lived a hundred years during the war. And now, when every day something recalls a hidden memory, it all returns to me with such vivid force that I feel almost a sense of physical pain." In Belle's case, they were her acquaintances such as Turner Ashby, Jeb Stuart, the wounded who she had nursed at Martinsburg and Front Royal, young men who she had witnessed death, but most of all, the death of her Southern hero, Stonewall Jackson. They were all dead and gone, but Jefferson Davis was the one who was still living and still represented the old Southern Confederacy legacy and the Lost Cause.

Belle's letter to Jefferson Davis was written from Philadelphia on May 10, 1882. She wrote:

A long time has passed since I had the pleasure of meeting you from my Northern home. I can look back through the vista of years, in memory I see you at the head of our government. I would so like to have a chat with you. I am not the merry light-hearted girl of 'bellum' days but I hope a good wife and mother. I have a dear good husband and four beautiful little children. My boy Eddie, the only one alive for I lost my oldest little boy when I was so ill years ago, he was named 'Arthur Davis Lee Jackson' his little grave is in 'Lone Mountain' San Francisco. My baby is only seven months old so that my eldest daughter (Grace) is in her teens another eight and the other four. My boy a baby, I am very happy in my home and my husband was a good soldier of the South, an Englishman by birth. I should feel so honored if you will call and see me. I frequently have a visit from our ex officers and their families, and you for whom I have always cherished such high regard and esteem, I should be so more gratified to have my friend. You know my only crime is I was a Rebel. My heart was with my Country. I have laid a marble slab over the grave of the past and the epitaph is 'En memoriam.'

Mr. Davis won't you write me one little kind line of remembrance? I have letters from Genls Lee, Jackson, and Benjamin and many other of our people. I have put them away as precious heirlooms for my children, and may I have yours to put with them? Would I ask too much that you give me a photograph? Now dear Mr. Davis please fully appreciate the motive that prompts my letter. Remember me kindly to Mrs. Davis and with profoundest respect."

Belle signed her letter: *Marie Isabel Hammond nee Belle Boyd.*

Why did Belle write Jefferson Davis and inform him her husband had been a former officer in the Confederate army, while some newspapers were fueling the speculation by previously reporting that he had served with the famous Louisiana Tigers from New Orleans? Or was it because she wanted to show her loyalty to the South by pretending to marry a Southerner after marrying Samuel Hardinge? The reason may likely be that she wanted to impress President Davis. Even after the war, she was still devoted to the principles, culture, and cause of the Southern Confederacy and still looked to him as her hero and leader.

After Belle and John left Philadelphia, they moved to an upscale northwestern Dallas, Texas area. In Dallas, John took a position as vice president of the Commercial Traveler's Protection Association, but marital troubles were nearing for Belle and John. The *Dallas Herald* and later republished in the local West Virginia newspaper, the *Shepherdstown Register,* reported that after several years of marriage to John Hammond, Belle discovered he was still married to another woman. According to the newspaper, "she then separated from Hammond until the divorce was procured," and then she remarried him. According to Belle's first biographer, Louis Siguad, in his interview with Belle's daughter, Maria {Belle Jr.}, she denied that her father was married to another woman. But that was still not the end of Belle and John's troubles.

Belle and John's marriage began to deteriorate quickly. A physical incident occurred in Dallas in August 1884 between a young attorney named Ray Sheppard and John Hammond. Hammond accused young Sheppard of being intimate with his wife and "destroying his home and happiness." The article published, "Hammond made the blood flow freely from Sheppard's nostrils, but did him no serious harm." When the newspaper interviewed John Hammond about the incident, he said, "My wife ran me into debt overwhelmingly, and used the money which she well knew was not mine and has behaved as a true wife or woman would not in entertaining male friends of hers, strangers to me, and against my expressed wishes. Among the number is the man, Sheppard, whom I to-day assaulted." Hammond had divorce papers prepared and declared that "there can be no reconciliation now between myself and Mrs. Hammond."

The day after the incident, Belle filed for divorce and said in a newspaper interview, "I have left him for good. We have not lived happily together for some years. He became jealous of me, and became cross and crabbed, and rendered me most miserable. I have sued for a divorce, alimony, and the custody of our four children." She continued, "Sheppard has only acted the part of friend and gentleman and that he was a pupil of hers in the study of elocution." Belle also claimed John had been physically abusive toward her, that he had intimacies with other women, and had made false accusations against her.

According to Grace, she took her mother's side and said that her stepfather had "boxed Momma's ears," and he had made one comment "reflecting on her chastity." But Maria {Belle Jr.} Hammond Michaels always denied the physical allegations and did not believe they took place. She believed that her father, John Hammond agreed to the divorce because it is what Belle desired.

Belle was granted a divorce from John Hammond on November 1, 1884, by the United States District Court in Dallas, Texas. Belle won her divorce decree on the grounds of "cruel treatment" and won the custody of the children. Hammond also turned over their plush Dallas home on Pocahontas Street to Belle, which she sold on July 29, 1887. This gave her a substantial financial settlement. After the divorce, John Hammond wanted to place his children in a convent. At first, Belle resisted the idea, but eventually, the two girls, Byrd, and Maria, were educated at Hammond's expense at Indianapolis and St. Louis in Roman Catholic convents of the Ursuline Sisters and Sisters of the Sacred Heart. At the time of their divorce, John Hammond was 58 years old, and Belle was 40 years old.

Eventually, John Hammond returned to Syracuse, New York, where he died in 1886. Belle claimed he was ill with "softening of the brain," or as it is called today in modern medical science, Encephalomalacia.

In September 1884, another adventure took place in Belle's life. She shot and wounded a young man by the name of Jason Collier.

Collier was accused of betraying his promise to marry Maria Hammond, Belle's third daughter, whose age was given as eighteen-years-old. According to the newspapers, Belle sent for him because she wanted an "interview" with him. Collier came from a wealthy family and was successful in business and well-connected in the Dallas social circles.

Sometime during the interview, Belle's daughter "begged him to marry her, or at least to provide her with money so that she could leave the city and hide her shame." He denied the engagement story and claimed that he was innocent of any wrong doing on his part in the matter. Collier informed Belle and her daughter that he had no intentions of marrying or giving her any money. When Collier refused to marry Belle's daughter, Belle pulled a pistol and commenced shooting. The first shot missed, but the second shot wounded Collier in the left arm just below the elbow. At once, Collier grappled the gun and quickly left the house. Belle recovered the weapon and pursued Collier from the house, firing at him several times, but the bullets missed their target.

The Dallas shooting incident involving Belle was republished in national and local newspapers in the United States. The story was republished in the Austin, Texas *Weekly Statesman*, October 16, 1884, the Alexandria, Virginia *Gazette* October 14, 1884, the Lancaster, Pennsylvania *Daily Intelligencer* October 14, 1884, and the Dallas *Daily Herald* September 14, 1884.

There is one problem with the articles. Belle's daughter, Maria, whose name was referred to in the newspaper articles, was only six years old when the incident occurred. Grace was the oldest at nineteen. Grace was being betrayed by Jason Collier and not her younger sister, Maria.

Three months later, on December 29, 1884, in Dallas, Texas, Belle's oldest daughter, Grace, married a twenty-one- year-old man from England named Ray Charteris. Charteris claimed the title of "Earl of Linwood." For about a year, Charteris had been employed as an instructor of elocution in Dallas.

The article about Grace's wedding was published in the *Omaha Daily Bee* on December 31, 1884. The article also revealed plans to organize a comedy company. Belle announced "she, together with her daughter, the Baroness, and the noble son-in-law" would appear behind the floodlights in leading roles.

Since Belle and Ray Charteris endeavored in the same occupation, elocution, this may have been how Grace first met him. Whatever happened to the dream of organizing a comedy company between the three of them did not materialize. After this article, Grace disappeared from Belle's life. From then on, Belle referred to Grace as "being dead to the family." There must have been some disagreement that Grace had with her mother for her to alienate herself from her family and no longer maintain contact with any of them. What event or circumstances would cause Grace to leave her mother and siblings and disown them? Since Maria Hammond was still living when interviewed by Louis Siguad about her family, she never gave him an answer. It may have been because the comedy company never came to fruition. Was money invested in starting up the company that was lost because they could not get the project off the ground? It was both. An article appeared on the January 27, 1885 edition of the *Fort Worth Gazette* that sheds the lightest on the fallout between Belle and Grace. The article confirms that it was both the collapse of the company and money: "Miss Belle Boyd Hammond, the Confederate spy of much renown, has left the city. Her departure is commented upon by a few on account of her naughty actions since her residence in Dallas. Herself and Mr. Hammond are strangers, Mrs. Charteris, her daughter, Mr. Charteris, are also strangers. The Belle Boyd Comedy troupe, which collapsed a short while since involved the lady in a number of debts in this city which were neglected when she left."

Shortly after her divorce from John Hammond, Belle met Nathaniel Rue High, Jr. Her acquaintance with High was short, and there is no mention of their early relationship. Still, she married him in Texas on January 7, 1885. Twenty-four-year-old Nathaniel Rue High was from Toledo, Ohio. High was the son of an Episcopalian rector, the Reverend Nathaniel Rue High Sr., and Hattie High. Nathaniel had mostly played juvenile lead roles for theatrical stock companies, and he was considered handsome and possessed a charismatic personality. Belle's first biographer, Louis Siguad, wrote of High: "he was considered to be in his youth roles even more fascinating than John Barrymore, the great idol of a later generation."

286

Source: *Author's Collection*

Nathaniel Rue High Jr.

By June 1885, Belle and Nathaniel lived in Little Rock, Arkansas, where Belle taught elocution, and Nathaniel continued his acting career. According to an article published in the *Little Rock Democrat,* she became destitute and ill. According to the *Memphis Dailey Appeal,* both members of the Union and Confederate army veterans' groups held a benefit for her to raise money to help her in her poverty-stricken state of life. Her illness was the recurrence of typhoid fever.

Even though Nathaniel High was an up-and-coming successful actor, his money was insufficient to support Belle and her three children. Belle decided to return to the stage, although she knew her chances of obtaining leading roles were slim because of her age, and she had been away from professional performances for sixteen years. So, for Belle, it was starting over again from the beginning and trying to get her name again in the public limelight.

In October 1885, Belle obtained a supporting role as Daisy Brown in the comedy theatrical production: *The Professor.* An article published first in the *Atlanta Constitution* and later in the McMinnville, Tennessee *Southern Standard* published, "This will bring her prominently before the country again, and her career during the war will be the subject of renewed interest."

Well after America's Civil War, articles were still being published and republished by news periodicals across the country in both the North and South about the bloody four-year conflict. Many of those articles were written about Belle Boyd or someone who had an association with her during the war. The memories of the war were still a matter of importance to the old-timers who had participated in the bloody conflict, and they were still reliving the past. This kind of interest played an essential factor in Belle's life when she would soon take the stage, portraying herself as a rebel spy for veteran groups across the country.

Belle always made national news and stayed in the newspapers of something dramatic happening in her life. There was an incident that had occurred when she passed through St. Louis, Missouri, on her way to Chicago, Illinois, where again she was scheduled to perform in the theatrical production: *The Professor.* While in Chicago, the *Tribune* newspaper printed a story that had previously occurred in St. Louis. The incident that occurred in St. Louis involved Belle moving from the Hurst House Hotel to the St. James Hotel, leaving a trunk behind at the former hotel. When the proprietor of the Hurst House Hotel trunk opened the trunk, it was discovered she had left behind "a pair of old corsets, a slipper, a plug of tobacco, and a God Bless Our Home motto." The *Chicago Tribune* did not publish that she had eluded a "board bill but left that to be inferred." Belle immediately sued the *Chicago Tribune* for $5,000. When Belle was interviewed, she said, "I am opposed to the newspapers publishing my private affairs with the object of making me ridiculous. Not only has that story, which was entirely false, wounded my pride, but it has done me great injury here and elsewhere." According to the correspondent, she began to cry as she continued, "If I am poor, it is not my fault. It was a matter between the hotel people and myself." There were no follow-up articles to indicate if she dropped or won or settled her lawsuit against the *Chicago Tribune*, but the story made national headlines.

By the beginning of 1886, Belle again left her acting career to develop a narrative to perform her life and Civil War adventures on stage. Her husband Nathaniel acted as her business manager and agent for booking her performances. Her first performance of *NORTH AND SOUTH; or The Perils of a Spy* occurred on February 22, 1886, at the People's Theater in Nathaniel's hometown of Toledo, Ohio. From her first performance until the end, she mostly appeared in her Confederate gray uniform from Civil War days with a broad, low-crown hat and a large flowing black plume such as Turner Ashby, Jeb Stuart, and most Confederate cavalrymen wore during the war. Her stage scenery was of battle and war. Her recitals were a stirring and emotional eyewitness account of events in which she participated as a conflict participant, primarily based on her book, *Belle Boyd in Camp and Prison*. Belle covered her career as a spy, her "hair-breadth escapes," her two imprisonments, twice being sentenced to be shot, running the blockade, being captured, banished, and personal memories of President Abraham Lincoln. She always finished each performance stressing the importance of unity with "One God, One People, One Flag Forever." In an interview with a correspondent from the *Toledo Blade*, Belle said she did not want to be remembered as the "Rebel Spy" but as someone who had "learned the true beauty of the stars and stripes" and "would be willing to take her life in defense of that government that I once sought to destroy."

The following year, Belle remembered her first performance at Toledo, Ohio: "I gave my first recital of my life as a rebel spy and scored an unqualified success."

It must have revived past war memories for Belle when she returned to Front Royal, Virginia, for a performance at the Presbyterian Church on Chester Street. When she looked at the Fishback Hotel, she must have recalled to her husband how she overheard General Shields's plans for defeating Stonewall Jackson's army during the early days of the Shenandoah Valley Campaign. She had many fond memories of spending evenings conversing with her cousin Alice Stewart and her Grandmother Glenn in the cottage where she lived. Her midnight ride to Colonel Turner Ashby with valuable information. The field she crossed to encourage Stonewall Jackson's men to enter the lightly defended village during the fighting on May 23, 1862.

A Belle Boyd performance cost the public twenty-five cents and lasted two to three hours. She was always billed as "The Original Belle Boyd," and Belle carried certificates of authenticity signed by Superintendent William P. Wood, Senator Charles Faulkner, former Minister to France, and General John D. Kenny. She carried these letters because of the Belle Boyd imposters who had previously attempted to use her fame or some who were still attempting to reproduce the authentic person.

Throughout the remainder of 1886 and into 1887, Belle lived for a short time in Detroit, Michigan and according to the *Kansas City Journal* she also lived in that city for a short time. Through 1886 and 1887, she maintained a busy schedule of performing tours through Illinois, Nebraska, and Missouri to any group or organization who wanted to hear her stories of her adventures during America's Civil War.

By 1888, Belle returned east to give performances. On May 18, 1888, she participated in the Confederate Memorial Day parade in Norfolk, Virginia. Riding at the head of the parade with a mounted escort was Governor Fitzhugh Lee, who was a former general commanding a cavalry division under Jeb Stuart. General Bradly

Johnson rode in an open carriage and "Belle Boyd, the Confederate scout and spy, mounted on a spirited horse and also with a mounted escort."

By the early months of 1889, Belle Boyd was again the center of national attention when she was mistakenly identified as the female outlaw Belle Starr. Belle Starr, whose real name was Myra Maybelle Shirley, was a rustler, horse thief, and bootlegger. During America's Civil War, her family was Southern sympathizers who were closely associated with Quantrill's guerillas, where she made the acquaintance of the James and Younger brothers. In 1880, Belle married a Choctaw Indian named Sam Starr. When Sam Starr was killed in a gunfight, she married again to Jim Starr, a relative of Sam's who was fifteen years younger than her. On February 3, 1889, while riding from a neighbor's home in Eufaula, Oklahoma, she was ambushed and killed by an unknown assailant. Immediately, the national newspapers picked up the story. The story rose to greater fame when it was published and publicized by Richard K. Fox of the *National Police Gazette*. The problem with the stories was the newspapers were reporting that Belle Boyd was the outlaw and was the woman who was ambushed and killed near Eufaula, Oklahoma. A newspaper article published first in the *New York World* and later republished on February 21 by the Andersonville, South Carolina *Intelligencer* reported Belle as the villain, and the lady married to Jim Starr. The article said, "A telegram from Eufaula received here tonight confirms last night's dispatch that Belle Starr, better known as Belle Boyd, had been shot by unknown parties, who fired upon her from ambush, and left no clue."

The reason for so much confusion between Belle Boyd and Belle Starr is because they were both about the same age. Belle Boyd was forty-five-years-old and Belle Starr was forty years old. Both Belle Boyd and Belle Starr dressed almost identically in a Confederate uniform with a plume in their hats. And since Belle Boyd dealt in treachery and covert activities during America's Civil War, most Northern as well as Southern newspapers associated Belle Starr's deeds with those of Belle Boyd's during the war, but others came to Belle Boyd's defense.

Denials almost immediately were published not only by Southern newspapers, but also by Northern newspapers. On February 9, 1889, the *Wheeling Dailey Intelligencer* wrote, "Belle Starr, the female outlaw shot near Eufaula on Sunday, was not Belle Boyd, the Rebel spy."

Belle even wrote her own defense that was published nationally, beginning with her early life, war service, and theatrical career, which she was currently pursuing with her husband. At the time of the Belle Starr incident, an old friend of Belle's, Congressman Tom Ochiltree, who represented the state's 7th District was in New York, and gave greater creditability to Belle's defense. He said and it was published, "Belle Starr, who was recently killed in Indian Territory, could not have been the real Belle Boyd."

The newspaper that came to Belle Boyd's defense and vindicated her was an article that appeared in the *Pittsburg Commercial Gazette* and later republished in other national newspapers such as the *Wheeling Dailey Intelligencer*: "The news that reached here today that Belle Boyd, the famous Rebel spy, had been murdered in Indian Territory, was somewhat of a surprise to people who are acquainted with the woman. Belle Boyd, who claims the title of the famous Rebel spy, is located here, and is to-night lecturing at Johnstown." The Pittsburg article was confirmed by the local *Johnstown Times*, which published, "The original Belle Boyd was then in that city with her husband, Nat. R. High." The city of Johnstown referred to in the article is located east of Pittsburg, Pennsylvania.

The confusion created through misidentification by various national publications faded and was another episode in the life of *Belle Boyd: The Rebel Spy.*

Source: *Author's Collection*

Belle Boyd
(Belle used a Confederate uniform for performances)

Chapter 34

1890 1899

The 1890s found Belle continuing a heavy schedule of performances and traveling throughout the Northern, Southern, and Midwestern areas of the United States. Belle and Nathaniel High traveled once more through the Deep South, back to Ohio, and then north to Massachusetts. Belle's performances did not only feature her but now her husband, Nathaniel doing comedy. Her two daughters, Byrd and Maria were performing song and dance.

In 1893, Belle and Nathaniel were in Boston where she was interviewed by a journalist. In her interview, Belle appeared to have long separated herself from the bitterness, animosity, and partisan emotions that arose from America's Civil War and the Reconstruction Era that followed the war's conclusion. She appeared reflective, happier, and mature and looked at her life differently. When interviewed, she said, "I am living now in the delightful memories of my past, of rambles among the old, historic cities of the East and journeying up the Nile. For the past eight years, I have been traveling, lecturing for the Grand Army post, and learning more of your Northern people. I want specially to know your women, to get at their heart."

After Belle finished a theatrical performance in Fall River, Massachusetts in 1893, a former sailor named Fred Hammer approached Belle. Hammer had served on the U. S. S. *Connecticut* during America's Civil War when the Union Navy captured the *Greyhound*. Hammer was one of the sailors of Samuel Hardinge's prize crew, who sailed from Virginia to Massachusetts. During their conversation, Hammer revealed that he had been ordered by Commodore Almy before leaving Virginia to watch her without her knowledge. Belle jokingly replied, "Well it was lucky for you at the time that I did not have a revolver, you wouldn't be here talking to me today."

By 1894, Belle toured the Maryland Eastern Shore with performances in Parksley and Onancock before traveling south to North Carolina. At Goldsboro, North Carolina, many of the old Confederate veterans called upon her while she lodged at the Hotel Kennon. Belle and the veterans met in the hotel lobby and "talked over the days and events of the war." The journalist from the *Goldsboro Weekly Argus* found Belle to be "very conversant and accurate in her recollections of incidents with which they were themselves familiar and entered cordially into conversation with them." The Confederate veterans and journalist were impressed that even though Belle, now fifty-years-old, was still "the spirit and fire of Southern chivalry and the fidelity of Southern interest that were the ruling characteristics of her young womanhood and that have made her immortal."

After her appearance in Goldsboro, she traveled to Durham, Hendersonville, and Wilmington, North Carolina, before returning to Virginia. In Wilmington, North Carolina, W. M. Creasy remembered attending one of Belle's performances, later recalling, "I listened to her tales of hairbreadth escapades; all else was forgotten but the woman and her words. Her sparkling eyes would glow, and her expressive features portray every motion she recounted. Her hands made an indelible impression on me. She literally talked with them." "Belle still had the spirit and fire to ignite enthusiasm among the veterans of the Union and Confederate armies" at her performances. One newspaper journalist observed that even though Belle was now "51 years of age, remarkably well preserved for a woman of her years, still looking good, tells her story in such realistic and dramatic style, as to chain the attention and arouse the enthusiastic admiration of her audience."

After so many Belle Boyd imposters had roamed the South in the 1870s and even still in the 1880s, those who knew Belle stepped forward to continue to ascertain her identity. The *Atlanta Constitution* August 19, 1895 edition proclaimed, "She is the original." In Georgia, Clement Evans of the U. C. V. said, "Mrs. B. B. Hammond-High as the true Belle Boyd, the Rebel Spy," and still another gentleman John

H. Leathers from the Confederate Veterans Association in Kentucky, wrote, "Mrs. Nat. R. High, is the genuine Belle Boyd of Confederate fame." Leathers was from Martinsburg, Virginia {West Virginia}, and could personally vouch for her identity. The organization commended her for her service to the Southern Confederacy and formally recognized her as "the genuine Belle Boyd." Still, at times she had individuals challenge her identity as the real Belle Boyd, but after finishing her performance, she spoke to them privately, proving she was the 1 original Belle Boyd.

In September 1895, Belle appeared in Griffin, Georgia, but the attendance for her performance was meager. The show had been "extensively advertised," but she had little money after paying for her expenses. Belle left her luggage behind at the Chambers Hotel in Griffin while she went to Barnesville to arrange for another lecture. The hotel proprietor became alarmed and concerned that she had left without paying her hotel bill. The hotel proprietor had a warrant issued for Belle's arrest for not paying her hotel bill. When Belle returned to Griffin, she had the hotel proprietor arrested for false imprisonment. While waiting on the court trail, Belle moved to the Goddard Hotel, but before she departed, she "proceeded to give the proprietor at the Chambers Hotel a piece of her mind." Police Chief Shackleford was sent for and asked to "make a case of disorderly conduct" against Belle, but nothing came of the incident.

In 1896, Belle's troubles did not end. While touring the South in Montgomery, Alabama, law enforcement arrested Belle and placed her in the county jail for larceny. The *Atlanta Constitution* published that "they had no money and when they left their baggage remained behind." When her luggage was searched by manager Bailey of the Merchants Hotel, he found several pieces of "his linen and he swore out a warrant against Belle Boyd."

The son of former governor, Thomas Jones remembered the first time he met Belle. He later wrote she appeared to be "under pathetic circumstances," and he remembered "very distinctly and particularly the indignation of Confederate Montgomery at the treatment Belle Boyd received while in Alabama."

Belle sent for young Jones's father. Belle had been accused of stealing some napkins and towels worth $2.50, and she wanted

Thomas Jones as her attorney. When young Jones's father arrived at the jail and began to interview the prisoner, he soon learned from talking to her of "having seen her two or three times when he was serving in the Valley under Stonewall Jackson"; that she "was Belle Boyd, the famous woman spy of the Confederacy."

Belle had paid her hotel bill by a draft in Montgomery before leaving for Talladega to lecture but did not know the draft payment had been refused. She was arrested at Talladega and returned to Montgomery. Thomas Jones signed for her bond and Belle lodged with them until the court trial.

At Belle's court trial, Thomas Jones proved the napkins and towels that Belle had been accused of stealing were actually the possessions of her two daughters. As a result, Belle was acquitted of all charges against her. But that did not calm the anger of the thousands of Confederate veterans, who were living in Montgomery and the surrounding area. Not only were they embarrassed by the incident, but one of their own had been falsely accused of a crime which she did not commit. To show their appreciation for her, they sponsored a benefit for Belle. At the conclusion of the performance, they gave her the money they had raised from the benefit. Belle was deeply gratified by their generosity.

During the first half of 1897, according to the Shreveport, Louisiana newspaper, *The Progress*, Belle performed at St. Landry, where survivors of two Louisiana brigades under Stonewall Jackson were living, and "recalled some of the daring deeds of Belle Boyd in the Shenandoah valley campaign."

In December 1897, Belle was celebrated with some of the highest honors that she had ever received when she appeared in Richmond, Kentucky, at the courthouse for a performance. At 8:00 in the evening, when her performance was about to begin, a detachment of cadets with muskets marched onto the stage with drums beating and flags waving, doing different military maneuvers under the command of Lieutenant Vestol of the United States Army. When the cadets were finished with the military maneuvers, they stacked arms, draped the colors, and stood at attention. When the cadets were finished, according to a journalist with the *Richmond Climax*, "directly on the arm of Major-General J. M. Poyntz, of this city, the lady speaker walked down the left aisle and was received with applause." Belle mounted the platform and looked over her audience "with evident pleasure." The journalist continued his article by praising Belle for the way she "spoke with marvelous power and directness." For an hour, she "held her audience in pleased astonishment at her narrative of the war and her thrilling personal experience. Her description of the battle of Gettysburg was superb, {and} her stories of hospital life were touching in the extreme. A thousand letters home she wrote for the sick and dying men of both armies, blue and gray."

Belle was not at the Battle of Gettysburg, but instead at her home in Martinsburg. She could have only known about what occurred at Gettysburg by the battle descriptions from soldiers who had fought in the fight and then piecing it together for a narrative. While nursing the sick and wounded at Martinsburg and writing their letters home, this is how she also learned about the battle's dramatic high points.

Belle continued to receive praise for her performances. On February 7, 1898, she appeared in Greenfield, Ohio, before a large audience of Union veterans. Even though Belle was fifty-five years old, her performance that evening was received with enthusiasm. Congressman Henry Luther Dickey, the representative for the 7th Ohio District, wrote a raving review of Belle's performance: "It may be safely stated that no audience in Greenfield was ever more charmed and pleased than the one which {who} sat under the wonderfully thrilling and eloquent power of Belle Boyd, in her graphic descriptions of the scenes and battle through which she passed. Mingled as her lecture with sparkling bits of wit and humor, changing again to a pathos awaking the tenderness sensations, I most cheery commended her, feeling sure the public who hear her will be delighted."

Belle's audiences were primarily men who had served in the Union and Confederate armies. But through the 1890s, their numbers decreased because of dying or being too sickly to attend her performances. Even though Belle continued to show the fire and spirit of her youth, another generation was born who did not want to hear the old war stories. It left Belle almost destitute, but she continued to perform, not realizing that the final curtain was soon ending on her performances and her life.

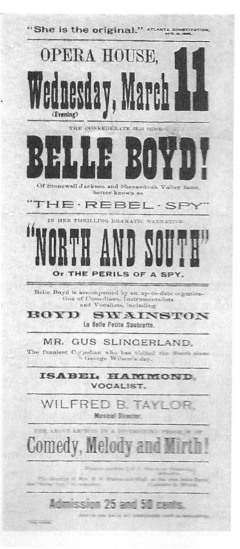

Source: *Author's Collection*

Play Ticket

Chapter 35

Taps

By the spring of 1900, Belle had rented a seven-room home, with a bath for $8.00 a month in Evansville, Wisconsin. She felt content with her location and believed it was a good choice.

On May 21, Belle wrote her daughter, Marie {Belle Jr.}, who lived on Groveland Avenue in Chicago, Illinois that she was living near lakes and in a "lovely town." She wrote about the satisfaction of living in her new home and she would be there all summer with the possibility of steady theatrical work. Belle also informed her daughter she had been under a "Dr.'s care" and she was in "bad shape," for a while, but felt better and believed the physician could do her "a lot of good." Marie might have been unemployed when Belle wrote this letter because she informed her, "You know darling, what it means in Chicago to hustle, don't you?" And then, she asked Marie if she needed money and advised her to learn the millinery trade.

On May 22, Belle performed at Magee's Hall in Evansville, Wisconsin. A journalist for the *Tribune* found her performance very believable and professional, writing, the entertainment "was good, especially Mrs. Boyd's story as a spy is very good and full of thrilling incidents and narrow escapes, picturing the deceit practiced and embodied in some persons."

After her performance in Evansville, Belle, and Nathaniel journeyed to Portage for a performance before traveling north to the resort town of Kilbourn {Wisconsin Dells} to give another performance for Union veterans of the Grand Army of the Republic, which was scheduled for June 13.

When Belle and Nathaniel arrived at the Hile House Hotel in Kilbourn, the clerk's first impression of Belle was that she appeared to be regal and sickly. He was not impressed by their appearance because he later said they appeared to be in "dire straits," and "Miss Boyd and Mr. High's clothes were old, out of fashion, and threadbare." Although the hotel clerk did not feel that Belle was properly dressed, he still remembered that "there was something beautiful about her…something a man never forgot."

On Monday, June 11, 1900, Belle appeared to be in her usual good health, but for some reason, she appeared despondent. Belle may have been despondent because she had just sent one of her daughters the last two dollars that she had and was concerned over her daughter's welfare.

On the evening of June 11, Belle "was taken with a sinking spell due to heart trouble." Belle confided to Nathaniel she believed she was dying. A lady only identified as Mrs. English was sent for as well as a physician; by the time the physician arrived, Belle had died.

The news of Belle Boyd's death at Kilbourn, Wisconsin on June 11, 1900 spread quickly and was published in newspapers throughout the United States. The St. Paul, Minnesota *Globe* published on June 17: "The story of her life reads like the weird tales told in yellow-covered novels." The *New York Times* published and later republished in the Wheeling, West Virginia *Daily Intelligencer*: "The sudden death in Kilbourn, Wis., on Monday, of Belle Boyd, the noted spy of the confederates recalls another leaf in {the}history of the civil war. It recalls the thrill, the danger, the triumphs, the reverses, the many ups and downs in the life of the most determined woman foe the Union ever had." The Manning, South Carolina *Times* on June 20 published: "In fifty-seven years of her life, there had come more adventure, more excitement, more romance, more danger than a score of lives possibly of other active women of modern times."

Most of the newspapers reported that Belle died from "a heart attack," "cardiac arrest," and "heart disease." The physician who examined her said the cause of death was attributed to a heart attack. As we well know, heart attacks usually come from a blood clot or coronary artery disease {Heart Blockage}. During Belle's time, there was no cure or way to resolve the issue, as modern science has provided us today. But she had been battling illness for some time, as she revealed in her letter to Marie on May 21. Since she had suffered her first battle with Typhoid Fever while in prison in 1863, she had suffered additional recurrences of the disease throughout the post-war years, it is possible that the damage and effects suffered from the Typhoid Fever caused problems with her heart, such as Myocarditis, which is an inflammation of the heart muscle, leading to possibly congestive heart failure or Endocarditis, which is an inflammation of the lining of the heart and valves or Congestive Heart Failure. The *Kilbourn Mirror Gazette* published that she had a "sinking spell," which means that death for Belle was almost instantly.

After Belle's death, Nathaniel discovered a pistol under her pillow. Crying, he said, "My poor Belle! You won't need this anymore. Nobody can hurt you now, ever." The previous day Belle told a hotel housekeeper that the weapon was her "best protection."

Immediately after Belle's death, Nathaniel sent a telegram to Belle's children in Chicago that their mother had suddenly died and asked them to come to Kilbourn by Wednesday, June 13.

When Belle's children arrived, The *Mirror Gazette* published, "Her three daughters and a son came out from Chicago, and when they saw the beautiful cemetery at Kilbourn, at once they decided to buy a lot here." Grace must have resolved her differences with her mother. She was living in Chicago at the time of her mother's death. Her genealogy reveals that she lived in Ward Three, the south side of Chicago, at the time of her mother's death. Grace lived with her husband Lee Bennett of Iowa, who she married in 1896. They later moved to Moon Creek, Montana, where they lived according to the 1920 and 1930 census, but her death is listed in California. However, that is not valid. Grace died in February 1934, Miles City, Custer County, Montana; age sixty-nine. Lee Bennett was six years younger than Grace and he died in October 1940, also in Miles City; the author has viewed the grave sites.

The burial lot that they chose, according to the *Mirror Gazette*, had a panorama view, "much like the field at Gettysburg." Old soldiers of the war who fought at Gettysburg often remarked on its similarity.

The Reverend Arthur Gorter officiated Belle's funeral service at the Kilbourn Episcopal Church. The church was full of mourners who came to pay their respects to a woman who was a stranger among them. The *Mirror Gazette* published, "The church was filled with people who thus expressed their sympathy for the strangers who came to bury their mother among strangers."

The mortal remains of *Belle Boyd: The Rebel Spy* were lowered into the ground by four veterans of the Union army and two veterans from the Spanish American War.

Belle Boyd, *The Daughter of the Confederacy* was fifty-seven years old when she died even though she still looked much younger.

Belle's obituary was published nationally in major as well as local newspapers. Below is one of those obituaries, the Greenbrier, West Virginia *Independent*:

Belle Boyd, the famous, of Confederate fame, died suddenly of heart disease, at Kilbourne, Wis., some time ago, where she had gone to lecture. She was 57 years of age, and known all over the country.

Belle Boyd was born in Martinsburg, W. Va., in May, 1844, and is descended from Revolutionary ancestors. She was at home when the Civil War broke out, having just returned from school, near Baltimore.

Patterson and Cadwalader's armies from the north invaded Virginia and swarmed around her home in Martinsburg. One of the Union soldiers, a drunken fellow, insulted in grossest language, her mother, who fainted. Belle was present and drew her pistol and shot him. She was arrested and carried to General Patterson's headquarters and a court of inquiry was held. Gen. Patterson said she did right, and under the same circumstances he hoped every Southern girl would do the same. The incident got into the Northern papers, and "like a white elephant," as she expressed it, she was pointed out as the thousands of troops came into town as being the most dangerous Rebel in the country.

Jackson discovered her merit as a spy, and gave her a permit to pass anywhere through the lines, and she often rode through the dark, lonely hours of the night to carry news to Jackson and Stuart of the movements of the enemy.

She sent information she had gathered from Union officers to Gen. J. E. B. Stuart. She was detected once, and an article of war {was}read to her, but it did not deter her from being a messenger between Beauregard and Jackson. While en route from Front Royal to Martinsburg she was arrested, and taken to Baltimore and handed over to General Dix, who quartered her at the Eutaw House, where she was kept a week and sent home.

Near Martinsburg she ran out of the Federal lines, across a field on which a battle was about to be fought, to the Confederate lines to carry them information. Shot and shell followed her, but she was unhurt. Soon after she was arrested as a spy, by order of Secretary of War Stanton, locked up in the Capital Prison and court-martialed. Her stay in jail gave an international fame. She was finally released and sent South.

Next, she bored messages from the Confederate government to authorities in Europe. She ran the blockade but was captured before she could get away by the United States man-of-war Connecticut.

She was carried to Boston and kept a prisoner for a few days in the Tremont Hotel. By reason of her being captured under the British flag, she was not shot but banished. She was carried to Canada, and ordered to never return her foot on United States soil again or she would be shot without trial.

A young lieutenant on the Connecticut, Sam Hardinge, fell in love with his fair captive. She got his signal book, which she sent into the South by way of the blockade, and then sailed to England from Quebec on board the Damascus, and arrived in London, carrying her dispatches safely through. She was followed across the ocean by her lover, Lieutenant Hardinge, and they were married at St. James, in Piccadilly. The Prince of Wales attended their wedding. They were afterward presented at five different foreign courts. By him she had one child, Grace Hardinge. She was left a widow and upon the dramatic stage in Europe and made her debut at the Theatre Royal, in Manchester. When the general amnesty was proclaimed she came back here and played a few engagements in this country and married Col. J. S. Hamilton, an English ex-army officer in March 1869. They went to California, where she was seriously ill, and, on recovering, returned East and settled down in her home.

In 1885, in Texas, she married her third husband.... Nat R. High, formerly of Toledo, O.

A few years ago, Belle Boyd took to the lecture platform, and told the story of the part she played as a Confederate spy.

There were a few mistakes published in the Greenbrier *Independent*. First the battle occurred at Front Royal and not Martinsburg, secondly, Samuel Hardinge did not die in England as reported and third, her second marriage was to John Hammond.

Belle's grave remained unmarked until 1905* when a marker was placed with the inscription:

One Flag
One Country Flag
Marie Isabelle Boyd
Confederate Spy
Born May 9, 1843
Died June 11, 1900

Years later, in 1919, another gentleman named Willis Everman, a private in the 3rd Missouri regiment, placed a marker on her grave, which is still present today. Everman wrote from Greenville, Mississippi, in a *Confederate Veterans* publication: "Some years ago, while visiting the dells of Wisconsin, I strolled through the cemetery nearby and to my surprise ran across the grave of Belle Boyd, who died in Kilbourne and was probably buried with funds contributed by the good citizens of that village. A short time ago, it occurred to me that I ought to put up a marker at the head of her grave. So, I took up the matter with a granite company, and after some correspondence, I have sent an order for them to put up a headstone with the inscription:

Belle Boyd
Confederate Spy
Born in Virginia
Died in Wisconsin
Erected by a Comrade

Union veterans, who were still living on Memorial Day in 1918 placed flags on the graves of their comrades who were buried at Spring Grove Cemetery, and they placed one on Belle's grave, a tradition that is still occurs to this day; they were assisted by the Women's Relief Corps. The local newspaper published that year, "this

305

shows that the bitterness is gone and that there is a growing brotherhood."

Over the years following Belle Boyd's death in Wisconsin, there was a conversation about exhuming her remains and bringing them back to Martinsburg to be interred alongside her mother and father. Still, even though it had the support of her son John {Eddie}, it never materialized. In a May 30, 1955 edition of a Wisconsin Dells newspaper, the residents of the town believed they had earned "the right to claim her for their own." The town received support that year from Belle's granddaughter, Mrs. Virginia Monique Hammond of Los Angeles, California. Mrs. Hammond wrote, "My grandmother shall rest forever in her scenic and eternal resting place in Wisconsin Dells, despite rumors that some misguided Southerners wish to remove her remains to Virginia."

To this present day, Belle Boyd's grave is still maintained by the American Legion of Wisconsin Dells.

Epilogue

The question is, was Belle Boyd who she said she was and were the events that transpired in her life during America's Civil War fictional or factual? Many of the old veterans of the Union army must have believed she was who she said she proclaimed to be because after the war they sponsored and attended her lectures about her experiences during the war. Most people after the war in the old Southern Confederacy believed her war experiences were true, especially the United Daughters of the Confederacy or they would not have awarded her the *Southern Cross of Honor*, which she always wore and displayed. The *Southern Cross of Honor* was given in recognition of a Confederate soldier's loyal and honorable service to the South and only a Confederate veteran was eligible to wear the *Southern Cross of Honor*. This was an award for worthy service for Belle Boyd but it does not in itself give her credibility. What gives her credibility are the facts that have been written and revealed and verified by other sources of the time period, who can collaborate her version of events in which she was involved. James D. Richardson of Murfreesboro, Tennessee wrote in a *Confederate Veterans' Magazine* article in 1900, that Belle was compared to "Joan of Arc" and she performed "fearless deeds of daring" and her "devotion" was "deeply rooted, more widely manifested," and "more generally felt." A former Northern Army of the Potomac journalist, Charles Carlton later wrote that Belle Boyd "was taken into Stonewall Jackson's confidence around Harpers Ferry, she was passed rapidly from one scene of exciting adventure to another until her final capture and banishment in 1864." Richardson and Carlton add to her credibility.

Many other sources in this book have documented Belle Boyd's war experiences. Through various newspaper articles published in both the North and South, as well as soldiers' diaries, civilians' testimonies, letters, the *Southern Historical Society Papers*, and the

Official Record War of the Rebellion are what gives us the truth. The events Belle wrote about in her book, *Belle Boyd in Camp and Prison* are factual and were verified by those who she had personal acquaintance and others who were her foes during the war, plus the other sources mentioned. Individuals who she wrote about and proclaimed that she interacted with can be proven and verified, such as when she was at Front Royal with Lieutenant Henry Kyd Douglas, General Richard Taylor, Captain David Strother, Major Harry Gilmor, and Colonel Robert Gould Shaw. I have revealed many of these sources and many more in the book who interacted with her during the war and following the war while she traveled the country and lecturer.

Belle wrote her book much like a novel, it reads like a romantic adventure, but her participation in the events in the Shenandoah Valley of Virginia have been verified over the years by several other biographers as well as this current historian. Over the past years, I have read many diaries, letters, and eyewitness accounts of the war. Out of most of those accounts, women have always been the most truthful as well as emotional telling their narrative. I do not imply that men were not truthful, but at times they could either hype up or downplay a narrative of a specific incident that they were involved.

Many years after Belle's death, she is still remembered for her daring deeds and her ability to deceive her foe. Immediately after Belle's death, the *Richmond Planet* wrote, "It would take a book to tell all the adventures of Belle Boyd and all the hardships she endured in her later life while carrying on a heroic struggle to support her children. Another newspaper, the Washington *Evening Star* remembered, "Many an old soldier remembered her as the most daring woman in the Confederate army." And last, an article published in the Washington *Evening Times*, "She gloried in the fact that being a woman, she was more abled to outwit Federal officers, whose gallantry got the better of their discretion."

Over the past 123 years since Belle Boyd's death, interest has remained about her life and experiences through articles, books, and Websites. Her life is still a fascination to those in the Civil War re-enacting community as well as those who study and read about the war. Since the war, boats, streets, organizations, race horses, and children have been named after her. And even there was a theatrical play written and staged about her life during the war and after the war.

Hopefully, history and historians will take another look at Belle Boyd's life and war experiences. With the material I had access to for this book, and I made every effort to discover as much as there was available, I believe I have presented her life as objective and as fair as I can present and publish.

The Washington *Evening Star* newspapers best summed up Belle's life when it wrote "she was a mystery while yet she lived, and she remains a mystery today."

Belle will always be remembered as **Belle Boyd: The Rebel Spy.**

Appendix A

Hardinge & High

****

Samuel W. Hardinge

By now, you may be asking what finally happened to Samuel Hardinge. After much time and research through *Family Search Genealogy*, the most extensive database and resource of names in the United States, and old newspapers, I came across some answers. According to the 1870 census, Hardinge lived in Brooklyn, New York, and registered his occupation as a purser, living with his parents, and remarried to a lady named Helen. Helen may or may not be the woman who rode on the train and spoke about Hardinge with Marshal John Keyes; there were no children by Hardinge's second marriage.

While married to Helen, Samuel enlisted in the United States Navy. He "was one of the crew of the United States warship *Juanita,* which was dispatched to the Artic region in 1873 in search of the Hall-Polaris castaways." The *Juanita* is the same ship that Belle was placed on when she was exchanged in 1862.

According to the July 6, 1903 edition of the Washington *Evening Star,* Samuel Hardinge had filed a lawsuit in the Court of Claims for his pay as a lieutenant after discovering he had been neither "discharged nor dismissed from the navy" in 1864. His counsel for his lawsuit was General Benjamin {The Beast} Butler, but I did not find any record of the case's outcome.

According to the March 8, 1879 edition of the *New York Times,* Samuel Hardinge died on March 6, 1879. The newspaper did not give the cause of death, and his body was returned to Portsmouth, New Hampshire, where he was born and interred on March 11, 1879. At the time of his death, he was thirty-six-years-old, and his residence with his wife was listed at 166 Montaque Street in Brooklyn, New York.

310

Nathaniel Rue High Jr.

There is little to be found on Nathaniel High. Nathanial disappeared from the public domain after Belle's death. Guy Glazier, a Kilbourn resident, claims that on the day of Belle's death, Nathanial had nothing to do with disposing of her body. It is with mere speculation on the author's part, but it could have been possible that Nathaniel experienced significant grief that other individuals were willing to help him, provide for his comfort, and arrangements to remove Belle's body from the Hile House Hotel.

Nathaniel and Belle were married for fifteen years. After reading and researching her life, it appears that Belle's third marriage was her happiest. Nathaniel showed an undying devotion to Belle and her children. Despite their age gap and financial struggles, it appears Nathaniel and Belle's marriage was a successful relationship.

After Belle's death, Nathaniel returned to Detroit, Michigan, where he still resided in 1902. As of the publication of the second edition, I have not been able to find any additional information on High.

Appendix B

Belle's Second Marriage Children

****

Mary Byrd Swainston Hammond

Belle once described Byrd as "tall, graceful much resembling her mother." Also, like her mother, Byrd {Byrdie} Swainston Hammond became a very successful theatrical actress performing in *The Little Minister*, *Darkness and Daylight* and appearing in many more theatrical productions during her career.

In 1891, at seventeen, Byrd married James Williams, and they had one child, a daughter, Nana, born on March 19, 1897. James died, and Byrd remarried in 1906 to Harold Mowery, a salesman with the American Steel Company. The following year, Byrd retired from the theater.

Harold and Byrd were married for fourteen years, with their marriage ending in divorce on March 30, 1920. Byrd did not remarry.

Byrd resided at 175th Street in New York City when she suffered a severe stroke. She lived about two weeks after the stroke before dying on December 16, 1932. She was fifty years old.

Marie Isabelle Hammond

Marie {Belle Jr.} was like her sister Byrd, a theatrical actress and professional singer. Of all of Belle's children, Marie was much like her mother, especially in her dynamic singing voice.

On June 24, 1903, Marie married Charles Chase, a well-known artist and writer. Marie and Charles lived in Chase, Florida, for some time, but their marriage ended in divorce. Marie married again in 1913 to Adolph Michael and was still married to him when he died in 1942, and there were no children by either marriage.

312

Marie joined the Warren Rifles Chapter, United Daughters of the Confederacy in Front Royal, Virginia. One of the "greatest satisfactions" of her life was the "honor paid to her" mother.

Belle's first biographer Louis A. Siguad had the opportunity to interview Marie about his book, *Belle Boyd: Confederate Spy*. Siguad's impression of Marie was that she was much like the description of her mother, "forthright, impetuous, vivacious, and courageous." While growing up, she was called "Little Hell" by her sisters Grace and Byrd. Siguad's final evaluation of Marie was "as long as she lives Belle Boyd cannot be said to have died." After a lengthy illness, Maria died June 16, 1961, and is buried in the Lutheran Cemetery in Brooklyn, New York.

John Edmund Hammond

John {Eddie}received his education at the private Episcopal {military} school in New Jersey. After school on September 18, 1899, he enlisted with Battery O, First Artillery in the United States Army, but medically discharged several months later, December 19, 1899, due to disability. When the United States became involved in World War I, he served on a escort ship, transporting troops and supplies across the Atlantic Ocean to Europe.

In 1920 there was an interest in returning Belle's remains to Martinsburg. The *Shepherdstown Register* published on September 16:

Belle Boyd, the famous woman spy of the Confederacy, daughter of Benjamin Boyd, will most likely rest in Green Hill Cemetery in Martinsburg. Her body now lies in the cemetery in Kilbourn, Wisconsin, but recently arrangements have been started for its removal to Martinsburg. F. P. Staley, secretary of Green Hill Cemetery Association, is in receipt of a letter from one of the dead woman's children, John E. S. Hammond of Tompkinsville, N. Y., in which he voices his desire. John had visited his mother's gravesite and addressed his letter to Staley if there would be enough room at the cemetery for his mother's remains and he was assured there would be enough room for her reburial.

John had given his full approval, but it did not materialize. According to an article in the Washington *Evening Star*, "evidently the plan was abandoned." No reason was given.

While John's mother was making the newspapers, he was a judge in Tompkinsville, New York.

John married and had two children, John Jr., and Ned Boyd.

When Louis Siguad published his book *Belle Boyd: Confederate Spy*, Marie Isabelle, John's older sister, had not communicated with her younger brother for twenty years. She believed he was already deceased.

Appendix C

What Happened to Eliza Hopewell Corsey

Eliza Hopewell Corsey was Belle Boyd's most trusted confidant before and during America's Civil War. Eliza was born in Virginia in 1834 because she gave her age in the 1870 census as thirty-six-years-old. She stated in the 1880s census that her parents came from Virginia. Eliza was first enslaved at Belle's Grandmother Glenn's estate "Glenn Burnie" or "Glennburnie," eight miles east of Martinsburg in Jefferson County, Virginia {West Virginia}. When Eliza learned she would be "sold south," she escaped and sought refuge with Belle's family in Martinsburg. Eliza had been used to working in the "big house" rather than toiling in the fields when she sought refuge with the Boyds. Eliza must have already been acquainted with Belle and her family because of the Glenns visiting the Boyds and vice versa. Most likely it was Belle who became instrumental in Eliza remaining with her family in Martinsburg and working as their house servant and helping Belle.

Belle and Eliza became close because Belle taught Eliza how to read and write; Eliza's granddaughter, Ann Berry verified this fact. Eliza assisted Belle during the war by carrying dispatches of information on the Union armies' designs, helped her nurse the sick and wounded Confederate soldiers and removed incriminating papers during Belle's arrest at Front Royal in 1862. And it was Eliza that removed Confederate flags from Belle's bedroom in July 1861, when Union soldiers arrived at her home in Martinsburg and it was Eliza who sought the assistance of General Patterson when his troops threatened injury and the destruction of the Boyd home after Belle mortally wounded a drunken Union soldier. It is evident that Eliza's loyalty to Belle stemmed from the fact that Belle had been instrumental in Eliza remaining with the Boyd family instead of being "sold south," and they had bonded over the years in close friendship.

After Belle's arrest in July 1862, Eliza disappears from Belle's life. What happened to Eliza? First, Eliza was married to Samuel Corsey because they had a son, John, born in 1851, and Laura Lee, born in 1857; they are not mention on the trip to Front Royal. Therefore, they must have remained in Martinsburg. Second, the *Emancipation Proclamation* was issued by President Abraham Lincoln to take effect in January 1863, which proclaimed that all enslaved people were free. Also, Western Virginia became the thirty-fifth state to join the Union, June 20, 1863; Martinsburg was now a city in West Virginia. By the time Belle returned to Martinsburg in July 1863, she still fails to mention Eliza in her memoirs. Did Eliza and her family leave Martinsburg?

Samuel Hardinge may have given us a clue when he wrote about his visit to Belle's Martinsburg home in 1864, and when he was confronted by a servant while looking around in Belle's bedroom. Hardinge was "told by a servant" that no one had used the room in Belle's absence. Could he have been writing about Eliza? Maybe. However, the most significant evidence of what happened to Eliza through the remainder of the war points to Eliza's obituary as the most significant source. According to her obituary she returned to Berkeley County after the war. She may have lived in Edgewood, Pennsylvania, or the surrounding area because her granddaughter still lived there at the time of her death. After all she had endured before and during the war, it is most logical to want to get out of harm's way and keep her husband and two children safe.

According to the 1870 census, Eliza lived in Martinsburg with her husband, Samuel and their two children John nineteen and Laura Lee thirteen. In the 1870 census, Samuel is listed as a "Barber," as is John. Eliza's occupation is listed as "Keepinghouse." In the 1880 census, Eliza and her family are still living in Martinsburg. She listed her occupation as "Washwoman." Sometimes, she worked as a midwife and assisted local physicians. Eliza's grandchildren, John, and Anna, and by 1900, their son John lived with Samuel and Eliza. Eliza and Samuel's wealth was estimated at $150.00, considered prosperous before the turn of the century living in rural America. Belle Boyd and Eliza maintained contact with each other because Belle sent Eliza's a high chair, plate and later a cat and white shawl when her first grandson was born.

Eliza was eight-two when she died in December 1916. The local *Martinsburg Evening Journal* newspaper published her obituary on December 26, 1916:

Aunt Eliza Houewell {Hopewell} an old-time colored mammy who for many years has been well known here, and who had many friends died Monday night at 10 o'clock in the King Daughters hospital, her death being due to old age. Her exact age is not known but her descendants believe that she was at least 101 years old and possibly older.

Aunt Eliza was an ex-slave and before the Civil War she was owned by the prominent Glenn family, at Glenn Osbourne {Burnie}, in Jefferson County. Belle Boyd, the famous Confederate spy, was her last mistress. After the war, she came to Berkeley County, where she had since resided. She was taken ill as she was about to leave for Edgewood, Pa., with her granddaughter. She is survived by two grand-children---Prof. Randolph Ramer, principal of the local colored school, and Nannie Coleman of Edgewood, Pa. The funeral will be held Wednesday afternoon at 2:30. The services will be conducted by the Wilen undertaking establishment with the Reverend J. T. Reid, pastor of Ebenezer Baptist church and interment will be at Mount Hope cemetery in Martinsburg.

Appendix D

Who was C. W. D. Smitley

C. W. D. Smitley was born on June 6, 1839, in Cumberland, Maryland, and later raised in Johnstown, Pennsylvania, before moving in 1859 to Boothsville, Marion County, Virginia {West Virginia}. At the beginning of America's Civil War, Smitley joined Company B of the 2nd West Virginia Infantry before becoming a chief scout with the 5th West Virginia Cavalry. During the war, Smitley served under Union generals Milroy, Averell, and Sigel.

Almost two years after his encounter with Belle Boyd, Smitley and fellow scout Spike Harris from eastern Hampshire County, West Virginia, were scouting when Confederates captured them on May 11, 1864. Harris was killed, and Smitley was captured during the incident.

After nearly dying from a fever in a Confederate prison, Smitley escaped and joined Major General William T. Sherman's army as it entered Columbia, South Carolina, in 1865.

After the war, Smitley moved to Burlington, Ohio, with his wife, Elizabeth Ruth Fancher of Boothsville; they had ten children. Later, Smitley and his family returned to Eldora in Marion County, West Virginia, where he died three months after Belle Boyd's death on September 23, 1900. He died from pneumonia and is buried in Clearmont Cemetery in the Boothsville area.

Appendix E

About Belle Boyd's Gravesite

One hundred and eighteen years ago, on Memorial Day, May 30, 1905, a young man entered Spring Grove Cemetery in Kilbourne {Wisconsin Dells}, Wisconsin. Painted on the plank of wood he carried, were the words "One Country, One Flag," along with a depiction of the American flag. The cemetery's Sexton assisted the young man in digging a hole two feet deep over the unmarked grave of a woman, and they set up the plank. She had died five years previously while on a lecture tour in Kilbourne, but the grave remained unmarked. As the two men finished their task, they were approached by three Union Civil War veterans. After a brief argument, the leader of the group, banker Thomas Coon declared, "Well, comrades, I guess the boy had beat you. I guess you won't haul the plank down." Flowers were placed on her grave, along with ten Wisconsin Union veterans, "local boys who had fallen in battle." The rebel grave was *Belle Boyd: The Rebel Spy*. According to the young lad, Gus O. Glazier who had challenged the Union veterans "feelings against the South still ran high. I certainly stirred up a hornet's nest when I suggested the marking of Belle Boyd's grave," Glazier later said.

Glazier had experienced opposition previously when he submitted his plan to mark Belle Boyd's gravesite to the Grand Army of the Republic Post and the Women's Relief Corps Auxiliary in Kilbourne. "No one knows with certainty what Belle hoped to achieve at Kilbourn because she was strongly resented by the community."

On the day of Belle's death, Glazier lived in Sauk County, near Kilbourn and had arrived in town after her death. "I know a lot about her death and burial and aftermath of erecting of the first head board," Glazier wrote. Glazier remembered that "Nat High did not claim Belle's body or have a part in its disposal, nor is he mentioned again." However, as I have written, Nathaniel High was too distressed to give his attention to details. Intentional negligence or animosity on his part was not in character with him.

Glazier had previously prepared a newspaper article that was published on October 6, 1905. After reading the original article published that the Grand Army of the Republic and the Women's Relief Corps Auxiliary had assisted in her burial, Glazier decided to write a rebuttal. Glazier remembered, "On the day of her death, the Grand Army of Kilbourn were appealed to. No, not one red cent would they give to bury that rebel, and so the body lay all day at the Hile House. Late in the day, Rev. Fr. Arthur Gorter, an Episcopal minister lent his assistance. Word was sent to her relatives, also the Theatrical Union, both of whom sent money by telegraph." The following day, a lot was purchased in Spring Grove Cemetery and Belle was buried, "Father Gorter conducting the funeral services." "I was told by Father Gorter that there was not a single member of the G. A. R. or W. R. C. {that} attended the funeral," Gus Glazier remembered.

Since 1918, Belle's gravesite has been decorated with a United States flag as well as Union veterans.

In 1919, most of the animosity surrounding the war had faded and Willis A. Everman, and ex-Confederate soldier, who had served in the 3rd Missouri Infantry erected the permanent headstone that I wrote about earlier.

On the 107th anniversary of Belle's birth, the Confederate flag was flown over her gravesite and Virginia soil was spread over the site. A Virginia delegation came for the occasion, the Wisconsin American Legion participated, and an excursion boat was named in her honor. The local newspaper published: "The Legion post of the Dells is to take part in the ceremony and it is to include dedication of a new excursion boat to be christened the *Belle Boyd* by Mrs. Phillips for the Riverview Boat Company. Pans include a rose arbor and a fence to be placed at Belle's grave.

Today, Belle's grave is maintained by the Wisconsin Dells American Legion.

Places of Interest

Belle Boyd House

The Berkeley County Historical Society owns and operates the Belle Boyd house. The Belle Boyd House is located at 136 East Race Street in Martinsburg, West Virginia with operating hours from 9-5, Monday thru Sunday. The house, originally built in 1850, was Belle Boyd's home until her family moved to South Queen Street in Martinsburg. The house on South Queen Street does not exist any longer.

The Berkeley County Historical Society is where historians, authors, and researchers may obtain access to the Belle Boyd archives as well as historical records and newspapers of Martinsburg and Berkeley County. Check their website at www.bchs.org for appointments and fees. Their staff is most knowledgeable.

A visit to the Belle Boyd House also includes a costume room, Black History, Industry, war and military, and a toy room. A visit is highly recommended.

Belle Boyd Cottage

The Belle Boyd Cottage is owned and operated by the Warren Heritage Society, located at 101 Chester Street, Front Royal, Virginia.

Belle lived in the five-room cottage prior to and during the Battle of Front Royal, May 23, 1862. Tours are provided of the cottage for a $3.00 admission; children under ten are admitted for free. The Belle Boyd Cottage is open from 10-4 weekdays and 10-4 on Saturdays from October thru April.

The Warren Heritage Society also houses the Laura Virginia Hale Archives, which includes material on Belle Boyd while she lived in Front Royal.

For historians, authors, and researchers, contact www.warrenheritagesociety.org for appointments and fees. Their staff is most knowledgeable. A visit is highly recommended.

Belle Boyd Gravesite

The Belle Boyd Gravesite is located at Spring Grove Cemetery on Route 23, past the intersection of Routes 13, 16, and 23 in Wisconsin Dells, Wisconsin. The GPS coordinates bring you in on the lower road. The GPS coordinates is 43.62569-89.75407.

Warren Rifles Confederate Museum

The Warren Rifles Confederate Museum is operated by the Warren Rifles Chapter of the United Daughters of the Confederacy. The museum is located on 95 Chester Street in Front Royal, Virginia. Their hours of operation are between 9-4 weekdays and 12-4 on Sundays, April thru November. The museum displays relics and records of America's Civil War, cavalry equipment, rare documents, and photos. They also have a Belle Boyd display of memorabilia that would be interesting to anyone who desires to know more about her.

Acknowledgments

Belle Boyd: The Rebel Spy would not have been made possible had the author not received the assistance of others willing to give their time and talents to the project. First, I would like to thank the Berkeley County Historical Society, the keepers of the Belle Boyd House for their assistance and for allowing me to use their archives and a tour of Belle's childhood home. I want to thank the Warren Heritage Society, the keepers of Belle Boyd's Cottage, for giving me an excellent tour of her cottage and some of the photographs used in this book. Finally, I would like to thank Judy Bushong of the Culpeper Museum for answering questions regarding Belle Boyd while she stayed in Culpeper County in 1862, and I would also like to thank the staff of the Library of Congress, Chronicling America, for using its vast collection of newspapers and resources.

Any author needs good editing and feedback on their work. I want to thank my wife, Rhonda Whitehair, for reading the first draft and for her input into the project, and I would like to thank Arlene Pombo for reading and giving her input on the final editing. And for Mosby Whitehair, my six-pound latte poodle, who kept me company while writing ***Belle Boyd: The Rebel Spy***.

Belle Boyd References

Belle Boyd in Camp and Prison

1) Chapter 1, pp 69, 71
2) Chapter 3, pp 80-83.
4) Chapter 4, pp 86-87.
5) Chapter 5, pp 95-96, 98, 102.
6) Chapter 6, pp 105-107.
7) Chapter 7, pp 113-115.
8) Chapter 8, pp 118.
9) Chapter 9, pp 129.
10) Chapter 9, pp 140, 147.
11) Chapter 12, pp 152-153, 155.
12) Chapter 16, pp 178.
13) Chapter 20, pp 202.
14) Chapter 21, pp 204, 207.
15) Chapter 22, pp 212.
16) Chapter 23, pp 229.
17) Chapter 27, pp 260, 266.

⌞SEP⌟Primary Sources & Diaries

1) *I Rode with Stonewall*. Henry Kyd Douglas, pp 6, 51.
2) *David Strother Diary*. David Strother, pp 36, 37.
3) *Destruction and Reconstruction*. General Richard Taylor.
4) *Lucy Buck Diary*. Lucy Rebecca Buck, pp 17, 34-35, 79.
5) *Kate Sperry Diary*. Kate Sperry, pp 140.
6) *History of the 5th West Virginia Cavalry*, pp 249, 257.
7) *Belle Boyd's Letter to Abraham Lincoln*. Library of Congress.
   Jan. 24,1865.
8) *Reveille in Washington*. Margaret Leech.
9) *The History of First-Tenth-Twenty-Ninth Maine*.
   Major John Gould, pp 108-109, 154.
10) *Reminiscences of Martinsburg*. Ann Elizabeth Stribbling.
11) *The Valley Campaigns*. Thomas A. Ashby, pp 53, 56-
   57, 80. 114-115.
12) *Private John Robson Diary*, pp 37.
13) *A Southern Perspective; Belle Boyd and Lucy Rebecca
   Buck of Front Royal*.
14) *The College Cavaliers*. Samuel Pettengill, pp 39, 44-47.
15) *Prisoner of State*. D.H. Mahony, pp 269-281.
16) *History of the Old Capitol*. James J. Williamson, pp 50-53.
17) *A Virginia Girl in the Civil War 1861-1865*. Mytra Lockett
   Avary, pp 51-59.

18) *Frederic D'Hauterville Diary*, June 10, 1862.

19) *Robert Gould Shaw to Sarah Blake Shaw*, July 28, 1862.

20) *G Campbell Brown Diary*, pp 367.

21) *Four Years in The Stonewall Brigade*. Pvt. John Casler. pp 153, 165.

22) *Four Years in The Saddle*. Maj. Harry Gilmor, pp 77-78.

23) *Sarah Wakeman letter to her mother*. Date unknown.

24) *History of the 5th Connecticut Infantry*. Capt. Edwin Marvin, pp 144-146.

25) *Observations of the North*. Edward Pollard, pp 13-24.

26) *Memoirs of Marshal John Keyes*, pp 214-218. Unpublished.

27) *Stories of our Soldiers*. Carleton, pp 43-50.

28) *Captain John Molyneaux Diary, 7th Ohio Infantry*.

29) *Boyd's letter to Lincoln*. Smithsonian Institute.com.

30) *Belle Boyd in Camp and Prison*. George Sala Introduction,

31) *Confederate Veterans Magazine* 1919. Willis Evermore

32) *History of the United States Secret Service*. L. Baker, pp 53-54.

33) *History of the 1st New York Cavalry*. Lt. W. H. Beach, pp 275-276.

34) *Battles and Leaders of The Civil War*: Volume II, pp 299, 301.

35) *Belle Boyd Letters*. Rosenback Collection.

36) *The Valley Campaigns*. Thomas A. Ashby, pp 53, 56-57 73-74, 139-140.

37) *Virginia Cavalcade*, Spring 1961, W. H. Creasy, pp 39.

38) *Confederate Veterans' Magazine*, 1900.

Newspapers

1)	*Valley News Echo*	July 4, 1861
2)	*Philadelphia Inquirer*	July 6, 1861
3)	Washington *Evening Star*	November 6, 1861
4)	*New York Times*	May 27, 1862
5)	Washington *Evening Star*	May 31, 1862
6)	*Frederick Examiner*	August 6, 1862
7)	Washington *Evening Star*	August 29, 1862
8)	*New York Tribune*	June 4, 1862
9)	*Richmond Daily Dispatch*	July 26, 1862
10)	*Richmond Daily Dispatch*	September 3, 1862
11)	*Richmond Dailey Dispatch*	October 13, 1862
12)	*New York Times*	October 25, 1862
13)	Knoxville *Daily Register*	February 14, 1863
14)	*New York Times*	February 23, 1863
15)	Memphis *Daily Appeal*	February 24, 1863
16)	*Richmond Enquire*	July 21, 1863
17)	*Alexandria Gazette*	August 21, 1863
18)	*Alexandria Gazette*	August 28, 1863

19) *Rockingham Register*   June 5, 1863
20) Cleveland *Morning Leader*   May 12, 1863
21) Washington *National Intelligencer*   May 24, 1864
22) *Dailey National Republican*   May 25, 1864
23) Cleveland *Morning Leader*   May 25, 1864
24) Washington *Evening Star*   October 1, 1863
25) *Alexandria Gazette*   October 3, 1863
26) *New York Tribune*   December 2, 1863
27) *Camden Confederacy*   November 6, 1863
28) Washington *Evening Star*   May 14, 1864
29) *Montreal Gazette*   June 4, 1864
30) *Montreal Daily Transcript*   June 1864
31) Washington *Evening Star*   June 8, 1864
32) *Daily National Republican*   September 8, 1864
33) *New York Herald*   September 8, 1864
34) Wheeling *Daily Intelligencer*   December 10, 1864
35) *New York Herald*   February 27, 1865
36) *Clearfield Republican*   March 15, 1865
37) *Columbia Daily Phoenix*   March 15, 1865
38) *Orleans Independent*   March 24, 1865
39) *The Daily Phoenix*   August 11, 1865
40) *The London News Illustrated*   August 19, 1865
41) *Norfolk Post*   September 13, 1865
42) *Pulaski Citizen*   May 11, 1866
43) *Spirit of Jefferson*   June 26, 1866
44) *Boston Traveler*   July 7, 1866
45) *Memphis Daily*   September 17, 1866
46) *Public Ledger*   September 17, 1866
47) *Alexander Gazette*   October 20, 1866
48) Columbus, *Ohio Statesman*   October 23, 1866
49) Newcastle, England *Chronicle*   November 3, 1866
50) Brooklyn *Daily Eagle*   January 30, 1867
51) Memphis *Daily Public Ledger*   September 23, 1867
52) Portland *Morning Oregonian*   October 1, 1867
53) Memphis *Daily Public Ledger*   October 3, 1867
54) Nashville *Union Dispatch*   October 10, 1867
55) Charleston, SC *Daily News*   November 4, 1867
56) *New York Herald*   January 18, 1868
57) *New York Herald*   January 25, 1868
58) *New York Tribune*   May 22, 1868
59) *Dallas Herald*   December 19, 1868
60) *Spirit of Jefferson*   February 2, 1869
61) *New Orleans Crescent*   February 12, 1869
62) *New Orleans Crescent*   February 18, 1869
63) *New Orleans Crescent*   March 7, 1869
64) Staunton *Spectator*   June 1, 1869

65)	Washington *Evening Star*	July 15, 1869
66)	*Shepherdstown Register*	July 17, 1869
67)	*Shepherdstown Register*	November 6, 1869
68)	Carson *Daily Appeal*	November 28, 1869
69)	Baton Rouge *Sugar Planter*	December 25, 1869
70)	*Memphis Daily Appeal*	April 18, 1870
71)	*Spirit of Jefferson*	November 24, 1874
72)	*New Orleans Bulletin*	November 28, 1874
73)	*Alexander Gazette*	December 5, 1874
74)	*Alexander Gazette*	December 12, 1874
75)	*Yorkville Enquirer*	July 1, 1875
76)	*New York Herald*	October 29, 1876
77)	Jefferson City, MO *Statesman*	February 18, 1876
78)	Jackson, TN *Whig & Tribune*	February 19, 1876
79)	*Memphis Daily Ledger*	February 23, 1876
80)	Tarborough, NC *Southerner*	March 3, 1876
81)	*Alexander Gazette*	August 8, 1876
82)	*Spirit of Jefferson*	May 8, 1877
83)	*New York Times*	March 8, 1879
84)	Staunton *Spectator*	January 9, 1881
85)	Staunton *Spectator*	September 9, 1881
86)	*Shepherdstown Register*	August 8, 1884
87)	*Dallas Daily Herald*	September 14, 1884
88)	*Alexander Gazette*	September 21, 1884
89)	Lancaster *Daily Intelligencer*	October 14, 1884
90)	*Shepherdstown Register*	October 14, 1884
91)	*Alexander Gazette*	October 14, 1884
92)	Austin *Weekly Statesman*	October 16, 1884
93)	Omaha *Daily Bee*	October 31, 1884
94)	Fort Worth *Gazette*	January 27, 1885
95)	*New York Times*	April 4, 1885
96)	Staunton *Spectator*	June 17, 1885
97)	*Memphis Daily Appeal*	June 30, 1885
98)	Andersonville, SC *Intelligencer*	October 15, 1885
99)	*Toledo Blade*	February 22, 1886
100)	Goldsboro *Weekly Argus*	September 20, 1864

Newspapers Continue

1)	*Yorkville Enquirer*	April 17, 1895
2)	*Atlanta Constitution*	March 18, 1896
3)	*Alexander Gazette*	October 1, 1896
4)	Shreveport *The Progress*	March 13, 1897
5)	*Richmond Climax*	December 22, 1897
6)	Hillsboro *Traveler's Herald*	February 17, 1898
7)	Evansville *Tribune*	May 22, 1900

8) Kilbourn *Mirror Gazette*	June 12, 1900
9) Washington *Evening Times*	June 13, 1900
10) Washington *Evening Star*	June 14, 1900
11) *Richmond Planet*	August 11, 1900
12) Wheeling *Daily Intelligencer*	June 16, 1900
13) Greenbrier *Independent*	July 5, 1900
14) Washington *Evening Star*	July 6, 1903
15) *New York Times*	April 4, 1915
16) *Martinsburg Evening Journal*	December 26, 1916
17) *Shepherdstown Register*	September 16, 1920
18) Washington *Evening Star*	November 7, 1926
19) Washington *Evening Star*	May 14, 1943
20) *The Oakland Republican*	February 1, 1945
21) *BaraGoon News*	May 22, 1952
22) *BaraGoo News*	May 30, 1955
23) Washington *Evening Star*	May 7, 1961
24) *Martinsburg Journal*	May 22, 2011
25) The *Monte Vista Journal*	December 15, 2006

Official Records of the War of the Rebellion

1) OR Series II, Volume IV {S# 117} Prisoner of War, June 13th to
   November 30th, 1862.
2) OR Series I, Volume XV {S# 15} Operations in the Shenandoah
   Valley Report #1, Major-General Nathaniel Banks. Battle
   of Front Royal May 23rd, 1862.
3) OR Series I, Volume XV {S# 15} Report #5, Captain George
   Smith, Company H 1st Maryland Infantry. Battle of Front Royal,
   May 23rd, 1862.
4) OR Series I, Volume XV {S# 15} Report #4, Colonel John Kenly
   1st Maryland Infantry. Battle of Front Royal May 23rd,
   1862.
5) OR Series I, Volume XV {S# 15} Report #8, Lt. Charles Atwell
   Knapp's Pennsylvania Artillery. Report of the Battle of
   Front Royal.
6) OR Series II, Volume IV, Pages 310, 349.

Southern Historical Society Papers

1) Volume II, Captain Robert E. Park, 12th Alabama Infantry.
2) Volume XXVII, Private J. C. Goolsby, Crenshaw's Battery[SEP].
3) Volume XXVIII, H. C. Wall, 23rd North Carolina Infantry.
4) Volume XXVIII, Letter Thomas R.R. Cobb, September 3,
   1862.

Secondary Sources

1) *Battle at Bull Run*. William C. Davis, pp 47, 52-53, 65.
2) *Stonewall Jackson: The Man, The Soldier, The Legend*.
   James Robertson, pp 398.
3) *Stonewall in the Valley*. Robert Tanner, pp 258-260.
4) *Belle Boyd Siren of the South*. Ruth Scarborough, pp 6, 9, 19, 26, 107-
   175, 177-179, 180-181. SEP
5) *Battles and Leaders of The Civil War*: Volume II pp 299, 301.
6) *Secret Missions of the Civil War*. P. Van Dorn Stern, pp 102, 103.
7) *Belle Boyd, Southern Spy of The Shenandoah*. Laura Virginia Hale,
   pp 2, 8.
8) *Aler's History of Martinsburg and Berkeley County*. F. Vernon Aler, pp
   211,212.
9) *History of Pennsylvania Volunteers 1861-1865*. Samuel Bates.
10) *Mosby: The War Years*. CW Whitehair, pp 22-23.
11) ead.lib.virginia.edu. William R. Denny.
12) *Spies of the Confederacy*. John Bakeless, pp 143.
13) *Rebel Chronicles*. Steve French, pp 93.
14) Delaware State Archives, 3rd Delaware Infantry.
15) *Belle Boyd: Confederate Spy*. Louis A. Siguad, pp 103,104-105-107,
   121, 169, 178, 183.
16) *Stonewall Jackson*. G. Henderson, pp 152.
17) *Berkeley County and Martinsburg in the Civil War*, Vernon Aler, pp
   4.
18) *HMS Civil War Project*. Annie Jones.
19) *The Life of Abraham Lincoln as President*. Robert J. O'Connor, pp
   202.
20) *Maryland Historical Magazine*. Carroll Curtis Davis.
21) *Wikipedia*. George Augusta Sala.
22) *Wiki Tree*. Samuel Hardinge geology.
23) *Civil War Historian*. CW Whitehair.
24) *Beleaguered Winchester*. Richard Duncan, 89, 119.
25) *WVRA Trans-Allegheny Dispatch*. September 2009.

Books by CW Whitehair

Northern Fire

Escape Across the Potomac

Gettysburg: The Field of Glory

The Bloody Harvest

Libby Life

Mosby: The War Years

Fire Along the River

The Struggle for Harpers Ferry

William H. Carney & the 54th Massachusetts Infantry

Jackson's Valley Campaign in the Newspapers

Sheridan's Valley Campaign in the Newspapers

John Brown in the Newspapers

Antietam & Gettysburg Campaigns in the Newspapers

Prayer & Valor

Quiet Valor

Book of Presidents Volume I

Book of Presidents Vol II

The Presidents' Ladies: First Ladies of the United States 1789 to 1933

The Presidents' Ladies: First Ladies of the United States 1934-2021

.

Made in United States
Orlando, FL
20 April 2024

45842082R00183